# How 'Bout That for a
# "Crack Baby"
## *Keys to Mentorship and Success*

### by Shawn T. Blanchard

Cover Design by Timothy Paule II
MarsPaule Advertising Agency

Edited by Diane Proctor Reeder
Written Images

ISBN-13: 978-1534680043
ISBN-10: 1534680047

**Speaking Engagements and bulk book orders**
LaVonne Turner
LT@iamshawnblanchard.com

Press and Media
Akilah Flynn
akilah@iamshawnblanchard.com

Office Phone: 313.355.4724

**Website:**
www.iamshawnblanchard.com

# TABLE OF CONTENTS

**PHASE THREE: CREATING CONSCIOUSNESS / 167**

# Dedication

To Denise Thomas, my mother. Without you I wouldn't have life or any of the extraordinary experiences that have contributed to the man I am today. Even in your absence your presence is always felt. Never feel guilty for your mishaps. Your every decision was a blessing in disguise for me and any and everyone who reads this book. I sincerely thank you.

To Terry Blanchard, my father. At times I'm your spitting image; physically as well as the positive characteristics that I never witnessed. You're forever a giant in my eyes! Salute and thank you sir.

# Acknowledgments

*Thank you to the following individuals who without their contributions and support this book would not have been written:*

Juanita Higgins, M.C. Higgins, Terry Blanchard, Denise Thomas, Che Stuckey, Terry Stuckey, Sky Blanchard, Ty Blanchard, Tisha Tyson, Doug Little, Michael Thomas, Tila Thomas, Tracey Stuckey, Makia Macklin, Bernard Tyson, Andy Thomas, Brian Higgins, Anthony Stuckey, Shannon Stuckey, Yolanda Stuckey, Kevin Stuckey, Melvin Forman, Trey Zackery, Thomas Bell, Jimmy Higgins, Menree Stuckey, George Stuckey, Virginia Edwards, Corky Stubbs, Bernedette Blanchard, Nancy Roy, Tyrone Winfrey, Denise Lee, Dr. Patricia Gurin, Jerry Gurin, Bryan Dameron, Roland Gainer, Anthony Bomar, Kimberly Jenkins, Barbara Johnson, Reggie Lane, Dr. Creflo Dollar, Ronald Dickerson, Phoenix Wright, Lizette Alvarez, Sharif Rucker, Tiana Millen, Aaron Bjerke, Ryan Glass, Kofi Dawson, Charles Bryant, Adrian Brooks, Karim Lannaman, Josh Woods, Keith Campbell, Rog Walker, Kwaku Amuti, Carlos Walton, Chris "Kazi" Rolle, Eyan Edwards, Shaun Derik, Edward Ewelle, Robert Earl Thomas, Jessica Babridge, Sebastian Jackson, Armond Harris, Terrence Reeves, Dr. Ken Harris, Bryan Barnhill, Drew Leahy, Ryan Leahy, LaVonne Turner, Akilah Flynn, Kanetra King, Monica Neal, Jason Wilson, Trabian Shorters, Ben Evans, Shawn Dove, David McGhee, Dr. Alex Ellis, Janirah Scott, Carl Schronez, Stephanie Dyer, Gail Perry Mason, Diane Proctor Reeder, Detroit Mayor Michael Duggan, Timothy Paule, Marv Neal, Jerami Roy, Ray Richards, and Melinda Johnson.

# Introduction

## The Struggle is Beautiful

Blood, sweat, and tears have been poured onto these pages. This book illustrates my story of humble beginnings to an influential community leader and entrepreneur. Life experiences have enabled me to unveil keys to leveraging mentorship for success. I'm excited to share them with you through my interesting journey.

At this point in life I'm comfortable enough to display that I, like many of you, live a versatile lifestyle. It's not a mask; it's an authentic self that makes me proud to understand the world from a diverse perspective. It's the moments in life that give us the most pain that tend to shape our character as we push through tears and doubt. We all have a story to tell and we become encouraged to navigate through the issues of life when we know we are not alone. Let your test be a testimony of hope for those that silently endure their own brand of hardship.

God will never give us more than we can bear. If times are rough, that just means God thinks highly of you. Push through.

## The Truth about Mentorship

It's one of life's best kept secrets to be led by the Gurus. Mark Zuckerberg was mentored by Steve Jobs and Big Sean was mentored by Kanye West. Even in the days of Kings and Queens a King's duty was to mentor the prince and the Queen's duty was to mentor the princess. One day we will all transition to eternity and our greatest aspects of self will be left through those that have believed in us and our value as mentors.

Mentorship is not a choice. It's a birthright to receive it and liferight to give it.

## Words from My Brothers

I have seven brothers. Among them there are two that have served interesting roles as it relates to mentorship: My first mentor and my first mentee. Ironically, both of them are currently incarcerated. It's because of their roles in my life that I'm actually able to write this book. They penned the words you see below. Keep them in your prayers.

I love you bros! Thanks for blessing us with your words.

## My First Mentor—by T. Stuckey

When my father departed this world his name was Terry Blanchard.

The surname Blanchard belongs to my great granny, Lula D. Blanchard. You see, my father managed to get into some trouble and was forced to change his name. He chose Blanchard to keep the integrity and true bloodline of our family intact. This introduction was not written to take anything away from Shawn's identity; his father would be very proud of him if he was with us today. In fact Shawn's full name is "Shawn Terry Blanchard." Ironically, my father almost had two juniors... So with that said...

What up Doe?

The world knows me by T. Stuckey. But most of my family members call me Terry. I got that from my pops. His birth name was Thelmon Felton Stuckey Jr. Same as my birth name but I'm the "III'd". Me and Shawn share the same father. We are blood brothers. So I would like to introduce the world to Shawn Terry Blanchard.

I watched Shawn grow from a boy to a man. And I'm very proud of him. Shawn's like a sponge, he soaks up all the game you throw his way. I am his protector, "my brother's keeper." I never gave my brother more than he was able give himself. It was always a method to my madness. For instance, it was easy for me to give him all that his heart desired. But it was always a lesson in my blessings. I remember one time Shawn asked me to buy him a new chain. But instead of me going out and buying him a chain of my choice, I took him with me and let him upgrade the one he had on his neck. He used his own money. Funny, he never knew why I did that and I never told him. But my reason was to give him some type of input and financial interest in his new chain. So when he told his story to those who asked about his new chain, it wouldn't be just "my brother bought it for me." He upgraded himself as a man should.

I didn't want to spoil my brother, I wanted him to be independent of the street life and the easy-come/easy-go mentality. Things mean more to us when we work for them.

Believe me, Shawn is a well-rounded human being who understands more than most. Just ask him a question and most likely he's going to know the answer. I love you Li'l Bro' and I wish you the world and God's Blessings.

*T. Stuckey*

P.S.: You don't need to look to the sky for a star because Shawn Terry Blanchard is a star. Now watch him shine!

# My First Mentee—by Douglas Little

I would like to introduce myself. My name is Douglas Little and Shawn Blanchard is my older brother. For as long as I can remember he has always been a great inspiration to me.

As I sit and write these words I'm in the midst of a storm, incarcerated. Whenever the rough waves of life come my way, Shawn B. has always been there as a life jacket. Even in the midst of my darkest hours, losing our mother, Shawn helped me keep my mind right and stand tall.

Like telling me not to blow, while I'm locked in a cell behind a fence 24 hours a day. Here, people care only for themselves. It's easy to lose yourself in a place like this. Shawn, being the brother/father figure he is, gave me encouragement and a voice when no one else could or would. How did he do this? Well...

He set up a surround sound system at our mother's funeral, in secret, and allowed me to speak and share my thoughts and memories with our family and friends from behind bars. This blew me back! This act of Love was nothing short of preserving my sanity. This one act of selflessness saved me months, no, years of turmoil. I was in a place of sorrow. Just imagine, being stripped from seeing the one human you care about the most. Death. Not being able to say your good-byes. This was my darkest hour and Shawn's sole act of love helped me through it all. He has a way of always being there whenever I need him. Even if I didn't realize I needed him.

1996 was the year our older brother Mike was murdered. He lost his life to the streets, selling drugs on Michigan Avenue in Inkster, Michigan. This is when Shawn, at 14 years old, really started being my official mentor. He stepped up to be a male role model for me at a young age. Unfortunately, my father was either in prison or absent. I was looking for a figure to follow and Shawn provided the guidance as a father/big brother.

Shawn observed the hurt and pain in his little brother's eyes after our brother Mike was killed. Initially, Mike was like a dad to me. Losing him, I felt alone. But that wasn't the case. Shawn had my back and noticed the potential in me at a young age. Big bro' would take me everywhere. To all the hoop games around the way, homecoming events, despite the fact that I'm five years younger than him. I was there and he never left me out or played me like the lame little brother. That meant a lot to me. It heightened my level of confidence. Shawn always played stylist on his little bro' Doug-E-Fresh. He gave my nickname life!

Shawn made sure I was the flyest little dude around the way. No wonder he's a co-owner of a custom suit company. I saw that one coming miles away! Hahaha! I'm sure a bit of that came from Mom too, but I'll let you read about that part. The way he would set trends with fashion in high school was dope. Along the way he taught me the value of keeping my things up and looking sharp. It was bigger than clothes too, because from day one he was on my head about learning and growing in school.

At times I would ask myself, *How does Shawn keep his grades up so high…* knowing that he stayed out late most nights? I didn't understand it. But he did! School was a place Shawn used to hone his skills and take him to another place, mentally. It was his escape outside of the negative ills of the street life until the bell would ring!

Speaking of how life was in the hood after the bell would ring…I remember one summer night me and Shawn was out on the block on the west side over one of his lady friend's house. I remember Shawn getting into it with a guy named Jake, a big bum-looking dude. It was about some money from a dice game from Mackenzie High School.

Jake had all his goons around, they were super deep! So Jake got to poppin' off at Shawn about some money, from what I remember. And he was the one who owed Shawn money! Anyway, dude had the clean-cut smooth, popular guy mixed up as if Shawn was going to back down! Mistake number one! Shawn socked Jake in the middle of the street and they got to fighting and went at it! Bro' held his self down and rocked out with dude. Jake was twice his size! After the fight was over we went in his home girl house…where she showed me a gun!

So I told Shawn and he went to get it from her. Shawn didn't do what you think. This simply displays how Shawn thought and how he showed me to think outside the box. My advice to him was, "Bro let's go air this out (shoot) all of them lames!" So he thought hard about it and said, "You know what… I'm not going to shoot this guy. I'll catch him on the rebound in the 'hood."

Shawn made a major choice to be a leader then, and he made the best choice: not to go shooting at dude! That one situation could have been real life changing, and the Shawn Blanchard story would be wayyyyy different today. I look up to the fact my brother never played off his emotions or ego and kept it real modest, humble.

The summer of 2000, after Shawn graduated from high school, I returned to our grandfather's house. I went down the stairs into the basement, which was our old room and it was empty. As soon as I saw this I ran upstairs to ask Granddad, "Where is Shawn?" he said, "You didn't know boy, that damn Shawn up in Ann Arbor at the University of Michigan!"

At the age of 17 Shawn stared life right in the face and didn't fret at the unknown. He was determined to better himself. Along the way he was still pulling for his younger brother. I listened to my brother's wisdom, but I also chose to follow my own path.

I'm currently two years from my earliest release date. I see now that Shawn had this life thing figured out. How? Hell if I know… I'm still asking myself that question. At this point I'm all ears! For years now, I've been educating myself with the knowledge of self to understand how I can impact the world for social change. My brother Shawn has laid the foundation, which motivates me to work by my brother's side in the business world and in the world of mentorship. While big bro' is mentoring outside the wall, I'm mentoring inside the wall for the forgotten. In closing this out I would like to say a few words to my brother.

You've always been cut from a different cloth bro'! You've always been a great mentor, even though sometimes your pupils will have to bump their heads along their own journey. Your work will never return void! Thanks for not giving up on me and the many young men and women you have helped. You've brought the best out of all of us. Bro' you did it again! You're a genius! It's the takeover; I'm on my way! Let's get it!

Peace and blessings,

Doug-E-Fresh (Your First Mentee)

# UNCONSCIOUS MENTORSHIP

# CHAPTER 1

## Family Dynamics

Dee Dee?! Her back was hunched over the table while her head moved from left to right like a typewriter. Her movements were halted, awkward, jerky; the child in her belly made moving difficult. He stood there and watched for at least two of her full left-to-right head strides in disbelief. But she didn't hear him; the snorting, inhaling noises she made drowned him out.

Then, she snapped out of it. Startled, she knocked the white-filled powdered canvass off the table. She didn't dare look at him with blotches of powder smeared across her nose. She was caught! He stormed after her and she ran towards the stairs screaming. He caught her at the top of the staircase. In haste he lifted his leg and kicked her in the lower back. Her 5'9" body was frail compared to his athletic 6'3" frame. She screamed as her body connected with the metal-tipped ledges of each step, and she was silenced when her body made a loud thump at the bottom platform. "What the hell is wrong with you woman?!" Her arm was cut, and her cocaine-blotched nose was bleeding. Slowly she rolled over, looking at the top of the staircase with wide eyes and pressing both hands against her five-months pregnant stomach. Her voice wavered as she answered in kind: "What the hell is wrong with you?!"

The child in Dee Dee's belly was me. On August 17, 1982 I was born in Detroit, Michigan to Liola Denise Thomas ("Dee Dee") and Terry Blanchard. After I was cleaned up, the doctors gave me to my mother. She held me and smiled. "Ms. Thomas," said the nurse, "the baby's left eye is swollen completely shut. It looks like the effect of some sort of trauma..."

I lived with my mother for the first three weeks of my life. Before I was born, she'd already had three kids: a pair of twins, Michael ("Mike") and Andy, and my sister Tila, the oldest. At that time, Dee Dee was staying with her mother, Virginia Edwards better known as "Grandma Virginia." I'm sure that she never dreamed something like this would happen: that her baby would bear the marks of her decisions.

Dee Dee was a hard worker; she worked all hours of the day and night. It wasn't too hard for her to do that; she had a built-in babysitter. "Mama, I need to go out. I'll put the twins to bed so they won't bother you." Dee Dee never asked permission. She just did whatever she felt she needed to do. Her feelings of entitlement would not prepare her for what was to come.

Early 1975, before I was born, Dee Dee walked into the bedroom where she kept Mike and Andy. She was not one for cooing and fussing over babies, even her own. She put Andy in his crib on his stomach. Mike too. These days, the medical professionals all seem to agree that a baby should sleep on his back but back then, the common medical wisdom was that sleeping on the back could cause a baby to choke to death—he might spit up—and so here Andy was, safely on his stomach. Or so my mother thought.

Dee Dee went out, and then came back to check on the babies. She looked in on Andy, and what she saw made her heart cold—colder than it already was.

"Mama! Andy is blue! He's not breathing!" Dee Dee snatched Andy up and got into her light blue 1975 Lincoln Town car. She drove to the emergency entrance of Oakwood Hospital and ran into the lobby. The staff took one look and went into action. They didn't even ask her name or his name. "Here ma'am, let me take the baby," the on-call nurse said, then ran to the triage room. Running with the hospital staff into the room, they gently helped her out. "Please, let us work on him...we'll do everything we can."

"My baby!" Dee Dee cried. "Andeee!"

The nurses and doctors looked at each other. They placed Andy's tiny body on the table and began pushing his chest up and down, breathing into his mouth at the proper intervals. After five minutes, they stopped, and looked at the clock. "Time of death: 9:14 a.m.," said one of the physicians.

They came out to talk to Dee Dee. She took one look at their faces and crumpled to the floor. "I am so sorry," the doctor began. Dee Dee pulled herself up and sat down, head bowed, eyes staring at the floor. "Sometimes children just...stop breathing and we don't always know why. We've named it SIDS, Sudden Infant Death Syndrome. You can't blame yourself; it's not your fault. There are still some things we just don't understand." His voice wavered. "I am so sorry for your loss."

Much, much later, Andy's twin brother, Mike, would die too. I'll tell you about that later.

I think that's the reason my mom gave me away when I was three weeks old. It's the only explanation that makes sense to me. For some reason, my other grandmother—my father's mother, Juanita Higgins, better known as "Grandma Juanita"—felt the need to explain my mother's absence.

"Your mom was attempting to get Mike and Tila ready for school," Grandma Juanita began. Tila was dragging her feet, Mike was whining, and you were crying. Dee Dee was never cut out to take care of kids. She ran from one kid to the next trying to address everyone's needs. Your Grandma Virginia was busy doing her hair and your Mom snapped!"

Why she told me what happened next, I'm not sure. I can't explain why any grandmother would tell her grandchild something like this:

"Then your mother said, 'I can't take this s—t. Get this little b—ch out of here!'

My mother is talking about me. This is too much for my child-sized brain to process: I am the b--ch. I am crying like any newborn that wants his mother or nourishment, and she is calling me a b--ch. She is mad at my dad for leaving. She is mad at herself (maybe at God?) for Andy's young, harsh, sudden death. She is mad at my grandmother for not wanting to be the enslaved grandmother that she apparently cannot be.

My mother, "Dee Dee," was an only child. Her mother, Grandma Virginia, worked at the Ford plant and made pretty good money. Her biological father cheated on Grandma Virginia, and left without a trace while Dee Dee was an infant. The only father she knew was Leroy Edwards. He was her step-father that worked at the Ford plant with Grandma. They met and married shortly after Dee Dee's biological father left.

Leroy was abusive to Dee Dee—verbally, physically, and sexually abusive. He hurled curse words, called her stupid and ugly, and never gave her an inkling of positive affirmation. Grandma was aware of the verbal and physical abuse. After all, she was verbally and physically abused too. Then one day, Dee Dee told Grandma about the sexual abuse. That was the last straw.

Grandma Virginia was up early, pressing her hair in the bathroom mirror. Leroy came home drunk, stumbling into the doorway. He called her name, but Virginia was accustomed to his drunken behavior. She closed the bathroom door, hooked the metal chain latch on the door, stared in the mirror, took a deep breath and exhaled. She continued pressing her hair. Leroy abruptly kicked the door screaming, "Virginia! Open the door!" Virginia silently backed away from the door clinching the pressing comb in her right hand. He kicked the door again and the chain popped off the wall, swinging the door open. Virginia charged at him and swung the pressing comb at Leroy's toupée-topped head. "Arrrghhhg!" He fell to the ground and crawled away from the bathroom door on his back. Virginia stood still in the bathroom as Leroy squirmed on the ground.

That was the last day Leroy would try Grandma Virginia. He left without a trace, never to be seen or heard from again. Dee Dee's long nightmare was over—except for her memories.

So Grandma compensated. Whatever Dee Dee wanted, Dee Dee got. At the store, all my mother had to do was "point and click" at something and sometimes whine, according to my Aunt Corky, and she would walk out of the door with it.

The compensation of material goods, however, could not heal Dee Dee's soul. She was upset with her mother for not protecting her more. Things are not protection. And mothers are hard-wired to protect their children.

Why didn't Dee Dee's mother, my grandmother, do more to protect her child? I don't think I will ever know.

Dee Dee's response was to rebel. She never finished high school, but she found her chosen profession early: shoplifting. My mother actually made a good living as a booster. She boosted for herself and for others, and the "others" had to pay. She had her rationalization: "The white man needs to pay for all the stuff they're not giving us anyway, so we're going to take from the white man until he gives us our forty acres and a mule." No matter what she did, she had rationale, a reason, and rhyme for it.

Except for one thing: Why did my father leave her?

According to Dee Dee, my father never left her at all. With Mom, everything that related to my father was sunshine and rainbows. She never told me about the time he kicked her down the stairs. Her mother did.

Dee loved him more than any of the four fathers of her children. She'd look at me, even after leaving me to others to raise at three weeks, and break out into a wide, beautiful smile saying, "Look at little Punchy; doesn't he look just like his father? Little Terry," she would call me.

"Oh, you should have seen the parties," she would tell me. "We were

7

decked out. We went to the best places from the Jackson 5 concerts at the Fox Theater to the Pontchartrain Hotel, and I would get your father Gucci and Hugo Boss and made sure his feet looked good in his Ferragamos." She didn't say, but by then I had figured out that all the clothes she got for him were from the "five finger discount" store. Terry Blanchard had the best clothes shoplifting could buy.

"And our house was decked out," she continued. "Leather couches and fine china and plush carpeting." She was so proud of the way they lived, and the home they had made together.

One thing she left out, though: he was rarely in it.

---

Dad, Terry Blanchard, was born on 9225 Cameron, between Westminster and Owens on the Northend of Detroit, famous for being the epicenter of the 1967 Rebellion. He was the oldest of four boys and one adopted girl and, if you ask Mom, she says Dad's mother, Grandma Juanita, neglected all of her children.

"Your dad told me they were not well-cared for," Mom would say to me. It's almost as if she and my father's mother were in competition as to who was the best mother, and Mom wanted to make sure that she had the edge in that department.

Dad grew up sucking stalks of sugar cane and playing games like *Mumblety-Peg* with ice picks, *Top Gun* with rubber bands and bottle caps, and pitching horse shoes with his brothers George, Menree, and Jimmy. In the 1960s, they would go down to Pork Chop Hill at Eastern Market to get pig parts that well-to-do people didn't want. You know, the slave food: pig feet, pig ears, and chitlins (chitterlings). Those parts were free until white people noticed how many black people came to pick up the scraps. Afterwards they would go to the Vernors factory on Warren and Woodward. "Here boys, take these cans and give your moms some too," the black janitors would say, giving them as much Vernors as their hands could hold. They knew the boys didn't have much.

Dad was a big man to many, both in stature and in reputation. He was a working-man; what some people might call a *working thug*. When he went to the Navy right out of high school, all of his brothers followed: two to the Navy like him, and one to the Marines. Of course, the Navy made him even stronger, at least physically.

My dad was 6'3" and weighed about 220 pounds in his prime and for the duration of his life. He had the kind of aura that made men self-conscious and ladies stare. His skin was caramel with a hint of gold in the sun. Deep baritone voice, like a television announcer or lounge singer. When Terry Blanchard spoke—just like Barack Obama—people listened.

Dad had a cool, effortless "Black man" stride that said, smoothly and quietly, but firmly: *Power*. The power reflected in his reddish brown eyes, his thick, wavy 'fro-ed hair, jutting two-and-a-half to three inches into the air, and his full mustache coupled with a goatee-style beard. He had a contagious, jumpy laugh that staccatoed into a series of deep yet jumpy breaths. When Terry laughed...well, you just felt you had to laugh, too, whether you knew what he was laughing about or not.

Terry was a man's man. He did man's work, including riding on—and working on—his motorcycle. His nickname, "Punchy," came from those big calloused hands. You would never want him to put those paws on you. Just looking at those hands was intimidating. But interestingly enough, he wasn't the scary kind of threatening that other men in the neighborhood could be. Maybe it was his high-wattage smile, or the smooth stride, or the gentlemanly demeanor. Whatever it was, people were attracted to his imposing power, not afraid of it or offended by it.

It helped him on the job. He moved quickly up the supervisory ladder at his job at the Budd Company plant, where everyone considered him a friend. I remember hearing how he was always getting a raise; he always had money.

Mom used to love to ride on the back of his motorcycle, an extension of Terry's power, and his "A-Team"-style black van with the painting of orange and red flames on the side. When he rode up in that van with his black jacket, goatee'd and grinning from ear to ear—you can just guess why Mom fell in love with him.

Everyone I talked with who knew my dad said the same thing: "Punchy" was a protector. If you were with him, you were OK. You were safe. Got an issue with someone? If you had a relationship with Punchy, you could go to him and he'd take care of it for you. Not just with words, but with action.

One day, my Dad and Uncle Jimmy (Dad's brother) went to McDonald's in my Dad's black "A- Team" van. As they closed the van doors and walked towards the entrance, a little boy, about five years old, ran past Jimmy and stepped on his foot. "Watch out little fella, I could'a been the wrong one." The boy's father, trailing behind, felt the need to play *Superman* as he hurled sharp, vulgar words at Jimmy.

"Don't talk to my son like you crazy m----f----!"

Terry was confused. Jimmy didn't say anything. He simply didn't want the "little fella" to run around the parking lot alone, bumping into strangers. Without hesitation my dad grabbed the man's neck with his left hand lifted him slightly off the ground and punched him square in the chin. He released the man and his limp body fell with a loud thud, right there in the McDonald's parking lot. The poor boy stopped running and slowly walked over to his dad while keeping his eyes on my dad.

Jimmy said, "Welp! I guess these niggas won't be having McDonalds!"

My dad picked the guy up and laid him near his car. Terry told Jimmy, "Buy the little fella a happy meal." The poor kid ate his fries while his dad lay there for another 30 minutes unconscious. As soon as he came to, Terry and Jimmy pulled off.

That's one of the many instances that he lived up to his nickname

10

"Punchy." With his stature, and his massive hands and physique, people knew: Don't mess with Punchy. Even though I didn't spend a lot of time with him, whenever I was in his presence, I felt two things: Safe. And invincible.

I think in retrospect I was mostly impressed with my dad's style and physical stature, as well as his status within our family. Whenever Punchy came to his mother's house—my Grandma Juanita, where I lived—I would hang at the door just to be physically close to him. In my eyes, everything he did was larger than life. If he bought me a sucker, I announced it to the world! If he took me to the store, I stood tall the entire time! If he said, "good job" on my report card, I didn't need to show anyone else!

It wasn't that he ever really talked to me a lot as a kid. He didn't interact with me in any substantial way. I regretted not having those father-son conversations. Even though I never knew what they were like, I missed them anyway.

I took whatever I could get.

As complicated as they were, I loved—still love—my mom and dad. At a young age I was even blessed enough to see them in the same room, once.

At my dad's funeral.

# CHAPTER 2

## At Least She Tried

I remember a big sky blue Lincoln Town Car. The driver was a pretty lady, and her hair was in a sleek, wavy ponytail. The pretty lady got out of the car and came toward me. "Hey Baby," she says as if she thought I should know her.

I thought: *That's her*!

I started running for my life. Maybe a better word is "pedaling." Pedaling on my Big Wheel past my Grandma Juanita's house, past the neighbor's house and down the street, fast as I could pedal.

Unfortunately, I looked back, and any tenuous balance my short legs had on each pedal was lost. When I fell off my Big Wheel, the woman ran toward me. Even from afar, I could now clearly see that she was in fact, beautiful. She had in tow another boy and a girl. They were both older than me, but still kids. I would find out later that they were my brother Mike and my sister Tila. I tried to get back on my vehicle, but somehow I couldn't. It's all a blur now, but I remember mentally preparing myself to fight all three of them. They were bigger, but my little bony body was ready!

I was four years old. The woman coming toward me was my mother. I never remembered laying eyes on her before then, but I knew it was her nevertheless. Even at the tender age of four, and even with long separations, mothers and sons have a certain bond.

The Big Wheel was upside down and my knee was bleeding. As I lay in the grass, the woman was fast approaching and the girl and the boy too and I thought, *Oh, no!* I pushed the Big Wheel off me and just as I as was trying to get back in the driver seat, they caught me.

*Are you OK?* My mother asked. I began to cry, hurled jabs, flailing legs, and biting at the air, clothes, grass. *Get off me!* But I was too small and my mother placed my arms behind my back aggressively and took me back home, to my grandparents' place two doors down.

---

Like my dad, Mom has a presence. Mahogany brown, thick and wavy hair that turned reddish in the sun; she often wore an elegant ponytail. About 5'9", 140 pounds or so with the kind of face and figure that made men stand at attention. Regal.

She could hold her own in a conversation, and could talk with anyone from the average Joe on the street to a billionaire on the cover of *Forbes*. It wasn't that she knew a whole lot; she was just an expert at "chiming in" when people were talking. She would say just enough at the right time to impress whomever she was talking with. She was a clothes expert, a wardrobe stylist and a connoisseur of fine garments. She knew cut, color, fabric, and quality, and usually found a way to weave that knowledge into her conversation. She knew clothing so well that she could speak on it quite robustly, with an intellectual quality that gave people the impression that she knew about more than just clothes. So when the conversation moved on to other topics, Mom would smile and nod her head just enough to make people think she was engaged and understood whatever was being talked about. She might ask a pertinent question or two, but she never said enough to make people wonder how much she really knew…or didn't know. For her, conversation was an exquisite, tension-filled art, but she made it look easy.

As I got older, I would admire the quality in her that attracted other people, the side that knew how to adapt to any situation, and silently filed it away for possible future use.

For Mom, appearances were everything. She never graduated from high school, and she didn't take the "legal" career route like my father, who was a naval officer and then a plant supervisor. She just instinctively knew how to interact with people to get what she wanted. She was street-smart with one tragic flaw: paranoia. If she misplaced something, the first thing she wondered was *Who stole it?*

There was a reason for that: My mom was a professional shoplifter. She was a chameleon who could adapt to any situation. She could steal a $5,000 dress and walk straight out the front door looking like a million bucks. No one dared question her. She could be incredibly charming; she would have to be in her profession.

But she didn't just steal for herself. Shoplifting was Mom's business. Her clients were clueless—or maybe they just didn't want to know. Mom would come to their glamorous homes with a bundle of clothing custom-fit to their particular style. *I have to fill my catalogue orders,* she would say. That's what she called her product: "catalogue orders."

But she had another side, too. If you crossed her, she could stab you with a rusty screwdriver. She once got into an altercation with one of her boyfriends, Ed. I was never told the details, just that she stabbed him. She once tried to run over my sister Tila; another time, she left Tila stranded in another state just because she got pissed off. When she was angry, she had no problem showing it.

Even with me. She was my mom, and she took good care of me in the only way she thought she could. That "way" landed her in prison from time to time. There were periods of time where I didn't hear from her for years, and just thought she didn't care. When she got out, she told me what happened. For me, it was just another day in the life and times of a mother I never fully got to know. At least she tried.

---

Home is my grandmother's house. My father's mother and stepfather. *Grandma Juanita!* I ran to her and grabbed on to her cotton nightgown for dear life.

*Hey Juanita,* my mother says.

*What's going on? What's wrong with my baby?* And *What are you doing here?*
She looks down at me and says *Boy stop; that's yo' momma.*

I continued to cry while Grandma Juanita began packing my bags. *I'm not going with you!* I yelled at my mom with bloodshot red eyes while staring directly into her guilt-filled face. *You're going boy,* Grandma Juanita answered, as she continued to stuff clothes into the duffle bag.

I am four years old.

I was actually going to this woman's house, a woman I've never seen before, a woman who I am sure is my mother but yet not my mother. The only mother I have ever known is Grandma Juanita. Frankly, she's all I cared to know as a mother.

She is at once not the typical grandmother and the quintessential grandmother. Her false teeth smelled like spoiled milk, and she cooked more salty pork parts than they did in the South in 1817. Yuck! I hate potato salad to this day because I first tried Grandma Juanita's! I recall she stirred the mush or potato salad with her bare hands with red acrylic nails. One of her nails actually broke completely off while she was aggressively stirring the mush. Just like the lottery, you guessed it, I was the lucky winner who hit the jackpot and bit right into her potato covered red acrylic nail. My face grimaced the same way it does at the sight of potato salad today.

Grandma Juanita calls all the children who live in her house—a multi-racial mixture of the offspring of my father and his siblings—*nigger*. In fact, we knew whether Grandma Juanita woke up on the right side of the bed or not based upon the inflection in her *"nigger"* pitch. A casual mid octave *"nig-ger please"* with a slap on the knee was grandma enjoying herself. A slow and calm *"nigg-gerr"* was a sign of endearment as if someone received a good report card. Then there was the quick, high-pitched *"nigger!"* when she was pissed, which was code for run, clean up your act, and look for Granddad now!

But, like a typical grandmother, she let me sleep in the bed with her and lay my head on her soft and saggy breasts. Her hands, too, were soft,

16

and wrinkled, and they frequently gripped a glass of Pepsi and vodka to her lips. She wore really big glasses—and it wasn't a 1980's fashion statement; they were just big. She religiously sported cotton nightgowns around the house and was a stickler for order and neatness. She ironed everything—not just sheets, but all of our underwear too. She would even starch the towels and the comforters and quilts. She would starch the clothes and put them in the freezer to be ironed later. I called her the "folding Nazi."

Grandma Juanita's obsessive-compulsive disorder extended beyond the plastic runners on the living room floor and plastic covered velvet couches to financial matters too. She handled all of the money in the household. She checked the mail, wrote the checks, paid the bills, clipped coupons, and purchased groceries.

But the biggest thing is, she was a die-hard defender of her grandchildren. Everyone else said "She's mean," even some of my cousins who lived there with me. But when she said, *If you need anything at all, you know you can come to me* or *This is what you need to do Shawn...* or *You're my baby; if you have a problem with anyone, let me know about it* I felt about as protected as I'm sure Mom felt with my dad. Grandma Juanita was my provider, helper, protector and counselor. She was everything to me for the first 12 years of my life.

But don't get it confused; Grandma Juanita could deliver a world class a-- whoppin', which she delivered early and often. I remember once when I called my cousin, Anthony, a "turd" right outside the kitchen. Her eagle ears heard me as she was boiling a pot of pig ears. *What did you say nigger!?* I hung my head low and replied, "A turd." *Come here and Anthony go get me a switch. Yes Ma'am*, said Anthony as he giggled and darted down the steps into the back yard. I slowly walked towards her and she bent down near my face. *Stick your tongue out nigger*. Reluctantly, I halfway stuck my tongue out. She grabbed it with her acrylic nails and began to twist it like a wrung-out washrag! She shouted with spoiled milk breath, *Watch your mouth nigger! And pull those pants down!* To make matters worse, Anthony mercilessly came running through the back door giggling and holding the switch high. Grandma Juanita grabbed it

17

as I tap-danced, pants down around my ankles, from the pain inflicted from her vise-like hand grip, and whipped me with the other hand for about five long minutes. She whipped Anthony too for laughing. LOL. I never called him a turd again.

But she was good for a long hug afterwards. She was soft and I could just sink into her after I finished crying. Other people took her strength for meanness, but not me. The love just shown through her harsh ways and funky dentures.

My mother's mother, Grandma Virginia, tried to diminish Juanita's love for me. "She's so nice to you guys because she did her own children so bad," she would tell me. But it didn't matter to me why she was good to me. It just mattered that she was.

Plus, I had built-in playmates: cousins Anthony, Shannon, Brian and Rusty; and Che', one of my many sisters, all either lived there or came over often. Grandma Juanita loved all of us.

My grandfather's was a different kind of love, but love just the same. While I knew Juanita's love from her whippings, I knew M.C's love from the way he tried to prevent them. "Juanita, sit yo' a-- down and stop whopping on them damn boys"—that's the first thing he'd say when he came home from his job at the wastewater plant. I knew if I could hold Grandma Juanita off from a whipping until he got home I would be in the clear.

Granddad was a cool guy. Born in 1931, but you'd never know it by the way he dressed and looked. You could catch him with some black Reebok pumps with the little orange basketball on the tongue, some Nautica denim jeans and a complementing Nautica sweater, and a trucker hat with the fish net half cap and a gold rope across the front of it. The hat would sit right on top of his head; if the wind blew it would fall off. He probably didn't pull it down on his head because his hair might drip. Remember, this was the '80s and he had a jet-black perm that he combed to the side with the bald fade along the sides. He would always wear his gold watch and a thin gold chain. The only thing

18

that might have given away his age was that he had about 6 or 7 teeth missing, mostly in the front.

Granddad was 5'11" with a strong physique. He would stand on the porch, shirtless, holding some kind of alcoholic drink, and salute the neighbors. "Get somethin' in yo hand," he would tell Mr. Salter, which was his invitation for him to come over and have a drink with him. He would come home, give us "noogies" (twisting his fist playfully in our hair), and talk to us—really talk. Then we'd sit and watch *Tom and Jerry* together...with Crackhead Uncle Menry who lived in the basement.

"Crackhead Uncle Menry." It was almost like "Crackhead" was his first name, that's what we always called him. He was the youngest out of all Juanita's boys and unlike his three older brothers, including my Dad, who went to the Navy, he went to the Marines and so he was already a bit different from his brothers. Uncle Menry looked like Snoop Dogg. He was tall, about 6'3 or 6'4", with very fine jet-black hair that he wore in a kind of wet curly ponytail. He enrolled in the Marines to dodge his debt to a few drug dealers. Even in the Marines morphine was his friend. It happened with many of the soldiers who went to Vietnam.

The drug usage didn't stop when he came home; Uncle Menry moved to crack when it was dropped in our neighborhoods in the 1980s. Of course, drugs take all of your money, and Uncle Menry owed everybody. Once, a couple of drug dealers tried to kill him. When he didn't come up with their cash, they needed to make a statement. They bashed his head in with a bat until it was flat and as wide as Martin Lawrence's head when he fought Tommy "Hitman" Hearns. The doctors had to remove a large portion of the left side of his brain, leaving him even more diminished, and blind in his left eye. His head had a wicked dent on the left side if you paid any attention.

One day he shook me down.

*You got some money, nephew?*

*No Uncle Menry,* I told him.

19

Desperate, he started looking around. He spied my Atari game system then my new single toggle joysticks.

*You betta not!!* I yelled. He ignored me and ran out with the goods. We usually put up our video games so he couldn't get to them. He caught me slippin' that day.

*Menry, stop taking those kids' things! You ought to be 'shamed of your damn self, stealing from them little boys!* my grandmother would say…but she would never throw him out. I never dared tell her about how he would shake me down for money; I'd heard about his being in the Marines, I'd heard that when he was married he came home and held a knife to his wife's neck more than once, I knew that Marines killed people in Vietnam, and I was scared to death of him. When he asked me for money, I would just give it to him. I didn't want to be on his bad side. Later, he became more like the family joke, but then, I was terrified.

It was a good childhood—as far as I could tell. The best of times and the worst of times, as they say. But I didn't know anything different.

---

*I'm not going! I'm not going!* Sliding across the floor and pulling on anything I could grab as we headed out the side door. I was pissed at my grandma for packing my bags. I was actually going with this woman who everyone says is my mother and who I know in my bones is the woman who gave birth to me. I cried until this new mother took me to McDonald's. *You want some chicken nuggets?* Mom asked. I nodded *Yes* through my tears. Chicken nuggets worked on me every time; my Grandma Juanita must have told her the trick. How else would she know?

# CHAPTER 3

## Sponge

By second grade, I had developed a pretty nice identity for myself. But I didn't just pull that identity from the sky. Grandma Juanita handed it to me on a silver platter.

You know the movie *The Help*, where the domestic servant Aibileen tells her young white charge Mae, "You is kind. You is smart. You is important."? My Grandma Juanita told me something similar. Her mantra to me was: "You are smart and handsome." She started telling me that the day I had an "accident." I guess I should say one of the many times I had an accident.

Doctors say that the effects of drug abuse during pregnancy can result in a number of defects such as problems with sustained attention and behavioral self-control, like increased aggression, delays in learning, abnormal muscle tone, slower growth rate, language difficulties and an increased need for special education in school-aged children. My issue was my bladder. Every night for about seven years, I wet the bed.

My older cousins Anthony and Brian, eight and nine years old respectively, didn't make it easy for me. They had dozens of names for me; Master Piss, Piss Boy, Piss Pot, and Piss Trap, to name a few. This particular morning beads of sweat were on my forehead and my twin bed sheets were on the floor. I rolled onto my left side and the plastic bed cover was stuck to my leg from a wet substance. It was a mixture of sweat and hot piss. As I awoke the plastic rustled and I slowly peered over to the adjacent twin bed where Anthony and Brian slept feet to head and head to feet. It was no wonder why I slept alone. I cautiously crept out of the bed focusing on the obnoxious sound of the plastic bed cover. With one foot on the ground I attempted to plant my other foot, but it was too late. I paused. Anthony began to stretch and kicked Brian in the neck. *What the hell man! Get yo' foot out of my face!* yelled Brian. Anthony replied, *My bad, blame it on Piss Trap! Look at him, he did it again!* I stood there with He-Man PJ's completely soaked. *Tisk*

*tisk, man when are you going to stop with the piss facuet? Damn!* Brian replied angrily. The taunting began and I picked up my wet sheets and ignored them. I was pissed, literally and figuratively. I had a problem and none of us knew the source. We just knew I was pissy.

I stomped down the stairs and ran into the front room where Grandma Juanita and Grandad slept. I nudged my grandma and she woke up reaching for her big glasses. *What Nigger?* I whined, *Brian and Anthony are teasing me!* She glanced at me as I stood there shirtless in my wet pajamas. Grandma Juanita knew why I had bladder issues and didn't feel the need to discuss it with me. She simply empathized with me. *Baby, look at me. You are smart and handsome and I love you.* I smiled. *Now go clean ya li'l pissy a-- up Nigger.*

I took her words *Smart* and *Handsome* to heart. So grades were never a problem for me. True to my grandma's words, I got the best grades and was considered the smartest boy in my second grade class. Plus, my biological mom was a booster. She literally dropped off garbage bags full of clothes for me, clothes from expensive and trendy designers such as Used, Damage, Cross Colors, Karl Kani...you know, the good stuff. Really cool lunchboxes, too, with all the popular cartoon characters like *Transformers*. At such a young age, I never asked "Where did you get this from?" At such a young age, I didn't know what kind of money it took to buy those things.

But my mom knew. She had neither gone to college nor finished high school. Neither did she get one of those good factory jobs that were so plentiful when she was a young adult. I knew that much. So this was her way of supporting herself and her family.

Before I was born Mom had fallen down two flights of stairs in a hospital and laid there, unconscious. A guy named Michael Taylor found her at the bottom of a flight of stairs and immediately called a nurse to aid her back to consciousness. Mom appreciated men who were gentle and treated her with respect.

Michael was different. He showered her with attention and what she thought was love. He didn't abuse her, and I imagine it must have been such a relief to be with a man who treated her so differently to that which she had grown accustomed. My twin siblings Mike and Andy were the product of that relationship.

Among the distinctions that he possessed was a peculiar hustle. Michael Taylor taught my mother to shoplift.

She honed her craft, and became a creative entrepreneur. Later, I would find out that this is how I got all those fancy clothes. Later, I would find out just how she did it.

Later, I would do it too.

---

I'm sure the reason I was so popular in second grade had something to do with the fancy clothes and the lunchboxes-with-the-Transformers-thermos. I ended up with two pretty girlfriends: Tangamiqua and Janetta. They both agreed to be my girlfriends and each knew about the other—no problem there, right?

But Clay, one of my classmates, was jealous. He led a group of five boys including himself, and every day at recess, without fail, they would find me and "jump" me. Daily, I would play with Tangamiqua and Janetta momentarily at recess. That is, until the recess teacher would separate the boys from the girls. At that point, I would just go off to the side of the boys' playground, or try to hide in the tall grass and play with dirt and my pocket toys, alone. It made me somewhat of a loner.

But Clay and his crew never failed to find me. It took five of them, because even then, I knew something about fighting. I had older brothers, cousins, and friends to pick on me enough to understand how to hurt people pretty good. Clay and company knew that just one boy wouldn't do.

One day it got really bad. I was minding my business as usual, and they were coming at me again. As usual, I wasn't going out without a fight. I hit the first boy who stepped up square in the nose. He fell. When another one came right behind, I kicked him in the knee and the two of them crawled away. After that, another boy kicked me from behind on the right side, hard. I broke down to a knee and was kicked in the stomach on the left. I hit the ground and began rolling over in acute pain. They laughed. I began to get up to make a run for it. About ten feet away and closing in fast, eyes wide, I saw Clay running toward me holding a glass bottle high in the air. He swung, and broke it on my nose. I had gravel in my mouth and a bloody nose, and to add to the injury and embarrassment, the boys started kicking dust in my face. They left me there, writhing in pain and coughing.

*Why would they do this to me?* I thought to myself. I didn't understand. After that incident, every day my teacher, Ms. McMurray, would place me at the front of the single file line as we were leaving school to walk home. She knew what I would do, and she wanted to help. Before those boys had a chance to get to me, I would dart out and run home like the wind. Eventually my third grade cousin Anthony started to take up for me. His mere presence at the gate 20 feet away from the single file line was enough to frighten five second-grade boys; anytime he came their way, they would look at him and think better of messing with me.

At some point, I noticed that other kids' dads were different from mine. My cool grandfather was around, but he was a little older and he didn't do the things that other kids' dads did. My dad didn't do those things either.

I would silently observe my cousins Anthony's and Brian's consistent interaction with their fathers, playing basketball under their tutelage. Anthony's dad, who was my father's brother, came over one day and took him to the backyard with a basketball. He bounced the ball between his legs and spun it on his finger. Brian knew all the moves too, because of his dad, Uncle Jimmy. I would watch, but felt these were private, father-son sessions and seldom did I feel comfortable enough to come outside and join in. I just didn't feel I was on that

24

team. Most of the time, I wasn't even there when Brian's and Anthony's dads were tutoring them, giving them tips, putting their arms on their shoulders and saying, "There you go son, that's how you do it."

In retrospect, I probably could have joined the fun. In retrospect, knowing my situation, maybe my uncles could have been more proactive in inviting me. Maybe they thought I wasn't interested. Maybe they figured that my grandfather was "father" enough in the gaping absence of my own. I don't know. I just know that now, I look for opportunities to mentor young men and boys that are in the same position I was in then, but just need a person to tell them "There you go son, that's how you do it."

The cousins talked basketball all the time. I would try to get into the conversation from time to time, but I didn't really know the game and the most I could come up with was "Yea man, you were good." But I was the youngest and they would just tell me "Shut up, you don't know nothing about ball" and I never had a comeback to that. Nothing to say…

One day, my cousin Anthony's dad came over. *I got something for you* he said, grinning from ear to ear. Once he saw what it was, Anthony started grinning too. It was a black butter soft leather "8-Ball" jacket with white stitching and a man dunking a basketball on the back. Anthony was so happy and he started hugging his dad and he immediately started trying on his jacket. *Aw man I love it, Dad!* All I remember is this: *I saw them but they didn't see me.* And I ran upstairs as fast as I could, stomping as I went. I jumped in the bed and cried myself to sleep.

I didn't care that Anthony had the jacket I just wanted a dad.

---

*Shawn! Somebody wanna talk to you.* Grandma Juanita is calling me.

I pick up the phone and hear a familiar voice on the other end.

*—Shawn? Baby!*

*—Oh. Hey Ma.*

*—I miss you baby. I'm on a little vacation, but I love you and I'll see you soon.*

*—Aight.*

I didn't want to let her know that I cared. I did, but I thought she didn't care. So why would I care back? We had a few conversations like that during my formative, primary school years. Mom just wasn't very motherly in the way we normally think mothers should be. Later, I would understand that Mom gave me everything she was. She tried her best, she taught what she could, and that was love for her.

Later, I would understand...those times Mom called me in tears, those brief phone conversations that seemed so out of character for her...that she was in jail.

In 1903, author, activist and thought leader W.E.B. DuBois said that the primary problem of the 20th century would be the problem of the color line. What he didn't say was that "color line" extended, not only to the division between blacks and whites, but even further to the division between, to put it in classic "Black English," *light-skinnded* and *dark-skinnded.*

That was magnified in my family. Like so many African American families, we were like the *"Rainbow Coalition"* of black folks. My grandmother (father's mother) was very light and my grandfather, M.C., was very dark. And the hair texture was all over the place!

There were cousins Shannon and Anthony. Same mother and father. Straight hair, light vanilla skin, dark eyes and eyebrows. Cousin Brian: carmel complexion, curly hair, mother "mixed with Indian." And me: the brown-skinned bandit. The youngest. The butt of all jokes. *You used to be our color* they would tell me, *but you just so dirty*; or *You're a little monkey boy.* It didn't help that I was wetting the bed, even at seven years of age.

Even my grandmother, the one who called me "smart and handsome," got into the act. My sister Che' and I were considered the "dark" ones.

*Come in this house nigger. You're getting too black out there.*

*I don't care grandma* I would always say.

*Nigger I do.* I guess I was handsome, but not when I was too dark.

And so once again, as I had been when my cousins' dads played with them in my backyard, I would be on the outside looking in as I stayed inside looking out at other people my age having fun without me. I just thought it was something I was supposed to do because Grandma said so.

Yet, we were cared for. Bath at 7:30, bed at 8:00. Sometimes it was a little too much. When in the second grade, grandma was still giving me a bath and putting on my deodorant for me, I just decided I'd had enough. *You know what Grandma? I think I got it now,* I finally said to her. That was the last time she washed me. Sometimes you just have to speak up for yourself.

---

My grandfather was cool, but older. My uncles were my uncles—they didn't always include me in activities with my cousins. The cousins I was living with were young. I didn't really have anyone that I looked up to except my father, who was more of a legend and a perception that a real human person I could touch and see and emulate.

Until one day.

I was seven years old. I was going outside, out the back door. I see a man with a cool casual walk coming up the driveway, holding a small boy with one arm, as the other arm swung with every cool stride. I thought the kid was his. The man is wearing a blue velour *Fila* jumpsuit with red trimming, a white *Kangol* hat, and a thick gold rope chain. The kid is dressed just like him. He reminds me of a movie star.

*What's up li'l nigga?* He said. *You know who I am?*

The only person that's supposed to look this cool is…*My brother,* I answered. I had heard the stories about him by then and put two and two together. I overheard Grandma Juanita talking about how he was a drug dealer and that he had spent time in jail. He looked exactly the way I imagine drug dealers are supposed to look. Cool.

He looked at me kind of sideways. Then he started to play, boxing with me a little.

*Who's the little guy?* I asked.

*That's your nephew, Corey.*

*Whoa. I'm an uncle?* I hadn't quite put those two things together: my brother's son is my nephew. It made me feel like a cool kid, a big man, not the "baby" any more. I'm cool because he's cool and he's my brother and he has a kid and that kid is my nephew. My cousins had brothers too but none of them were that cool.

*You're real fresh.* My brother complimented me. The only other person that had complimented me was my Grandma Juanita. To have a cool man do it was huge. *Do you want an outfit like mine?*

What? I could dress like that too? *Yeah* I said, hiding my enthusiasm behind a poker face so I wouldn't look too eager, too…uncool.

*OK. I'm gonna get you one.*

*I got a good report card too.* I wanted to let this cool big brother know I was the whole package, no slouch.

*Let me see it* he answered. That's all I needed. I hurriedly moved toward the house, excited that a male person was taking an interest in me. It was exhilarating; it was not like anything I had experienced, I'm sure this is what Anthony and Brian felt when they interacted with their dads. The few times when I talked to my dad and the daily fun with Granddad; none of those experiences could touch this!

28

When I looked up to open the door, I saw Grandma Juanita. She looked bigger somehow. Her face was a stone. *Uh-oh.* She was clearly not happy. She's pissed.

*Get out of here nigger!* This was a totally new pronunciation of the word, not like any pronunciation of hers I had ever heard before.

He looked up. *Hey Grandma.*

*Don't call me Grandma! You-get-yo'-ass-out-of-here-don't-come-around-here-and-that-ain't-your-brother.* She said all this like it was one long word.

My new exciting world was already changing. *Yes it is!*

*Shut up nigger* (the pronunciation reserved just for me). *You get you're a-- in this house.*

So I went in the house, no further questions asked. But I overheard the end of their conversation.

*That's alright I still love you Grandma.* Then: *This is your great grandson.* Then he tried to make her feel guilty. *You're going to do that to your great grandchild?*

*I love you nigger but you got to get away from here.* He took my little nephew, his mini-me, with him, the one with the cool Filas and matching hat. I didn't see him for a while.

That was my brother. Terry Stuckey, AKA "T-Stuck." Allegedly one of the most infamous drug dealers in Detroit history. Made the cover of *Don Diva* magazine.

He's in Federal prison, serving a life sentence.

---

The summer after my second grade year I was hanging out with my mother's other son, my brother Mike. The twin whose brother died of SIDS (Sudden Infant Death Syndrome). His father is Michael Taylor, the one who taught my mother how to professionally shoplift. By this time, I have become accustomed to going to my mother's house. I have to wear a second persona there, a "badder" persona. You had to be a little bad, a little more assertive; you might get run over by all the powerful personalities in my mother's house.

I was watching my brother Mike, 14 years old, riding his bike up and down the street. *What are you doing?*

*Making these sales man.* He showed me a bunch of baggies filled with little white candlewax-looking balls.

*Are you selling people candlewax?* I asked in a way that only an innocent seven-year-old can ask. I was trying to figure out why people would want to buy such little balls; they'd never burn!

Mike explained patiently. *That's crack rock, bro.*

I said *You're a drug dealer* and he said *Yea I got to get this money.* He said *I'm a hustler man. Mom takes clothes, I sell crack. You got to have a hustle man* he said. *That's how we make money on this side. Check it out.*

Mike showed me the business. *See this baggie? This a twenty-dollar bag. This one* (it was smaller), *it's only ten.*

*This little bag cost 20 dollars?* I was fascinated. *What it do to 'em?*

*Get 'em high man.*

*Well, how much money you gonna make?*

He said *I'm trying to buy a car.*

Wow. I was impressed.

Mike pointed to this Camaro across the street. It was purple with a T-top and it had tinted windows and gold rims and when the guy started it up it was real loud and roared when the driver pulled off.

*Ain't you too young for a car?* I asked.

30

*Aw naw. You can be young with a car; you just got to pay for it.*

So I just sat back on the porch and watched him go up and down the block on that bike.

A few hours later: *You got that money for that car yet?*

*Almost.*

Later on that summer, he bought a Camaro. I saw Mike giving everyone money, even our older sister Tila.

One day, he came to Tila with a proposition. *Tila I want you to f--- this b--ch up.* Apparently this girl had hit Mike and Mike didn't believe in hitting women, at the time. But he didn't mind another one doing it.

Tila was down for it. By now Mike had the Camaro. We got in the car, I hopped in the back seat, and we drove off to where the girl was.

*What's up now?* Mike asked the girl. *Big Tila here gon' whup yo' a--!*

Wasting no time, Tila hit the girl twice knocking her to the ground. She wrapped her hair around her fist and dragged her over to a tree. Then she beat her head into the tree, securely lodging the girl's head between the two very large tree trunks that had grown together. After she was limp, bleeding, and the scream turned into a whimpering whine, Tila let her body drop to the ground.

Mike smiled. *Here's 100 bucks,* he said. Even though Tila was three years older than him, he felt like the oldest sibling to me now.

Mike taught me a lot that summer. The basics of selling crack, how to have sex with girls. He even let me watch. The girls didn't even seem to mind.

I didn't mind either. Grandma Juanita was not a "church lady," so I didn't get any of those values from home. That would come much, much later. I just knew that Mike paid attention to me, that he was cool, that he was a man and (I didn't really understand this yet) I needed an older male to emulate. In my mind, he and my brother Terry were perfect. Two cool guys. Two cool brothers.

# CHAPTER 4

## New Tricks

I noticed her doing it before. There were all kinds of clues. I would notice the large bags with clothes in them, tags still attached, which were always around her house. She was always bringing over clothes to my Grandma Juanita's house. I had never seen so many clothes in garbage bags. It got me thinking: if they came from a department store or mall, why would she need garbage bags? So between that, eavesdropping on Grandma's conversations—and then there were the times I saw her steal from grocery stores—I was able to piece the not-so-hard puzzle together. I heard the conversations and I saw the evidence.

So by the time she said:

*Shawn. It's time for you to learn the catalog order business...*

...it wasn't news to me at all. I had gone out with her so many times when she was shoplifting. She had always kind of acted as if she didn't think I knew what was going on. But there's only so much acting you can do with a kid when you're in a car and the kid can simply peer over the seat and ask himself, "What is that my mom is bringing out of the side of her dress?"

It made me feel grown, in a sense, that she could tell me something that I probably wasn't supposed to know. It made me feel like a "man".

But it also confirmed for me that, yes, my mom really was a thief. No question there anymore. No imagining there might be other reasons for the way she walked kind of bow-legged coming out of the stores, or the way she looked around as if she were "casing" the place. Wow. Disappointment mixed with a strange kind of pride. After all, I was "in" now. In on the secret. In on the intrigue. In on the excitement.

I was officially a part of the team.

Mom said she never would tell her children about her "catalog order business" until they were "half of 20," or ten years old. I didn't see her that much, so by the time she told me I was 11.

*I'm going to show you the Sandwich,* mom said to me one day prior to heading to Jacobson's in Grosse Pointe, Michigan.

The "Sandwich" actually requires two people to work together, one standing in front of the other. Each person is able to see their view— 180 degrees around. Together, you can get the complete 360-degree lay of the land in the store. Finger moves and throat-clearing noises signaled whether someone might be watching and you should 'slow your roll.'

She even told me that I would get paid commission based on how much we were able to acquire. That's when my eyes got wide!

On the way to Jacobson's, I was nervous. Plus, I had to drive—again, I was 11 years old. Mom taught her children to drive when they were young so that she could prep and package the clothes, especially on cross-country excursions. Her business was national. My younger brother Doug was in the back seat. He was six years old at the time, and he doesn't "know" what's going on yet. Or does he?

We drove past big homes with circular driveways. People weren't "running from threats," they were "running for exercise," they were "walking their dogs." This is a far cry from my westside Detroit neighborhood, and I'm taking it all in. So it's not just all on TV; there were really people who lived this way!

My mom was dressed and walking funny. Her butt looked bigger and she looked bowlegged, even though I knew she wasn't. She taught me well. And so we walked into Jacobson's. Mom wore her infamous ankle length flower print "boosting" dress. She stuck her butt out and walked bowlegged to match her exiting walking style when she has tons of clothes in her girdle between her legs. Doug and I were walking close behind her with blue jeans, belts around our waist, and neatly tucked button-down shirts.

34

*Remember*, says Mom, *sandwich*. *I got it, I got it*, I tell her. My younger brother Doug looks at us quizzically. *What are you doing? What is a 'sandwich'? We're just going out to eat afterwards*, I tell him. That sounded like something Mike would have told me.

We are on the women's clothing floor. Mom is looking around, and I finally understand for the first time what she meant by "John's." We are in Jacobson's, and I realized that "John's" just meant St. John's clothing. You can pay $3,000-$6,000 for a St. John's dress or suit. Her plan was to go in the store and lift about four to six of those expensive pieces. This is the first time I really am paying attention; despite my small stature, I have been upgraded from a tagalong son to a co-conspirator. So I look around, doing my "sandwich" view, feeling a little paranoid. What if we get caught? She sure was putting a lot of faith in a rookie. Where the heck is Mike or Tila when you need 'em?

Mom is grabbing multiple outfits from the clothes rack, and it was hard to see how many pieces she had. It was deliberate. After choosing different sizes and an array of colors, she puts all the clothes gingerly over her arm, then asks a woman, in a very familiar tone, *Hey girl, can I get a room?*

*Absolutely*, says the woman. Mom acts like she has been there many times before. She has. The fact that it was so natural seems strange to me somehow. It is as if I was looking at her doing this for the very first time. I really didn't pay that much attention before.

While in the dressing room, my mother asks the woman for several of the same pieces. *This size is too snug around my hips*, she tells her. It is clear that her "work" is well-thought out, systematic, planned, and intentional. In a way, I am proud of her. She is doing her thing. It kinda reminded me of Mike zooming up and down the street on his bike with those baggies.

At this point, I am outside of the "Ladies Only" dressing room. I am thinking about the operation, wondering what I would have to do next, preparing to look as innocent as possible if we got caught. Then Doug breaks my concentration.

*You know what she doin'?*

I laugh. *Whatchu talking about?*

*I know what she's doin'. We always do this.* Then he looked at me with a look that made him seem much older than six.

*Make sure you watch out for her,* he warns.

Doug had seen my older brother and sister do these excursions with mom. He clearly knows the drill as well as, if not better, than I.

But he is still six, and he has to use the bathroom.

Doug knows the seriousness of the moment. But he was young, and he has to "go." And Mom is taking all day in the dressing room.

I watch as Doug walks smack dead into the middle of a dress rack across the room. He disappears, making me even more nervous. About two minutes pass, then he reappears and sits right next to me. I ask him *What did you do?* He places his little hand on my shoulder and answers, "Well, you gotta do what you gotta do." He is far too advanced for his own good.

If my thinking is correct… He can't be serious and we better hurry up and get out of here.

Stoned-faced, he looks up at me. *Don't say nothing, it's all good. Be cool big bro.*

Mom walks out of the dressing room, even more bowlegged. She says to the lady she had spoken to, *I'm going to get this blouse, everything else just didn't fit right today.*

*What about this belt?* asks the saleswoman.

Holding the belt to her waist, Mom continues the charade. *Well, it does look good on me girl. I'll take it.*

Yeah… she'll take it alright. After all, she had about $30,000 worth of merchandise in that ankle length dress. What's a $100 belt to that?

Suddenly, we hear some commotion… right around that rack where Doug had mysteriously gone.

*Oh my god, that smell! Is that… s--t?* The store ladies had found out what Doug just "had to do." Doug plays right into it. Looking confused, he asks "What happened over there?" All of a sudden he is six years old again. He sounds much more innocent than before, when he had just told me to "watch out" for Mom.

*I'll see you later,* Mom says to the lady, walking out with her stash carefully hidden in her bowed legs and large hips. Just in case someone was watching, Mom drives the car out of the Jacobson's parking lot for me. We run to get gas and switch places, so I was driving again. Mom began to pull out the clothes; I drove to McDonald's and got Doug something to eat. When Doug and I come out she tells me, *I got five John's.*

A lot happened that summer, the summer of my 11th year. And it was all a bit unsettling and confusing. You see, I was living with my Grandma Juanita, my father's mother and her husband, my step-grandfather M.C., during the school year. At Grandma Juanita's house, there were rules. You have to be "good"—or at least look like you were. So at first, while I was proud that my mother was letting me in on her very confidential-adult activity—even if it was cool and exciting—stealing was hard for me. Grandma Juanita had put the fear of God in me about doing wrong, so I felt a tug of guilt. Just not enough to tell my mother "No."

Another thing: my Mom's "business" wasn't what you would exactly call "slick." I didn't necessarily mind being slick. But this… It was cut throat, bold, and "in your face" activity. I guess I was OK serving as the lookout, the one who saw the other 180°, but this hustle, I decided, was not for me.

At 11, I was making decisions about my future that were based on seeing what other people around me were doing. I was observant. I was making adult-level assessments and didn't even realize it.

Doug was another story. He had absolutely no problem participating with Mom in the business. He watched her closely enough that he got the hang of the strategy. That same summer, we would go out to the outlet malls like Birch Run and visit stores like Tommy Hilfiger and Nike. Eventually mom went against her own rules of "half of twenty". Doug was in on the gig younger than all of us. He was a natural hustler of all sorts.

"I want these shoes," I would point out to Mom, knowing that she knew how to get them for me. This must have been what it was like to be rich, I thought. You could just point to things and your parents would get them for you. Magic!

My brother was a bit different. *I want these Nikes, these Tommy Hilfigers…but I can get my own.* He would go into the dressing rooms and, just like he had seen Mom do, put clothes under his clothes. If it was cold, he'd wear a bubble coat, where he could slip some of those tiny children-sized gym shoes right into the sleeves, just under his underarms. No salesperson would ever know the difference. Not even the security guards took note of Doug. He was just so young, and so polite. *What a nice little boy,* people would think to themselves. Doug never gave them any reason to think otherwise.

Until quite later.

Meanwhile, I was serving as my mom's lookout, and asking for some of the nice clothes. I thought of myself as her helper, but not really deeply involved in wrongdoing. There was only one "wrongdoing" that I could really get excited about.

Touching girls. I was fascinated by girls, pretty much like any boy coming into manhood.

Touching girls was the only thing I would actually initiate on my own. In all other matters illegal or immoral, I was just someone else's helper. If I was with Mom, I was a lookout. If my brothers wanted me to sell something, I sold it. If someone needed me to fight, I would help them out. I was around a lot of initiators, and I was perfectly content to follow their lead…as long as I didn't have to get too deeply in their mud.

And on our "shopping" excursions, I was nervous EVERY SINGLE TIME. I remember once or twice trying to put something under my clothes in the dressing room, but I would always take it off. Too scared. Mom would say "I wish you were a bit more helpful…like your brother." Just as if she were saying, "I wish you would do the dishes more often."

Later, I would finally try to pull it off. It did not end well.

I was 15 and went into the Hudson's at Fairlane Mall just outside of Detroit. I was with my friends, and they had decided to lift some Girbaud jeans by putting them on under their pants in the dressing room. I went in and tried to do it myself. My friends and I were reaching under the stall, passing jeans to each other. They had done this countless times before, and many of them had a nice stash of the high-end jeans.

I came out with my Girbauds under my pants. I thought I was home free, walking through the clothes racks approaching the exit of the department store and the entrance of the mall…

"Hudson's LP (undercover police) m----f----." Two big guys hoisted me off the ground, each grabbing an armpit. They came out of nowhere! Two of my boys had already escaped the store and were looking down at me from an upper level with their hands over their mouths. Then they ran. The "Hulk" sized Hudson's LP twins drug me to the "back room," along with one of my homeboys.

It was my first time going to jail. I had never been slick at this and this time, my nervousness landed me in big trouble.

The guards had been watching our every move in the dressing room. They saw us passing clothes back and forth. They heard us talking and laughing. We were sitting ducks for them.

They had us in individual holding cells, intimidating us and trying to get us to snitch on each other. In time, my grandfather came to the jail.

Did he scold me? Threaten to beat me when I got home? None of that for him.

Boy, you gotta be slicker than that," he told me. Then he explained how he used to get away with it. "Put a number of pants together to mask the product and get your own size! Don't be passin' s--t under the dressin' room. Tisk Tisk."

*My baaaad granddad. Good look, comin' through for me.*

The police drop the charges thinking my granddad was going to take care of me. Yeah, he took care of me alright. He made sure I would get it right next time.

The times I really tried to be slick, it had just the opposite effect. Mom had decided to make a "run" to Ohio, to visit a department store there. We were looking for "Coogi" sweaters; any and everybody who had style rocked Coogi's in the early '90s. Even granddad had a couple.

I was doing the "sandwich," feeling very comfortable, and I cleared my throat. It wasn't that I saw anything; it was just a little "too" quiet. I wanted to be completely sure that we didn't get in trouble with law on my behalf.

My mother tried her best to ignore my signals to stop what she was doing. "This is a nice color, isn't this nice?" Always in hyper-cautious mode, she avoided saying my name.

Then she went back at it again. But I still felt something was not right. I couldn't put my finger on it, and kept clearing my throat and rustling my fingers.

Finally Mom said "You know what, as she smiled, I don't like anything here." She sounded a bit perturbed, but I felt good…like I was doing some "shot-calling." "Yeah" with confidence, "let's get out of here."

As we drove home, Mom asked "What's going on?"

"It was too quiet in there," I explained. "It just didn't feel right."

She looked at me, nostrils flaring. "That's because they were not paying attention AT ALL! You couldn't see what I saw…they were busy doing something else. I just need you to watch your side; I see everything else!"

So I messed up a couple thousand dollars. So what? I didn't dare say that out loud or let my eyes say it for me. I nodded in agreement… After all, she's the klepto guru.

My mother did not feel the same nonchalance as I. We got back to my sister Tila's, where my mom was living at the time, and Mom started talking about what kind of money she needed. "That m----f---- messed me up," she said downstairs while I was upstairs, hearing everything. "He's so damn paranoid. I just can't deal with this." I heard her come upstairs.

"Shawn!"

"Yes?"

"If you f--- up my money one more f---ing time."

"I was just trying to help."

Pow! She hit me right in the mouth, full fist.

It knocked me back and my lip was busted. A tear trickled down my face and I thought to myself, *I don't really like you much anyway, and I'm nearly 12.* I contemplated whether I could "take" her or not. But I just let her go ahead and curse me out and stood there. After she finished I went to the back bedroom, mad. I wanted to hurt her. I was frustrated

41

because I couldn't retaliate. I was used to whippings from Grandma Juanita for doing the wrong thing. But that even stopped a couple years ago. I couldn't deal with the fact that I was getting beaten for not doing the "wrong" thing, right.

Some kids wish their parents were present. I was not one of those kids. That day, and many days afterwards, I just wished that she were absent. For my money, at that time, she could have disappeared and never come back and it would not matter to me one bit.

My Grandma Juanita was all I needed. Bad cooking, bad breath, cursing, and all, she was my angel. This chick… She could kick rocks and watch the wind blow in a desert for all I cared.

I said it was an eventful summer, right? The very next day after my mother punched me in the mouth, I was out with my brother Mike. Mike was a "Boss" in the drug game. He showed me how to cut crack. I figured any new trick was better than my mom's BS.

I had seen the little baggies when I was seven, when Mike first started coming around. Now, Mike is 18. He has cars, money, Jordans—a cool guy. The 'hood star. Like everybody in my world, Mike had a hustle. Just like my mom. Just like my dad, who hustled in the factory. Just like my brother, T. Stuck who allegedly sold dope too. At least that's what I heard. The nice thing about Mike's hustle: it wasn't as "in your face" as Mom's. He did his a little more secretively. It just seemed cooler to me, less blatant.

I was at my sister Tila's house when Mike came in one day. He had some blocks of crack on the table. We called them bricks, Ya-yo, or Ya (Pronounced as Yay). The bricks look like huge blocks of plain candlewax, an off-eggshell yellow tint. I came in, and he stood up and said, "Hey man, go ahead, go in the back."

This time, I didn't want to go in the back. "What are you doing?" I said. I smiled knowingly. "You over there makin' some money huh?

"Yeah, you know me li'l bro," Mike said.

42

"Can I see?"

"Hmmmm... Ummmm... C'mon nigga," said Mike (I was used to everyone, from my friends to my grandparents, calling me that), "I guess you can help me a li'l bit."

"OK, so what is this?" Grinning I rubbed my hands together. "You've showed me this before."

"Yeah, but I ain't showed you how to cut it, I wasn't tryin' to do all that with you." This is how I make money fareal. I want you to keep doing what you doing in school, but this, only if you really wanna know I'll show you. I don't want you playing with Ya. But, it's best if you learn from me than somebody else." He showed just a little reluctance.

In the 'hood, most people can respect those in their community who want an education. Most people. There is a feeling of camaraderie in some circles and particularly with family. The feeling that your success is the community's or family's success, something the people can take pride in. It's just the level of desperation and hopelessness that keeps people like Mike in survival mode. There was an instinctual part of him that wanted to shield me from all of this, to make sure I would stay in school and do well.

Yet he still said, "If you wanna know I'll show you." Almost a kind of resignation, the kind that droops your shoulders and makes you throw up your hands. "OK. Remember this is your decision and not mine, come on and go with me." That's what desperation with a hint of creativity in the 'hood looks like. You don't know anything else, and you don't think your hopes will go any higher than in old trees lining the old streets. So you stop dreaming and start doing. Then doing becomes your dream.

Mike showed me how to use safety pins after the bricks were broken down to mold the Ya into little rocks called "20s." The rocks were stiff and crumbly enough to break easily. The 20s were little, about a quarter cubic inch. Mike used a "triple beam scale," a weighing device that could measure substances in grams. To me, he was like a mad scientist.

After hours Mike would put all the perfect 20s in baggies. The little pieces that were smaller than 20s were called "shake." They went into "shake baggies"—the "clearance" items. You could get a good deal on shake. The dope fiends didn't care, they just wanted to get high.

So I started helping Mike that very day. I cut really good 20s with precision. I had a Good pile, an OK pile and a Shake pile, but my "Good" pile was really good and plentiful. I felt good; I was helping my bro'. Not to mention, big bro' paid me for my services.

I started to really like the idea of having a hustle. Easy money!

One evening after I finished breaking down a brick of Ya, Mike said: "Yo. Come wit me." We walked out of Tila's house to his burgundy Camaro, with the gold rally stripes on the hood, spoiler, T-Tops, gold rims, tan interior, and the ground gear shift. Mike loved cars.

We hopped in the Camaro and the pipes yelled heartedly as the engine started and Mike revved the engine. *He had motor skills and loved to use them; He never stayed still,* Mike. He would just drive through the neighborhood, showing off his Camaro and seeing if there were any customers. There always were.

That day, we were both wearing black leather pants and black & white Jordan 9's, with Jordan t-shirts, and leather Pelle Pelle jackets to ward off the chill at night. We were matching! You couldn't tell either one of us that we weren't the coolest brothers on the planet.

Mike created a very simple communications system to exchange cash and drugs. Customers looking for what Mike had to offer would blink their hi-beams twice. In turn, Mike would pull up behind them and engage the exchange.

We pulled up behind a blue Ford Taurus. Mike said, "Go ask what he need," nodding towards the car parked ahead of us.

I opened the door. "I gotchu bro." and proceeded to walk across the front of the Camaro to the driver side door of the Taurus.

He was a white guy, 50-ish with a beard and a crew cut. He was balding at the top and kinda heavy. He manually rolled his window down. Peering into the car, I asked him "What you need?

"Give me two twenties."

"Alright, I'll be back."

Running back toward the Camaro I yelled at my bro'. "Pull off, he's 5-0!" (code for "police") my brother said "Aight!" and burned rubber as we pulled off.

He looked like a classic cop and I wanted to do something exciting and decided to say it because I'd heard it before. I thought: "We're not getting caught today!" It was just a hunch, just like I had with my mom when I would clear my throat to get the heat off of us.

It turned out that he really was not a police officer.

My brother's response, however, was a little softer than my mother's that day when I misread the signs at the clothing store.

"That's good that you had a feeling, but this guy was one of my regulars," he explained. "I just pulled off to let you know that I trust your judgment. So…that's lesson number one for you. Trust your gut! "

I appreciated the fact that he didn't punch me in the mouth like Mom did. That was respect. Not like her at all.

Every so often, in the drug game, there is something called the "Drought Season." It can last anywhere from a couple weeks to a couple months. During that time, bricks aren't available from big distributors.

But drug dealers aren't known for their honor, and money still has to be made.

"What's that?" I asked Mike one day during Drought Season.

"Candlewax."

"What for?"

"Drought Season. No dope. So you gotta do something to make money. When they light it up, they gonna be sucking on candlewax." Mike shrugs his shoulders.

My brother would actually sell candlewax to crackheads. He would break them into "20s," just like the real thing. I wasn't as good at breaking up the candlewax, so I left that job to the expert.

The crackheads didn't retaliate. They feared the drug dealers.

I recall witnessing some of the antics of Drought Season. I once saw a middle-aged black guy with grey hair pull up in the middle of the street to a trap house (house that sells drugs) driving a brand new, '93, cocaine white Jeep Cherokee. The dealer approached the vehicle and said "What you need?" As he asked him, another guy snuck up to the back of the truck on the driver side with a big metal fan. He crouched down and waited. The cage was removed from the front so the metal blades where exposed.

"I need three 20s," said the driver.

"Cool." The dealer reached in his pocket and pulled his hands out quickly reaching for the driver's neck yanking him out of the driver side window!  Instantly, the other guy with the fan ran from behind the truck bashing the crackhead's face in with the fan blades. They beat him pretty bad, took his money and drove off…in his truck. He laid there bleeding and squirming in the middle of the street. No one said anything. The drug dealers were feared.

I was playing basketball in the driveway with my brother when I saw the incident. I looked at my brother for an explanation as he stared straight at the squirming guy in the street.

Mike slowly shook his head and came back to reality he turned toward me and said, "Now let me school you. That was straight up theft. It

46

happens a lot during Drought Season when there isn't much Ya to sell. During the good seasons, sometimes a customer will lend his car or truck to a dealer to get some crack. It's called a "base rental." I'm cool with a base rental, but that hot crap right there…. That's just terrible." Mike looked back in the street. The grey haired man was still squirming. We kept playing ball.

I was proud of him that day. He might sell fake crack during drought season, but at least my brother never smashed a crackhead's face in with metal fan blades. He had some morals.

We continued playing basketball until it was too dark, and we went back to Tila's house, where my mom, he and I were all living. Remember, I was only there for the summer; I would be going back to Grandma Juanita's soon for school.

We walked in, and smelled a distinctive yet familiar sour-sweet smell. We knew that smell anywhere. He looked at me, head bowed down to the floor. I looked in the back to see who might be there. All my nieces and nephews were gone.

I called downstairs. "Ma."

"Huh?"

"Whatchu doing?"

"I'm comin up."

"What's up Mom. Who downstairs?"

No answer from Mom. Just footsteps as she walked up the stairs.

She didn't answer my question, so I went downstairs into the basement. No one else was there. But the air was thick.

Somebody was smoking crack down there. I knew it. Marijuana smoke was in the air meshed with the familiar smell of "51s." 51s are a

47

combination of marijuana and crack mixed together and smoked for a different kind of high.

I went back upstairs and looked at Mike. He looked at me. I shook my head. He was talking to Mom, and he kept talking as if nothing had happened. I was trying to get his attention, but he didn't look back at me.

Instead, he went off with Mom into another room. I heard his muffled voice, scolding her. "Two things... 1. I told you, you can have all the weed you want, but leave that crack s--t alone! 2. What the hell are you doing smoking that s--t in this house? Kids are in and out of here all day!" She was silent.

When Mike came out, it was clear he was trying not to appear hostile. But I knew he was angry. I followed him out of the house. I guess he was trying to get me away from the situation.

I guess he was trying to get himself away, too.

With Mom, you never know what you're going to get from one day to the next. Tila beating girls up. Li'l Doug, youngest hustler of all time, crapping on expensive clothes. Mike selling crack. Mom stealing clothes. Me? I just like the ladies, although I was gaining a strong appreciation for hustling in general.

My grandmother on my mom's side, Grandma Virginia, didn't care for my Grandma Juanita. She wanted to let me know that my dad's side wasn't as good as I thought they were.

One day, that same summer, I was down the street from Tila's house at Grandma Virginia's place and she told me: "I know you know about your mama. She been snortin' and poppin' dopes with you in her stomach. Your daddy didn't make it no better. If he wasn't snortin' dopes he damn sure drank too much." She told how he would abuse her on a number of occasions and even kicked her down steps, how he wanted her to stop stealing. They would even have snorting and drinking parties.

48

"Plus your dad wanted your mom to stay put at home and not put dopes in her while she was pregnant. He had a good job. But he was not a saint! Not at all."

As usual, she went on and on…

The difference in the two families gave me two distinct identities for myself. So on my mom's side, I was a "goodie-goodie." After all, they were stealing and dealing drugs, and in fact made a living strictly doing illegal stuff. So the fact that all I did was help out during my visits and try to get with the girls made me look like a saint.

On my dad's side, I was considered "slick," pretty much because I spent those summers at Tila's and my dad's family had a good idea what was going on over there. And my dad, even though he was supposedly abusive and enjoyed a strong drink, at least went to work every day and had what they would call a "good job."

It was a confusing time, and I was still looking for—in fact, thought I had found—my space in the world.

Mom had a boyfriend that we called "pops." One day I came in from riding my bike around the neighborhood, and Mom had a swollen black eye.

"What happened to you?" I asked her.

"This MF, I'ma tell you what I'ma do." Mom was clearly upset and angry. She told me: "Gone in the back."

Pops came in and they started arguing. She said "m----f---- if you hit me one more m----f---'n time, I'm gon kill you b--ch. I'ma f--- you up." He said "Dee Dee, you the one trying to hurt me. I got to get you up off me." Then he said: "I'm out. I ain't messing with you today."

I thought: she must have provoked him. After all, she had stabbed her old boyfriend Ed with a screwdriver. Mom didn't play around. "Pops" knew that about her. Although he punched her in the face, I think he didn't want to hurt her. I know for a fact he didn't want to get hurt.

That was my first time witnessing a domestic violence encounter, but it surely wasn't the last.

A couple weeks later my brother Mike landed himself in jail and stayed there for several nights. Some police had flagged and stopped him. He had crack in his possession, but swallowed all of the plastic baggies and threw up later in his cell. The police never found the crack, but the police did find a pound of weed under the passenger seat and locked him up. Weed wasn't a big problem, but crack would send you away for a long time.

Mike was dating a girl named Kenyatta. Upon release he came home to Tila's, he was pissed that his girlfriend didn't write him.

"I was in there and the b---- didn't write me."

He was only in there for four days. The officers wouldn't let her visit, so in Mike's mind, the least she could've done was write.

Kenyatta knocked on Tila's door, No one was home but Mike, my three-year-old nephew Jeril, and me.

"Baby," said Mike. Reaching out to her with both hands he embraced her head and kissed her on the forehead, holding her close. Then he aggressively grabbed her neck and threw her down the kitchen steps to the basement. She screamed all the way down. Mike ran down behind her. "B--ch if you ever don't come see me, after all I do for you, and you don't make sure I'm good, I'm gon f--- you up."

After he threw her down the stairs, I took my nephew Jeril in the back room. His eyes began to tear up. "They have some stuff to work out... Just watch TV li'l buddy," I told him, trying to downplay what he had seen. I turned the volume up and closed the door behind me. I went to the top of the steps and saw Kenyatta was still crying and was at the bottom of the steps, while Mike was standing over her. With my 11-year-old mind, I thought that I could de-escalate the situation. "Bro! Bro! Chill out man!"

50

Mike looked at me with these eyes I had never seen before. "Get you're a-- in the back room." The eyes were piercing and watery, as if he was hurt, and tight lipped. He pointed his finger towards the back room. "Yessir!" Without hesitation I zipped to the back room. There were vents throughout the house so I could hear him from any room. "You don't give a f---!" He was yelling. "You know you don't give a f---! You lied! For your lyin' a--, know what? I got something for you. Go get my gun!"

"No Mikey no." she said.

He wasn't moved. "B--ch, go get my gun!"

I'm thinking, 'Bro' I don't know what you're going to do, but I don't think you want to necessarily give HER the gun.'

Nonetheless, Kenyatta slowly walked up the steps whimpering to get the gun from the front closet. You could tell by the sound of her footfalls that she was limping. My nephew was crying. "Get under the bed," I told him. "Just calm down. You'll be protected here under the bed; nothing's gonna happen to you," I whispered. He stopped crying, and we got under the bed together. In the meantime, she's going to my brother with the gun, still crying.

"Hurry you're a-- up!" Mike shouted. She handed Mike the gun, saying "Please! Jesus!"

"You know what? What I'm 'bout to give you, Jesus can't help you." What I heard next was thumps and some tussling. When I next saw Kenyatta, she was bruised. He apparently wanted to just scare her. I could tell he maybe hit her with something. I just know that whatever he was doing, it worked.

When my mom got back, Kenyatta left. In fact, all three of them left— together. But they didn't break up, and my mother never talked about it, and I never asked.

A few days later—maybe a week—I saw cars racing down the street from both directions. I was in the front yard, and saw a black van with black windows, then several Ford Explorers. They screeched in front of the house and several men jumped out in police uniforms and vests. Jeril was with me. I grabbed him and went in the house. They went in the backyard armed with guns and dogs. Dogs snarled and policed yelled "sit down," so I did as they said. I was clean, no drugs on me. They tore up pillows, opened drawers, moved TVs and furniture, pulled items out of cabinets and threw them to the floor. I just wished they would find what they were looking for.

My sister Tila was cursing up a storm as the officer questioned her loudly. "Where is he? You know what we're looking for. Where is Michael Thomas, and where are the narcotics? We know you got it in here!" She said "Oh you gon' flip my couch over. Ain't this some s--t! OK, go ahead, flip it over. I'm 'posed to sit here lookin' at that?" They handcuffed her. "We don't want to hurt you," they said, smirking as they tightened the cuffs around Tila's wrist.

Then an officer yelled "Bingo!" He held a drawer in his hand from my nephew's room. The drawer was filled with a powdery substance. The officer licked the tip of his pinky finger and placed it gently in the drawer. He rubbed the substance between his pinky and thumb to check for the consistency, then placed it on his tongue. His shoulders dropped and he stared at Tila. "It's baby powder."

The police said "Oh. Sorry." They never found anything, just a couple of marijuana joints aka 'roaches', but they can't put you in jail for that. I waited for them to straighten the place back up. But that never happened. That was my first time seeing a police raid. "Why the heck would they do this?" I thought. I knew if they had been at my Grandma Juanita's she would have had a fit. She never would have stood for it.

That was the first of quite a few raids.

I never saw this at Grandma Juanita's house. And I couldn't wait to get back there.

# CHAPTER 5

## Surprises

Even though I couldn't wait to get back to Grandma Juanita's when I knew I was going back at the end of the summer, in some ways I was disappointed. Admittedly, I had fun with my bros and my mom and my sister Tila. I had more money, more clothes, hung with a bunch of hustlers. I felt like a "young boss."

But even with that, I preferred my grandmother's. It was a relief. She was my safe haven. I could breathe again at her home.

I got back to Grandma's in late August right after my 12th birthday, but before school started. She said what she always says when I return from my Mom's. "Time to re-program you nigger." I knew what that meant. There would be no examples of drug dealing, stealing clothes, or fighting. The only "bad examples" adults would exhibit at Grandma Juanita's house were drinking, a bit of card gambling, and a few choice curse words. Granddad goes to work and she irons and cooks bad food.

But my cousins are there. I can go outside and play with kids my age. I can be a regular kid—riding bikes, playing basketball, having fun. We won't be dragged into adult mess unless it's on our own accord. The missions are over and it's back to earth…for now.

It was early in the morning, about 8 a.m. on a Saturday. I overheard Granddad talking on the phone. I heard him say that my brother Terry, "T-Stuck," was shot in the head and the knee. He went to the hospital, but his head was only grazed and he was OK. "That boy like Superman," Granddad said. "He take bullets and spit 'em out. Get in trouble and then get out. Won't nothin' stick to that boy. That boy know how to make money, stay outta trouble, and dodge bullets. People aught to leave that boy alone. He a good kid and a hell of a business man." Granddad loved to talk trash.

I thought: 'My brother is a Superhero. He doesn't get into petty, small time issues.' For me, he was the big-time man. Especially since he started making music! He was my true role model, my idol. More than Mike. More than Grandma Juanita. More than anyone I had ever met. Ever since our first encounter. I was proud to call him "brother."

I was glad he was okay. Besides, Grandma Juanita wasn't going to let me visit him in the hospital. She made it her business to keep me away from him.

I needed to clear my mind. Fortunately, I had made a few bucks from doing household chores. I headed outside on a mission to the go cart races, skipping rocks in the neighborhood, walking down some old railroad tracks when I came to a break in the tracks and crossed the street. I looked to my left and thought 'that's Granddad's truck. Why is he parked there?' Random...

"Hey Granddad! Hey!"

His head was leaned back on the headrest as if he was taking a nap. He jolted at the sound of my voice. I saw glimpses of him adjusting his pants. "What the heck is he doing?" I thought. Then I saw someone lift up her head from his lap. It was a woman, a woman I had seen before. Now I wasn't a rocket scientist but I knew what was going on. That had to be broken up. Quick!

"Hey. What's going on?"

I recognized the woman. She would drive down the street in a pink Escort. I remembered that Granddad left the house every time she drove past. My grandma talked about that a lot. He even bought and resold guns from her son all the time.

I squinted my eyes and stared at her. I wanted to smash her head between trees like Tila did that chick that disrespected Mike. This broad was disrespectful on another level! I wasn't mad at granddad, but I didn't like HER. She was a fake looking grandma with freckles, definitely not MY grandma.

56

Granddad said, "Where you going boy?"

I played it cool. "To the go-carts."

"Granddad: Alright. I'll meet you there."

"Okay Granddad!" I smiled at him and snarled at her for a couple intense seconds before I headed to the go cart track. I went around a couple of times. I only had enough for two rounds. Then Granddad pulled up.

"Hey boy. Wanna go for some more laps?"

I sure did. I must have gone around fifty more times!

I was milking it now. "How about some video games?"

Then granddad said "How 'bout we go to Shopper's World?"

He bought me some clothes, music CD's (E-40's "Captain Save 'Em" to be exact), and a pair of sunglasses. "You know you gotta keep this between you and me."

Granddad saved me from a bunch of whippings. I didn't want to tell on him so he would get one too!

The go-carts were a good time, but I was still worried about my brother in the hospital. A couple days later, Grandma and I were in the kitchen. According to Grandma I was still in my "reprogram" phase.

Grandma made french fries from real potatoes. I loaded a bowl full of fries and grabbed the ketchup from the refrigerator. I pulled up a chair to the kitchen table and squeezed a healthy amount of ketchup in the bowl for dipping. I put the ketchup back in the fridge. She turned around and saw my plate shaking her head. When I finished she said, "Nigger, you mean you're going to sit there and waste all that ketchup?"

Why did I ever say what came out of my mouth before I even realized who I was talking to?

"What you want me to do, put it back?"

Once I said it, I thought: 'Damn. Said it to the wrong one.' I could do that on my mom's side, but not here.

Grandma said: "Nigger you're not going to talk to me like you're crazy! You bring your a-- back here. You think you're crazy?"

"No," I said, somewhat sheepishly.

"I got something for your black a--!" She walked aggressively towards me, took her forearm, and swung for my head. I ducked. She hit her hand on the wooden baby crib that was newly installed in the living room right outside the kitchen as she was now taking care of another granddaughter's baby. She swung pretty hard, and fractured her forearm. "G-dammit!" she yelled.

I wish I had let her hit me. I would rather that than see her hurt herself.

Grandma's attention then turned to her arm.

She hopped on the phone and the next thing you know, Granddad came home and uncles came over to see what was going on. I got about five whippings that day. Granddad gave me an earful. Then Grandma whipped me with her good arm. Two uncles whipped me too. And my cousins were shaking their heads.

I couldn't have felt worse.

---

After Labor Day, it was back to school. I was looking forward to it. I liked school. There were plenty of girls, I get to show off my fancy clothes, and I got good grades. Perfect place for me.

The first day was a half-day, I think. It's hard for me to remember because it was the day where everything changed.

I came back home, walking by myself, happy to be back home, but feeling bad about my grandma's forearm. I decided to cheer her up, let her know how good the first day of school was.

Grandma?

Grandma?

Went in the kitchen. Not there. Basement. Not there.

I went back upstairs. "Granddad, where's grandma at?

"She went to the hospital. She had a heart attack."

A heart attack? I don't know exactly what that is, but I know it's not good.

We went to the hospital and Grandma had tubes everywhere. There was a breathing machine next to her bed, an air mask over her mouth and I.V. bags flanking her sides. She was unconscious. Beep. Beep. The air was getting thick. The room seemed to be moving in a slow circle. I walked down the hallway, woozy, feeling faint and weak. Finally, I fell to the ground. Granddad came and picked me up. My eyes were wide open but I couldn't see.

Grandma came home after about a week, but things weren't the same. She wasn't talking or moving like normal. She was quiet, randomly starring off into space, not quite registering everything, but trying to be herself. As it turned out, she'd had a stroke too.

A couple of weeks later, she was back in the hospital.

Grandma died October 5, 1994. I was 12 years old.

You have to understand, she had my whole life set up for me. Granddad was there; he was a provider, but he didn't run the house. He was there but he didn't look at my report card. Just the funny guy, the card player, the one who kept Grandma Juanita from beating me to death on occasions. I didn't know what life would be like without her. At the hospital, I cried hysterically.

Part of my hysteria was due to the fact that I definitely did not want to live with my mom year-round. I had stayed with my dad for a little while too, but didn't want to stay there either.

*O my God*, I thought. *What's about to happen to me?*

Granddad came into the hospital family room and saw me curled up next to a vending machine with blood shot red eyes and a full wet face. He was not sympathetic. "Shut up nigga," he said, as he placed his hand around my neck, "she ain't comin' back." I looked at him, and realized that what he was saying was true. Wow. I gotta get used to this. I stared at the floor and started thinking about different scenarios. Not Mom's. Not Dad's. No Grandma Juanita... Where could I possibly go?

I was somewhat relieved when my Dad walked in.

"Hey son? You'll be OK."

I was not so easily convinced. Throughout my short 12 years he has never solved one problem for me. "What's going to happen to me?"

"You're going to stay with your Granddad."

Figures that he would punt me over to someone else again.

Hmmmmm... That wasn't an option that I considered, but it was just fine with me. I breathed a little easier, although my best friend, first love, and life guide was gone.

---

Living with my granddad after my grandma died was an interesting experience. I believe that I took on his power. He was unbreakable. He wasn't moved by anything, he surprised and inspired me. Grandma Juanita's personality was so big, I must have overlooked his strengths.

He is, for me, yet another kind of "Super Hero." I mean, married to a woman for over 30 years and I didn't see one tear fall? That's serious.

So now: there is a difference in the house.

There are no rules. Uncle Menry, the crackhead uncle, is still in the basement. I can stay out a little bit later. Past 8pm. Then 8:15, 8:30, 9:00, 9:30. I come in and the response is the same every time: "Hey boy!"

But granddad didn't cook. So I ate a lot more TV dinners. More ramen noodles and hot pockets. And I had to prepare the food myself. Frozen beef patty burgers were a new taste sensation for me. Ironing my own clothes became part and of my new routine. I became a super washer and ironer. I starched, everything, just like Grandma. Ironed Granddad's clothes too. I had more responsibility. I had to take care of myself.

And Granddad didn't check my report card, didn't go to parent teacher conferences. Basically, I did whatever I wanted to do. I engaged even more with girls and hung out with the rest of my friends who always stayed out longer.

But I felt it was important for me to go to school. Smart was the one thing special about me. My Grandma told me I was smart, so I had to keep that intact. It was my way of paying homage to my angel. I considered that an integral part of my grieving process.

There was a gaping void that only a female could aid. Thus, my friend Jessica became my best friend shortly after Grandma Juanita left. We met each other in the 6th grade and I thought she was cool then, but by 7th grade I emotionally upgraded her role when Grandma Juanita left. She was the most beautiful girl in Charles Drew Middle School to me anyway. We were in band together, and I sat next to her. Deliberately. I played trumpet. She did too. I would ask her for her number every other day. And she didn't give it to me. One day she said "alright" and wrote 1-2-3-4-5-6-7. Eghh. I think she couldn't have phone calls.

So we became good friends. I even hooked her up with my cousin to prove that we were good friends. I had to convince her as well as myself. I didn't want my deeply rooted emotional attachment to cause me to lose her over a silly middle school boyfriend-girlfriend relationship. Hence, best friends worked perfectly fine with me.

Jessica was the only girl I talked to regularly that wasn't a "play toy" girl. She was the first girl I'd opened up to. We both came from interesting backgrounds and I told her about my family. I shared with her how I had seen every man in my life cheat. She told me I was gonna be a cheater too. "No. Not me," I told Jess. "I'm never gonna cheat on my girlfriend. I'm never gonna hit her. I'm gonna treat her real good, buy her stuff. I'm gonna be a good man. Fa Real!

I didn't want her to get the wrong impression, though. "But if I don't have a girlfriend, I'll do what I want."

I was 12.

Jessica's mom and dad were emotionally abusive to her. She was one of the smartest people I knew, but nobody ever told her. She shared how her family failed to love her properly. While living with her Mom, she was left alone often while her Mom was off with her boyfriend drinking and getting high.

We dealt with our family baggage differently. I just decided I'd be tough like my granddad. Jessica, on the other hand, just vented and cried.

By eighth grade, we started liking each other. But we weren't boyfriend and girlfriend. We ended up going to high school together. Graduating from high school was a big deal for both of us. I told her, "When we finish high school, it's me and you."

Of course things didn't happen that way, but we're still friends today.

This period after my grandma's death is an adjustment period. I'm adjusting to being alone. To growing up. To checking myself. I still spent some summers at my mom's and the same kind of things happened there—the excitement, the feeling like an adult, all became simply knowing I was "grown" a bit too early for my own good. But since I'm on my own, things are changing. I can do more. I can have girls over whenever. I can leave Monday and come back Thursday.

But I never took advantage of my freedom to my detriment. At least that's how I rationalized my freedom. Most importantly, I never skipped school. Well, once or twice, but it wasn't worth it. Never needed to. My friends felt the need to skip to engage in activity with girls, gambling, and drinking or smoking—those activities that couldn't take place at their homes. Fortunately for me, I could do whatever I wanted at home, anytime.

---

# CHAPTER 6

## Phone Calls

The first day of high school I woke up to my new room…in the basement. Uncle Menry was the former occupant and it had been a dusty dungeon when he was there. Granddad decided it was time for him to go. It was all mine now. I swept, mopped, and painted the chipping grey floor jet black. I kept the wooden panel walls yellow and bought a queen-sized bed. Somebody gave me a couch. Somebody else gave me a rug. I got a wooden closet set with multiple shelves and compartments for my clothes, cologne, shampoo, and soaps. I bought a 32-inch TV and linked it with a Sony® surround system. There was an old functional fireplace along the wall that we use to actually chop wood and heat the house when I was younger. I figure using heat from the furnace was just fine, but the aesthetics of the fireplace was a cool antique piece that made a bold statement. So, I placed a golden cage in front of it. Finito! Feeling pretty good… I had a bachelor pad. I had even lost weight over the summer… to make sure I was ready for swim class.

I was excited to go to Mackenzie High School. Although my grades were high and I was an honor student, I didn't want to go to a special magnet school like Cass Tech or Renaissance. The majority of my friends from my neighborhood went to Mackenzie. It was walking distance, directly across the street from my middle school, Drew Middle School, and I didn't want to take the bus. I knew I would have a great time there.

With plenty of urging from my older brothers, I became girl crazy! And this happened to be girl heaven. I had never been around so many accessible girls in my life. Plus, many of my friends and cousins were older, and so I had access to the older ones too. In fact, in freshman year I was asked to go to the senior prom. I didn't have enough for a pair of gators (alligator shoes) so I declined.

But my favorite "girl" was Ms. Champion, my high school counselor. Whew! She was one of the most beautiful women I had ever seen. She was 5'6" with a light caramel complexion…and really smart. She had a southern drawl that came from her Atlanta upbringing—one of those elegant drawls of a refined Southern black woman. She was always carrying papers. Fresh out of college, Ms. Champion was helping save the world. Or at least in my mind, save me.

I had the classic schoolboy crush. She reminded me of one of Mike or Terry's beautiful lady friends.

After the first week of school Mike came to pick me up for a weekend to take me shopping and to handle a few hustle missions. He was buying another Camaro. The one he had was burgundy with gold rims and T-tops. "Man, you can have this one." I was excited; after all I was only 14 with my own Camaro! I remembered being seven years old watching him go up and down the block when he was 14 until he saved up enough to purchase a Camaro. Now I had my own at 14!

The following Monday bright and early we drove to my school. Well, I drove while Mike leaned back in the reclined passenger seat. He noticed me admiring his chain and told me he would get one for me based on my next report card. I wanted a herringbone like Tupac, who had just died. My brother had a herringbone too.

We parked in front of Mackenzie High School and JP, a friend of mine, was walking by.

"You want a chain right?" Mike said.

"Yeah."

"See that nigga slippin' right there? Go snatch it."

The "N" he was talking about was JP. He had on a 2-inch wide herringbone chain, exactly the kind I wanted.

But JP was my friend.

"Yeah, I want it, but I know him bro'."

"You want me to snatch it?"

I quickly hopped out of the car and ran over to JP and greeted him with a handshake and a "What up doe?" In haste I said to Mike, "yeah bro, we're about to go to class. I'll see you later."

As much as I wanted a chain, I couldn't steal it from my friend. There were some lines I just wouldn't cross.

Mike left. He understood. He just felt that I deserved a chain.

That was one of my last interactions with Mike.

A few months later, I got a phone call from my sister. She was crying hysterically.

"What's going on?"

"He gone. He gone. *Sniff sniff.* He gone." I knew Tila was talking about Mike. I stood in the stairway to the basement and slowly sat on the steps and listened to her voice, altered by her tears of pain.

Mike had gotten killed in a drug transaction. He was at the Twin Elms Motel on Michigan Avenue with his friend Boomer. They were making an exchange with a crackhead. Mike was a big dealer in Inkster, Michigan, with a host of enemies. The crackhead had been hired to take him out. As my brother approached 2 feet away from making the exchange, the dope fiend pointed the gun at him.

The gun went "click." Misfired.

He turned around, pushing Boomer to go faster while making sure that he ran directly behind him to shield him from the glaring bullets. He was a track star, but didn't want to run ahead of Boomer.

Four shots fired consecutively. Pop! Pop! Pop! Pop!

The gun was a 22'. Three bullets flew past and the forth hit Mike in his right shoulder. He stumbled and fell to the ground. He tried to get up while the bullet bounced around in his body and traveled to his heart.

Mike fell again, instantly onto his knees, then head first to the ground. Boomer turned around. Two more shots were fired as Boomer ran and swiftly crawled towards Mike's body that laid still on the ground. Boomer held him close. Mike took his last breath in Boomer's arms. The shooter fled the scene. Boomer was unharmed. At least by bullets.

It was December 2nd, 1996. Mike would have been 21 on December 23rd. Boomer was 16.

Mike took care of everybody on my mom's side: sister, Grandma, aunts, Mom. He was like a father to Doug. Funny, Mike. Doug. Tila. Me. None of our fathers were around. Mike was like a father to all of us.

It hit us all pretty hard.

A couple weeks after the funeral my dad was in the hospital. I went to see him.

I was guessing since I'm a teenager now, he would actually deal with me. He tends to prefer dealing with his older kids.

I enter the room and walk over to the hospital bed. His liver is going bad. He is not looking well at all. Still has the cool, deep voice though.

*You know, I'm proud of you son. I heard about your brother too. I loved that boy like he was my own. Good old Mike. He was a leader, ya know. It's your turn now.*

*I want you to be better than me and Mike. I'm sorry I wasn't there for you. Don't be like me. Don't have all these kids if you're not going to be there for them. Promise me…you won't be like me. Right?*

A tear trickles down my father's cheek. Mine too.

I hold his hand and look him directly in his eyes, *Yeah, I can promise that.*

*And don't be having sex with all these girls. They are going to like you, trust me.*

A couple of days later, I get the phone call from my stepmom. *Your dad has passed away.*

Two of my idols. Now they're gone. Everyone said I'm just like my dad. All my life I tried to emulate all the good things people said about him. I patterned myself after my mythical thoughts of him. Not anymore.

I returned to school the day after the funeral to finish my first semester finals. Shortly after I received my report card. I had a 4.0. Neither Mike nor my Dad had a chance to see it.

A month later, I lost my virginity. I thought, 'shout-out to you pops.' I kissed my fingers and threw the peace sign in the air for him.

You see, I was kind of mad at my Pops. He put things into perspective when he told me he wasn't a good father. My mythical dreams of him being so busy on some secret mission were tarnished. I thought: "Oh. You just said, 'Forget Shawn.' The hell with me. Okay…"

I wanted to be just like him, but that fantasy was over. The realization was sobering and angering at the same time.

At his funeral, that was the first time I saw mom and dad in the same room. 'That's how they looked together,' I thought. Oddly enough, it was kinda cool to have my parents in the same room. Despite the circumstances.

My brother was at the funeral. That's Terry. My last idol still standing. Mink coat. Fresh suit. Chain. Alligator shoes. I remembered what my granddad said when Grandma Juanita died: *She ain't comin' back.* Terry was my distraction from that truth. We had the same dad. I wondered how he felt. I wondered if he felt like me…after all, dad wasn't there for him either.

We had a brotherly embrace in front of our father's casket. "It's gon' be alright bro'." I agreed.

I still had a man's blueprint to follow and words of wisdom. Relief.

I reached out more after that experience. He took me shopping after I told him how well school was going. He knew I was by myself. He made time to hang out. He would have me babysit/watch his son, Corey, who was 4 years younger than me. I was proud to do that. My nephew and I were so close in age, I was more like his big brother.

A few months later, I received another phone call. Terry was in a shoot-out. He was at a gas station. A team of guys ran up on him and just started shooting. He was with Proof, the rapper, who was then on my brother's record label, Motor City Records.

Supposedly, Terry had a gun too. Proof too. An innocent bystander was shot from the bullets that the team of shooters fired. The police flooded the scene and my brother tossed the firearm and started running. No gun in his hand. The police shot him six times from behind in the legs. He went to the hospital a bloody mess. When they cut his leg open, miraculously his arteries stood up. And they lanced them together. Terry could hobble.

He came and lived with us for about three weeks or so. He was being charged with tax evasion and the murder of the innocent bystander from the gas station. While he was home, it was great to have him around, regardless the circumstances. His girlfriend came over often. They had just had a beautiful little girl.

I can remember conversations about girls. And cars. And how I was doing in school. He was always telling me that he had been a football player in high school.

"If dad was around, I would've stayed in school, played football, and none of this would've happened," he would say to me when we conversed about me being on honor roll. He would look away, far into the distance, as if remembering a better time. Then he'd shake it off and come back to himself, the way I knew him. A CEO of life in all of his endeavors.

Still hobbling from his gun wounds, Terry turned himself in to the Feds for the tax evasion charge. No one there now. Thinking about someone to encourage Shawn is the least of his worries, but a major part of mine.

I was 15 years old in the 10th grade, and I think: "I think they taught me enough. I can take it from here."

---

I received another phone call. I am still 15. A lot has happened in a year, and the drama continues. My mom got caught boosting again. She didn't have any money, and she is now in police custody. But I had money from my $400 per month social security check from my dad's death, and I am flipping it to make ends meet, doing petty drug sales and the like. I wasn't doing anything big, but I had about $2,400 stashed. That was a lot of money for me.

Two-thousand, four hundred dollars. Just exactly what she needed. Mike used to help her. Terry wasn't her son, not to mention currently he was inaccessible. Tila didn't have it. Neither did Grandma Virginia.

"Shawn, what do you have?"

"I got about $2,400."

"$2,400?!!" They couldn't believe it.

"Alright Little Mike, you're taking care of things now."

I was *so* pissed. And Mom never even said thank you. It was like she felt I owed her that. She needed the money for bail and a jump-start on her attorney fees.

I never got the money back. Ironically, I skipped a step... It's gone from "Who is going to take care of me?" to "We need your help to take care of us."

# CHAPTER 7

## 11<sup>th</sup> Grade

He stared at my hair. "You know how you got them waves, right?"

I was remembering being nine years old, and noticing my brother Terry's hair for the first time. It was the coolest thing: black, shiny, baaadass waves covering the top of his perfectly blended bald fade. They were uniform, as if they had been manufactured by a machine. They made him look like he could conquer the world. Or at least some girls.

"How you get those waves?" I asked him.

"You gotta brush 'em," was his answer. He pulled out his black "Diane" brush from his back pocket and stroked his hair from the swirl at the top of his head down to his forehead. He did it a few times before handing me his brush.

"It's yours. Just brush it the same way I just showed you."

I thought I hit the lottery! I thought I had the power to conquer the world. Or at least some girls.

So while on a visit to prison when Terry asked me whether I remembered how I "got them waves," I laughed because I could go right back to that scene: a wide-eyed nine-year-old, looking up at this cool-looking dude who seemed to have it all together and thinking, *this is the definition of cool... I'm the definition of cool.*

Terry's girlfriend Eboni and I would drive together to visit Terry in prison. I thought she was so much older, but in reality she was only about three years older than me. Our conversations were wide-ranging: clothes, cars, family... of course my brother; and the things she wanted to do in life. She liked the idea of being an entrepreneur and going to school for business. "Your brother is so good to me," she would tell me all the time. "He really takes care of me." We drove the new Infiniti

73

truck that bro' had gifted her. Eboni was always draped in the designer brands that he purchased for her. This day, she was wearing a pair of platinum wire frame Cartier glasses, a matching Rolex watch, brown Gucci loafers, Guess jeans, a form fitting shirt, and a brown and black swirled waist length mink coat.

We drove east to FCI McKean Federal Correctional Institute in Bradford, Pennsylvania. As we approached McKean it didn't seem like a prison. The buildings were modern with soft gray and salmon colors. We parked in the visitor's parking lot. As we opened the facility door, we were welcomed by the air-conditioned entryway with carpets over an impeccable tile floor. The employees were well-dressed and fairly respectful. It actually looked like a well-kept college campus. The year is 1998. I am now 16.

We gave our IDs at the front desk. A couple inmates were walking around with mops and a large rolling black plastic garbage bin in their khaki-colored jumpsuits, made especially popular today by the television series, *Orange is the New Black*. We had our bags of quarters to get food out of the vending machines and take pictures. We had to provide my brother's name and prison number, our license plate number, and our dates of birth. Then we locked our jackets up…, no hoodies, no phone, no two-way pager (remember, it's 1998).

"2-4-9-9-8-0-3-9, Stuckey. You have a visitor."

They called my brother and I, Eboni and the baby go through security. The people in this facility moved quickly; by the time he was in the visitation room, we were with security taking off our shoes and socks, lifting up our feet, opening our mouths and lifting up our tongues. Men search men and women search women. You have to document every single item you have on your person: watch, glasses. And you'd better be wearing the same glasses when you come out that you wore when you came in, because they make note of every item.

When we went thru the metal detector, we entered a corridor and gave the next checkpoint officer our ticket, our driver's license, and our hand. They slapped plastic wristlets on us, and a neon "X" or the symbol for that day. You could only see the "X" under a black light. In other words, the guards made sure that the same person who enters as a visitor was the same person who exits.

We walked into a large open room with plastic chairs positioned for visitors. The prisoners may not speak to each other; they can only speak with their own visitors. Last visit I inquired why that rule was in place and Terry explained that this made sure prisoners didn't provoke one another and get into fights during family visits; and to make sure they don't exchange information or contraband from non-prisoners that might aid them in an escape or continue illegal business dealings on the outside. There were more reasons as well, but I completely understood.

My brother stood in place at his seating station once we entered the visitation room, smiling. He wore tan khakis, some white Nikes, a neck chain with a small diamond cross, and a pair of wood grain and platinum Cartier glasses. "What up doe?" he says in his standard Detroit greeting. We shook hands and embraced one another. Then he immediately hugged Eboni and picks up the baby. I went straight to the vending machines and got food. All the driving, talking, and waiting to see bro' had built quite an appetite. Besides, I already know he wants the little frozen White Castle Burgers.

We sat in the larger waiting area with other inmates and families for a moment and then entered the glass-encased room with play toys for kids. Their little girl, about two or three years old, bounces in with us.

Fast-forward note: She graduated from a private high school outside of Detroit in 2014. I'm so proud of her!

"Wow bro'. You're walking really well." My brother is 5'10" and well-built, but I am nevertheless surprised that his horrendous wounds that Eboni and I so consistently worked to disinfect and cleanse have healed to the point that he can walk without a cane and even without a limp.

"Yeah. I guess they thought if I took a few bullets, they could handle me. But I'm on the basketball court like I never missed a beat."

75

*This man is not real!* I thought.

It never felt like we were in prison. It felt like we were just randomly visiting him away at school. And he never complained. I respected that. No time for complaining. Just embrace the moment.

"I'll be out of here soon and everything'll be fine."

I always observed whenever Terry saw Eboni and the baby, his body language would change as well as his pitch and overall conversation. He was very gentle with her. He would speak softer and stroke her back…and the baby would be playing right at their feet. She was really soft and gentle… more gentle than most women I knew. It reminded me of the standard "picket fence" vision of family that television bombards us with. The "picket fence" happened to be barbed wire but it was still sweet and intimate.

And here I am: Uncle Shawn. I felt proud to play with my baby niece, excited to see my brother smile, and sad that we would only be there for a few hours.

Terry was in for four years this second time. The first time had been four years, too.

The third time…

---

It was first semester, 11th grade, and I just decided to skip school. Although I never felt the need to skip, I figured I would give it a try. I went to my cousin Anthony's house where he skipped fairly often. He was so smart that it didn't affect his grades too much. There were a number of us, girls too, and Anthony was known for ordering Hungry Howie's pizza with garlic butter crust. We, Anthony, Li'l Tommy, Melvin, Roscoe, and each of our little ladies were all hungry!

Anthony had a sister, Shannon, who was supposed to be at work, but she just so happened to come home early to see the madness. She was livid!

Li'l Tommy and Anthony were downstairs on separate twin beds. Both were under the covers with their girls.

She heard giggles and peaked down the dark basement steps. "What're y'all doing down there." Silence…

Roscoe, Melvin and I saw her approaching the house and hid upstairs before she came inside. We were silent too. Waiting for the perfect moment to make a run for it.

Shannon took the cover off Li'l Tommy and his girl. "You nasty little hoe!"

"Shannon, wait!" Li'l Tommy yelled. Shannon grabbed a broom and started hitting Li'l Tommy and the girl. Anthony pulled his covers back. "Shannon, what're you doing?"

"Get these nasty hoes outta here! This is Daddy's house…how dare you!" Shannon was not having it.

Melvin, Roscoe, the girls and I snuck out of the front door while Shannon was being Super Hater! We ran up the driveway, through the backyard, jumped the five-foot gate, and darted down the alley to get out of Shannon's line of sight. I didn't really try anything with my little lady. I could do anything I wanted at Granddad's house anyway, so skipping turned out not to be for me. I could have gone to class and avoided all that mess. I even ripped my Girbaud jeans on the gate.

I never skipped again. It wasn't worth it.

---

At this point Grandma is gone, Pops is gone, my brother Mike is gone, my brother Terry is…well, not present, and my Mom…well, hmmm. I'm getting older, and I'm accustomed to having nice things. Not the kind of stuff my Mom steals. In fact, I've outgrown her area of expertise. The majority of the brands that I like have become too sophisticated for her boosting ability.

I want Cartier glasses. Gucci and Ferragamo loafers. Ice Berg clothes, and Pelle Pelle leathers. I want it all and I won't settle for less than what I have been always given. After all, this is part of my image, part of my self-concept and popularity. I'm that young smart and flashy guy. I need to feel like a young P. Diddy in my environment at all times. To do that, I would have to take matters into my own hands.

You see, there were these guys that would steal jewelry but couldn't sell their high end merchandise. They stole diamond rings, chains, expensive watches, and bracelets. They would cut the gum that connected the glass casing in jewelry stores, lift it up, and take whatever diamond-filled goods they could—all while another cooperating partner would distract the salesperson. In the end they would walk away with hundreds of thousands of dollars in merchandise without using any weapons. But: If you don't have a client who can buy a diamond bezel Presidential Rolex, why would you steal a Presidential Rolex?

That's where I came in. I had connections with people who had money. I was the middleman. The ones who stole lacked such a network; that's why they needed me.

It was pretty good money. I would set a meeting between both parties and attend the meeting to make sure contact information wasn't exchanged. The thieves weren't to be trusted and my network of wealthy individuals knew that. They preferred to go through me and keep the thieves at bay. The thieves would pay me for the connection and the buyers would pay me for the connection on the backend. I liked being the middleman. I do referrals. That's what I do. It's easier. Cleaner. Less risky. In a nutshell, I'm a connector.

Malcolm Gladwell talks about "Connectors" in his book *The Tipping Point*. For Gladwell, "Connectors" are people who build bridges from one set of individuals to another. In his book, he says that Connectors have a "very special gift of bringing people together." That was me.

On top of that I sold weed among other one-off scams. I did it much differently than my peers, but I'll explain more about that a bit later.

My mindset and demeanor was changing. My mother, a number of my brothers, and a sister have all been to prison. I've experienced one too many close deaths. My style of clothing and jewels had become more expensive. I was still in school, but I felt like a man. I was still attending class regularly, but the allure of education was not exciting me as much. Who needs education when you have the means to run your own operation? Especially, if you never get caught. Hmmm...especially, if you never think you will get caught.

As a result of all these factors, my grades began to slip. I wasn't turning in all my homework assignments. I had even slipped under a 3.0, to about 2.8 or so.

And oh, I was contemplating the prospect of taking charge of raising my younger brother, Doug. That would mean attending parent teacher conferences, making sure he was in class, and completing his homework, among whatever other interesting scenarios that may arise.

I was 16. My little brother was 11—"half of 20", as my mom says. I decided to call a meeting with my mother. In the past she hit me in the mouth and scolded me for not doing the wrong thing correctly. But that was some years ago. Being that I was 16 at this point she may not want to do that. I won't hit her back, but I will shake her up a little bit, restrain her, and probably force her to sit down.

I knew she had the conversation with my brother, explaining her hustle. "This is how I make my money," the classic keynote speech she delivered once her children hit "half of 20," the semi-adult life mark. "This is how I make money from the white man; after all, he's the one that put us down. So I'm kind of like Robin Hood. We just want to make sure we can spread the wealth among our people." Blah, blah, blah...

I am thinking about the time she had that conversation with me. But Doug has known for years. This can't go on. Mike is dead. Andy is dead. Tila is struggling to find her way. What's going to happen next? My head was on pretty straight, I think, but my little brother was with

79

her every day, exposed to her wrongdoing and her lies. I couldn't take it anymore.

"Mom, I want to have a meeting with you. Can you come by Granddad's crib?"

"OK." Mom sounds curious but open.

She comes into my self-decorated basement bachelor pad. "Hey baby!"

"What's going on Mom? Have a seat." She sat on my couch. I had music playing in the background to soften the mood, because I know my Mom can be a bit of a hothead. I felt the power shift that I needed—after all, we were in my space, a space that I made.

Mom feels it too. A role shift. "What do you want to talk about?"

"It's dealing with Doug, Mom. I know you had your 'half of 20' conversation with him. I'm not too happy about that."

She squints her eyes. "Really?"

"Really. So I'm going to tell you this, and I love you, but I gotta keep it real. Andy is dead. He was neglected. Mike is dead for reasons that you already know. He was a hustler—and we know where he got that from. Tila? She's really struggling right now and we know that you have directly impacted her life. Me, I'm trying and doing okay. However, Doug is the baby and he's there with you. Honestly, any of us that were around you during our formative years have been mismanaged. You're…ummm… a busy person. Only God knows what will come from this for Doug. I don't want him going out on shopping sprees and driving with you across the country. That's not what he needs. He needs to follow me."

In a split second her fist clinched, her eyes became red, and she erupted!

"Who the f--- you think you are to tell me what I should be doing with my kids?"

She stood up and looked down upon me.

"You can't tell me how to raise my kids. I brought you in this world and I can take you out!"

I stood, now two inches taller than her 5'9, and responded with clinched fist and red eyes!

"I'm going to make this easy. Get the f--- out. My life is OK without yo' dumb a--. You're not worthy to be anybody's mother!"

She continued to curse and yell.

"I don't care how many curse words you have to say or how loud you yell," I fought back. "B--ch, get the f--- out. I don't care what happens to you. I don't care! You destroy people's lives. Bye! Get the hell out. I don't want to see you or talk to you ever again."

Mom leaves. "I never should have had you. I don't give a s--t about you either. Disrespectful-a-- kids, don't appreciate nothin'!"

"You are worthless. You are a walking disaster...bye, have a good life."

Dang. I envisioned that scenario going much different. What am I going to do about my brother? I've messed up with my mother, which I really could care less about, but she's the only portal to him. I didn't accomplish my goal. My brother was still left to her influence, and, I thought, to his demise.

I gave things time to die down. It was a little over four months until I reluctantly spoke to my mother again. The only reason I talked to her at all is because I wanted to pick Doug up from her house. I just wanted to make sure he was OK and being steered in the right direction with school. People on my mom's side don't typically finish school with diplomas. I would be the first to actually get a diploma among my Mom and her children. I wanted to make sure that Doug got one, too.

I made the drive to Mom's place. She recently moved to the west side of Detroit from Inkster. Doug was coming out of the side door with his bike when he spotted me. He had a huge Kool Aid smile, dropped his bike, and ran immediately inside yelling, "Mom, I'm going with Shawn."

"Okay," Mom said reluctantly.

A friend of my mom's who is visiting peers out of the side door, and my brother jumps out in front of her. "Hey bro', just hold on, I'm getting my bag together."

In the middle of his haste he noticed he was being a tad bit rude and introduces me to a lady friend of my mother. I gave a limp "Hi" from the driver seat of the car. I didn't really care to know my mother's friends.

"This is Patty. Patty Pussy," whispers my brother to me.

"What?" I said.

"I'll tell you later."

Patty said, "Your mother's upstairs."

"I know. I'm here for my brother."

"This is her house." Patty thinks she's going to scold me into submission.

"Yeah."

"I'm going to tell her you're here."

"Go ahead. Don't matter to me."

"You going to say hi to her?"

"Chick, go sit down. I don't want to talk to her."

I felt she was doing too much. She wasn't.

"Dee Dee, your son Shawn is here."

"What?" says my mom from upstairs.

"Shawn. He's here."

"I know" replies my mother flatly. "He's coming to pick up Doug."

Patty Pussy is in the middle of something she knows nothing about. It's really not her fault. She just has no clue. She went upstairs and talked to my mom. And Doug was taking forever.

"C'mon Doug!" Honk Honk!

"OK." He hollered out of the window. "I just want to get my cars."

Patty appeared at the door: "Your mom wants to see you upstairs."

I turn the car off and enter the side door. I walk through the kitchen and pass the plastic covered fancy antique couches. I open the wooden door that leads upstairs to my mother's bed room. As I walk up the rickety steps, the air turns thick from marijuana smoke.

"Hi," says Mom.

"You wanted me to come up here or som'em?"

Patty comes up the steps behind me, "Actually I wanted you to come up here."

Mom starts crying, saying, "He doesn't love me, he has never respected me, he looks down at me, I'm his mother!"…and on and on from there.

I am silent. Finally: "Yes I do. I love you Mom. I'll start coming over. I apologize."

I went over and hugged her. We made up.

But honestly, I did it just to gain better access to my brother. After the apology, I said, "I think it would be a good idea if Doug came and lived with me." Mom agreed. I don't think it was hard for her. "He needs to be around men anyway," she reasoned.

Doug moved in with me that weekend.

I talked to Granddad. "Don't worry. I'll take care of him. He won't be a problem." I meant it.

I am starting to feel an essential moral difference between my mother and me. My mother was trying to bring him into her world. Don't get me wrong, I had my fair share of wrongdoing as well, but I absolutely refused to bring him into my business. I was insistent that he have more positive experiences than I did from my influencers. He was far from stupid and he knew what I was doing, but I never showed him anything. I never invited him to take part in any of my illegal activity. I just wanted him to go to school, dress nice on my dime, and interact with the ladies. Women had a positive effect on me; I figured it would have the same effect on Doug. I was willing to dress him like me, complete with the chains, the glasses, the designer clothes. Doug was to be a "mini-me."

It was the same when it came to school. Just like I wanted Doug to have my "look," I wanted him to have my same passion towards the books. I went to the parent-teacher conferences. The teachers thought it was "cute." But I could speak with them intelligently. I took the home phone calls. Remember: Granddad wasn't coming to my parent-teacher conferences. Even though the example wasn't put before me, I was just that much more determined to make sure the example is put before Doug—by me.

I had "really good bad examples." I may not have known exactly what to do, but I surely knew exactly what not to do. Gathering this wisdom was a way of life for me.

I regretted that Doug didn't make school as high a priority as I did. Nevertheless, I insisted on seeing his homework. I put the parent-teacher conference dates in my calendar. I bought him shoes for good grades, quizzes, and report cards. I took him to my high school homecoming. Harmless things that made him feel "cool," things younger kids couldn't do that were really innocent. I just did what made sense to me.

---

I needed about $200. Don't remember exactly what it was for, but I decided to go to my mom's house. I had been taking care of Doug for months, and she felt compelled to help whenever I requested anything from her. I rarely did.

"Mom, can I get a couple hundred?"

"Baby, I don't have it right now."

"Thanks anyway, I'll figure it out."

It was late, so I decided to fall asleep on her couch in the den.

Then I woke up in the middle of the night. I heard what sounded like a headboard crashing, panting, and some moans. Male and female moans.

WTH?

I stared at the ceiling with furrowed eyebrows noting that my Mom's bed was directly above the den where I was sleeping. Noooo... Is she??? I was disgusted at the thought of my Mom having sex upstairs. Who the heck is up there? I didn't want to know so I buried my head in the decorative couch pillows.

In the morning, Mom was cooking. "Hey Shawn, you hungry?" As if nothing happened. Nobody was there at that point except Mom and me.

"Sure Ma."

"I got that $200 for you." She smiled.

I took it out of her hands, slowly, brows furrowed again. "Thanks."

I didn't ask questions, and I didn't want to know the answer. I decided to leave it alone.

I didn't sleep well throughout the night so I went home to Granddad's to take a nap around 6:00 p.m. I never took naps, but I had to get some sleep after the disgusting thoughts that were rolling around in my mind. I was in my basement, asleep; an hour into taking a nap. It was about 7:00 p.m. I heard blurred voices and commotion. I thought I was dreaming. Then:

"Hey. Hey. HEY."

Flashlights were shining in my eyes. I put my hands up just in order to see through the bright lights. There were about eight people around me hovering over my bed.

"What the hell is this?"

"This is the Detroit Police Department. Are you Richardo Davenport?"

"No."

"Do you know Richardo Davenport?"

"No. What are we talking about here? I just go to school, I don't know Richardo and I'm sure nobody else in this house knows any Richardos."

They started flipping over furniture, just like before. Déjà vu all over again.

Fortunately, I did not have any illegal substances in the house. Neither did my Uncle Jimmy beyond his personal blunt or two.

The police let me put on my clothes and go outside, still wondering what's going on. Granddad was outside already.

"You alright Nigga?"

"Yeah Grandad. I'm good."

"Police need to get the hell on…f---ing up s--t. Need to gone somewhere."

"What's up Granddad? Who the heck is Richardo?"

"Hell if I know. Looking for somebody named Richardo aka Rico. I don't know no damn Ricos. Just want to cook my gizzards."

For some reason, apparently, the police thought a murder suspect was in the house. He wasn't.

---

Ms. Champion had a way of making me feel like a normal student. She paid me academic attention, the kind of attention I never got at home. She would ask me appropriate yet very personal questions as if she knew I needed a special kind of attention. She was the only one who requested to see my grades consistently.

Granddad was happy as a southern man who didn't particularly care about school could be with my progress in school…I guess. He never went to award ceremonies. I would show him my grades and awards and he'd say "Keep goin' boy!" But he never set foot in the school. That time I was suspended for being tardy to class one too many times, I caught hell trying to get him to come to the school to get me back in. They simply had to settle on talking to him over the phone. Honestly, he didn't realize the opportunities school provided.

One day, I noticed Ms. Champion had on a very bright, colorful outfit. "What's with all the pink and green?" I asked her.

She replied, "I'm an AKA."

"'Also Known As'…what?"

"No, it's a sorority."

"Oh. Like in the show *A Different World*."

"Kinda, more like *School Daze*."

"Ohhh… That Spike Lee flick with the Pops from *Boyz n the Hood*. Gotcha!"

Ms. Champion had pink-and-green and maize-and-blue artifacts and trinkets throughout her office. I wondered what it all was. Then, I found out: Fab Five. Chris Weber. She went to school with them. Charles Woodson. Tyrone Wheatley. All from the University of Michigan in Ann Arbor, a place I had never been. So I thought: *Alright. That's cool.*

All I knew about college was Michigan and Ms. Champion. College had never been on my radar. Funny, as much as I care about school it's pretty blind. *The Cosby Show*, *A Different World* and *The Fresh Prince of Bel-Air* were the closest things I know about transitioning from high school to college. I'd never known anyone to go through the process; so why would I want to do it?

That is until I met Ms. Champion… She forced college on my radar. Television is cool and all, but she was the real deal. She was the coolest person I'd ever met that actually went to college.

She was pretty. She went to Michigan. That was good enough for me.

Ms. Champion would always encourage me. "You're going to be my Michigan man, my little Kappa."

"Shawn," she would say. "You need to be in the Compact Program." You need to run for student government. You need to be on the debate team." Whatever she said do, I'd do it.

I don't think she even knew the influence she had over me. I rarely questioned her.

She took me on a field trip to Michigan my junior year. *Man, this is crazy,* I thought. We took a picture at Michigan Stadium. *This place is huge!* I thought. That's the trip I remember. *I want to go there somehow,* I remember thinking. I don't know if you have to take a test. I have no idea how it works. I thought I could just automatically go to Michigan.

I had no expectations, no knowledge of what it would be like. *This'll be cool*, I thought. *There'll be even more girls than at Mackenzie.*

I didn't even know that Michigan was a 'prestigious school.' They mentioned it on the tour. They said it was for "The Brightest and Best." I figured that's what they probably say at every college. I had no concept of what that meant either.

Going into the 11th grade I had about a 3.8 GPA. I had recently taken the State MEAP (Michigan Education Assessment Program) Exam. If you get a certain score they provide you with the Michigan Merit award, which grants $2,500 towards college. Whatever the score was a few of us in the honors class received it and I was among the few. The idea of college started to become real to me, considering I was getting money for taking test. My angel, my grandmother, told me I was smart and handsome and Ms. Champion confirmed that for me years later. That was enough confirmation that I would at least try to go to Michigan. On the strength of those two amazing women, my future was charted.

Ms. Champion will never know what she means to me.

All the mentoring I do today? That I owe to her.

---

It was the end of my 11th grade year. My sister Che lived in Southfield, a suburb right outside Detroit. Her condo has an indoor pool and she always let me use her crib and car. My friend Li'l Tom and I were going to Belle Isle for the '99 senior picnic, in Che's black-on-black drop-top Camaro.

Che's house is big and airy and open. Ever seen the movie *Belly?* Everything is black and white, just like that movie's opening scene. Her bedroom, kitchen and bathrooms are decorated with a mixture of modern and antique African art. The living room is wide open with no furniture and black and white paintings on the wall. There is a balcony in the living room that peers out into a sea of trees and greenery. Upon entry there are steps with metal plates that cover the edges and lead right up to the upstairs. I decide to get comfortable and take a shower.

BOOM! BOOM! BOOM! Comes a sound from outside the bathroom door.

"Li'l Tom! Get the hell outta here! You're always doing too much!"

"It's the police! Open the f---ing door now!"

My eyes were wide open despite the soap. That's definitely not Li'l Tom! I was completely naked and wet from the shower. I washed the soap out of my eyes quickly and quickly pulled the shower curtains back. I grabbed the door knob and announced that I was slowly opening the door. I cracked the door, deliberately showed my hands, and dropped to my knees as the police slammed open the door into the wall, knocking hanging pictures to the floor. Their guns were in my face and I stared back at them with wide eyes and a racing heart.

A couple police officers aggressively grabbed my arms and dragged me down the steps, face forward. My full frontal naked body parts hit and scraped the metal steps the entire way down. Yes, it was just as bad as you can imagine. My penis was scraped and bleeding, along with countless bruises on my chest and chin.

A loud thud rang when I hit the bottom of the steps. "C'mon man, damn!" I protested.

"Shut up!" the police hollered back. "Get him over there! Right over there!"

They put me outside, butt-naked, in the middle of the parking lot, hands cuffed behind my back.

My sister screamed, "Leave him alone, he's a baby."

"B--ch, you better settle your a-- down." Then, to me:

"Sit on this tire."

I was already naked and wet, now they wanted me to sit on a dirty old tire…

Then they asked me again, "Do you know Richardo?"

"I don't know no damn Richardo or Rico or whatever you call him! All I know is I'm going to the senior picnic tomorrow, and I'm at my sister's house."

"Ohhhhhh… we see you everywhere huh? I remember you from the house we raided weeks ago."

I stared back at him with the same sarcastic dumb look that he had on his face while talking to me.

Slowly I repeated, "I-don't-know-no-damn-Richardo. All I know is, I'm going to the senior picnic tomorrow."

Finally, somebody brought me a towel. I was still wet, cold despite the decent spring weather, and bleeding.

But I did make it to that Mackenzie High School Senior Picnic. I was a junior at the time.

---

I missed Mother's Day; Mom was out of town on one of her "excursions." She came to pick up Doug early the following weekend. I decided to connect with them later the same day. I wanted to make sure I connected with my mother to pay her homage for her special day. It can be hard shopping for a Mom that can take virtually anything that she wants. So, I gift-wrapped and gave her two ounces of weed. "My baby got the streets and the books. Thank you baby! Oooh, where you get this from? This some good herbal right here!" She smiled.

Happy Mother's Day Mom.

# CHAPTER 8

## Senior Year

Back to school. All my friends and cousins had graduated last school year. I was in 12th grade now and pretty much alone. My classmates saw me as a cool guy, but I didn't hang out with many of them.

Fortunately for me I had my new girlfriend Kim. I had been working on getting in good with her since the first day I saw her in 9th grade! I've never given up on anything in life and I wasn't going to stop at her playing hard to get. Needless to say she was my girlfriend senior year. This year she would certainly serve as my accountability partner. Not to mention Ms. Champion was always on me to do well and participate in everything.

Ms. Champion put me in an ACT prep course. I took it only because she said I should. But when it got to taking the test itself…

I fell asleep. It was after school, and I got through Math and English; but when I got to Science, I slept. When I came to, I just gave random answers.

My score was terrible.

"Shawn! You got a 16. You're supposed to be my Michigan man. I need you to take that test again. You did great on the MEAP test… I need you to give me that kind of score!"

I am getting closer to graduation, and I am finding Ms. Champion is on me more than ever. "Are you turning your stuff in? Are you going to class?" "Yes, Ms. Champion."

She made me run for Treasurer again. I told her I wasn't going to do it. "You have to. Even if you don't score as high on the ACT, colleges need to see you as the well-rounded student and active leader that you are. Just think about it Shawn: Compact (that was a program that aided students in studying for the college entrance exams and awarded scholarships based upon obtaining particular test scores). Debate Team. Senior Class Treasurer. Employment. Raising your younger brother. Raising yourself. And you still have approximately a 3.5 GPA. That's going to look good to Michigan admissions counselors."

I couldn't overload my schedule with too many after-school activities because my little brother was a handful. I was also working at Red Lobster as the head bus boy, which was the perfect cover for my weed sales. As I mentioned before, I like to do things a bit differently than my peers: I would only sell weed on payday at Red Lobster. Not at school. Not on the street. Just to the employees that I built relationships with.

I would buy a few ounces, go to work on payday, and sell my product. I'd make four to five times the amount on my check. Did it twice a month. It was clean, easy, and systematic.

Outside of schoolwork, extracurricular activities, my job, my girlfriend, and my hustles I had to make sure my brother was paid proper attention. School wasn't a pleasure for him as much as it had been for me.

I went to parent-teacher conference at Noble Middle School. I met with Doug's English teacher.

"He's a good kid, and he does good work. He just needs to be in class."

"What do you mean?" I was confused.

"Doug is one of my best students…when he's in class. He actually controls the class when he's here. He has a natural ability to make other students behave. And he's very respectful. He also does a great job on his assignments. Again, that is when he actually comes to class."

"What do you mean by that? I see him off to school every morning."

"Well," said the teacher, "he only comes to class two or three days a week."

94

Two or three days a WEEK! I was truly confused. "What is he doing those other times?"

"I don't know."

I found out Doug was chasing girls and smoking weed when he should have been in class.

I had a talk with Doug. "Dude: mess with girls at home, on your own time. Not on school time. And about this smoking weed? We don't SMOKE weed, bro'. I had always been emphatic about not using the merchandise I was selling. "That's for suckers. You don't get high off your own supply. That's wasting money. You're supposed to be a smart guy, a fresh guy, and a ladies man. That's it. That's what we do."

Doug explains, "I guess I been forgetting how many days I been missing."

"You should be missing ZERO days of school, bro'. ZERO days."

This is the first time Doug has been accountable for his actions to a man. A 17-year-old man that has to act like a parent. But to Doug, I am the man. A few years ago, it was Mike. But Mike died. So it had to be me.

But I was accountable to no one...except myself.

---

One day: the condom broke.

A while later, Kim called me.

"I missed my period."

*Oh no*, I am thinking to myself. *My sister Tila had to pass on a basketball scholarship and didn't go to school. We can't do this. This is not supposed to happen.*

Kim is crying. "You want to get rid of the baby?"

95

I have a better idea. "Look: I'm going to call my mom."

We decided to get an abortion. I toiled both with thoughts of being a father and the idea of having complete freedom to pursue my future. I would not be like my dad, missing in action. I would teach my child basketball. I would be there for him. Like my uncles were for my cousins…

But Kim had decided. And I agreed. I wanted my mom to take her.

"Mom, I got Kim pregnant, and she needs to go to a clinic."

That is Mom's area: navigating me out of trouble. Before I call a lawyer, I'll call my Mom.

But Mom didn't take her. Kim told her mom instead. And her mom was strict. I am now no longer the "golden boy" with her mom. So Kim's mom took her to the clinic.

I paid for the abortion.

Kim took it hard. I did not. I figured it would only make life rough. Besides all the young parents I knew had rough lives. I didn't want that kind of life for my child.

The second time I took the ACT, I stayed awake.

"I didn't go to sleep this time, Ms. Champion."

"Alright. My Michigan man!" Then she looked at me conspiratorially.

"I got a surprise for you. A treat. We're going to have on-site admissions."

What does that mean?

"The University of Michigan Admissions counselors are coming here."

"Really? That's huge… What should I wear? What should I bring? Who should I research?"

"And they're here today. And you're going to be first in line."

"Ohhhh… Okay cool. Where they at?" Trying to be cool about something I knew absolutely nothing about.

When I arrived, there was a line of students talking to the admissions counselors. Their parents were with them, and they had folders. *Oh. They were waiting for this*, I thought. *They know something I don't.*

They had their parents. But I had Ms. Champion. They were dressed for the occasion. I was wearing Girbaud Jeans, Cartier glasses, and a pair of Jordans.

We went to one of the tables. I was armed with a 3.5 GPA and pretty bad junior year grades. It is somewhat late in the game.

"This is Shawn Blanchard. He is one of our stars. He has so much promise. He will do well."

Ms. Champion is talking to Mr. Malcomb Luther, one of her mentors, and Serena Knowles, in financial aid.

"OK, said Malcomb. "Let's see your personal statement."

"What is that?"

"That's the letter you write telling us what makes you unique, why you want to go to Michigan."

Clearly I didn't have one. I'm typically prepared for these kind of scenarios, but I wasn't prepped accordingly. I played it cool looking for a que from Ms. Champion.

Ms. Champion chimed in. "Shawn, why don't you tell them in your own words your personal story?"

I begin.

*I was born a bastard in which neither of my biological parents felt the need to keep me. My grandparents raised me. My primary caretaker, my grandmother, died when*

97

*I was 12. So I really kind of raised myself. I have one brother in prison, another couple who passed away. I take care of one of my younger brother, get him ready for school daily, go to his parent-teacher conferences. I am class treasurer, on the debate team, work at Red Lobster, keep my grades up, I cook for my brother daily and I make sure that he stays out of trouble and in school. I'm basically a father. I never had the example that I would have liked to have. My dad died when I was in the 9th grade so I try my best to be a good example and steer clear of trouble. My mom is kinda around, but isn't the best example...nor did she graduate from high school. I've got a 3.5, I scored really high on the state MEAP exam and they gave me money for it. I also took the ACT again, I got a 16 the first time because I fell asleep... I didn't take it serious. I enjoy school and learning. It's a place where I can come and feel completely safe. Sometimes I have a lot going on at home...to say the least. At times it's hard to focus on school. Sometimes I wish I could focus solely on school like normal young people, but then again my life is what makes me...me.*

I hoped the conversation was impressive enough to earn a spot at the mythical school that Ms. Champion says I must attend. And so I continued.

*I am excited about life. Being in an uplifting environment that champions education is very positive for me. To be completely honest, until Ms. Champion and my girlfriend told me about college, I just wanted to sell dope and rap. I don't really know what's out there for me, but I know if I am presented with the right opportunity, I can do something good with my life...I know I can make the lives of others better as well. And from what I've been told, the University of Michigan is the perfect place to help me do that.*

"Could you put that on paper for us?"

"Yes sir, no problem." I wrote it all down, right there, in approximately 15 minutes.

They asked me to leave the room. Then Ms. Champion went to work.

"This kid has so much promise, you have no idea," she literally pleaded with her mentors. "He works really hard and has very little support...If you just give him a chance...I really don't know what will come of him if he doesn't have this type of chance. He just needs to be in the right place. Just like he said."

When I came in, they told me:

"You're going to the Summer Bridge Program."

A huge smile came across my face. I believe the trajectory of my life flashed across my face. My mind flooded with endless yet unformed possibilities that I had yet to understand. I hugged Ms. Champion and I thanked the admissions counselors. "Thank you. You're not going to regret this."

I heard Ms. Champion say, "Thank God for affirmative action! This is a prime example of why it's vital!"

I didn't know what she meant nor did I care at that particular moment. They give me the paperwork to fill out. I was excited, yet cool in the room.

I walked home after school and shed a few tears. I never envisioned this day in my life! Now it was a reality… I didn't know what to think. It felt like I had been drafted to the NBA!

When I made it home I checked the mail. I flipped through letters from a couple colleges, but my heart and mind were already set. Excited, I told Granddad. "Granddad! I'm going to college!"

Granddad's response was typical: "Boy…You need to do something with yourself nigga. House dirty. Need to be like your cousin. See he at Job Corps. You ain't doin' s--t. Talkin 'bout racking up loans and bills. We got that right now! You over here messing with girls and s--t. Need to go to Job Corps like your cousin.

"Granddad. I'm going to college."

"Go then. S--t. That's what you supposed to do. Y'all boys need to get the hell outta here. Do something with yo'self. Get you a job. Need to go to work."

"Alright Granddad." I reached under the kitchen sink to get a bucket and some Pine Sol. I figured cleaning the bathroom was the best way to get Granddad into a good mood. He had no clue what college I was referring to or what it meant to attend such a school. Heck, I barely knew myself!

Granddad worked all his life. Don't be mad at him. He just didn't know. To him, if you're not getting your hands dirty, if you don't come home tired, you're not making something of your life. Work is all he knew.

He was…and is still…one of my favorite humans. He showed me how to work. Hard. He also taught me about the necessity of discernment while taking words of advice. Some of the most loving and intelligent people speak from their own life experience—the only thing they know and not necessarily towards your best interest. This was certainly one of those scenarios.

I decided to go see my brother Terry. He was in the county jail at the time. Recall, he had gone to federal prison for tax evasion, but he was back for a murder case. The man that was gunned down when he was actually shot in the legs. It worked better for his family since we only had to drive downtown to see him.

The Wayne County Jail was filthy. The elevators were dusty and dark, and smelled of mold.

The officer says, "8th floor." I go to the 8th floor and show my visitor's pass.

"Stuckey. Number 2-4-9-9-8-0-3-9."

Bro' walks up to the glass. We talk through the round microphone hole in the wall separating us.

"What up doe?"

"Bro'. I'm 'bout to go to college!" I knew he was going to be more excited than Granddad.

"What?! Thas whassup bro! Where you going?"

"I'm going to Michigan. Wolverines!"

"You going to Michigan? Chris Weber, Fab Five and s--t?!" Bro' was clearly impressed.

"We 'bout to take over bro'."

"That's what I'm talking about! College boy s--t! You have to pave the way for the rest of the fam bro'! Give me a minute because I'm gon' get outta here in a few…Watch what I tell you!"

"I'm going to Prom and I'm about to graduate!"

"Bro 'bout to graduate from high school. Dig you. You always have gone hard with school. Nice and steady huh… I like that bro'!"

Our arms were pumping the air, braggadociously, as if we knew…just knew…that we could take over the world if we wanted. We had to believe that. Others tried to give us another message: that we were simply statistical failures destined for death or prison. Ironically, as we conversed we were actually in the county jail. But certain bright lights in our community have told us otherwise. Certain bright lights like Ms. Champion. Stuck had teachers too, some of whom probably told him the same thing Ms. Champion told me. Other bright lights like my grandmother, who told me I was smart and handsome. My girlfriend Kim insisted and pushed me to attend college. My brothers taught me how to run businesses—even if they were illegitimate. And even my mother, who in her own way showed me the respect due to a man, so I could command it later at will.

"You know I got you bro'," said Stuck.

"Cool."

Stuck sent me $1,000 and a black S Type Jag for prom. My sister Che rented a room for me.

"I want to buy the suit," said Mom.

"Are you going to actually buy the suit?" I admonished her.

"Yes."

"Then I'm going with you."

She bought the suit. I made sure.

I was all set with a black Jag and an eggshell linen suit with a mock turtleneck sweater. I gifted myself a gold Cartier chain, diamond pinky ring, a Movado watch, a pair of mustard big block alligator shoes and matching belt. Kim was stunning in a cream and gold dress, gold shoes. Her hair was whipped and her face was beat to the gods. (In other words her makeup was really nice.) Gorgeous.

And we were running for prom King and Queen.

Anthony, Bryan, Melvin, and Li'l Tom all graduated a year before me, but they came to my prom as well. We had an assortment of big block alligator shoes: mustard, black, grey, brown, and grape.

"The 2nd runner up!" It wasn't me.

"The runner up!" It wasn't me.

Finally: Prom King is…"Shawn Blanchard."

Then they went to the Queen. Kim won that one too. It was perfect.

Ironically, for a brief moment I couldn't help but chuckle at the thought of second grade when I wasn't the most popular guy. Funny how I haven't changed much, but the concept of what was popular simply changed. I always thought school was important, I've always appreciated women, always had a nose for fashion, and I enjoy good people. Back then I managed to get beat up for this sequence of thoughts and actions… Now I get crowned for it. Go figure.

The prom was held at the Roostertail, a swanky establishment along the Detroit River where we partied for hours.

On our way out I held Kim's hand and opened the passenger side door for her. She reached over to open the driver side door for me. She then began to reflect.

"You know what Shawn, you live in this fairy tale land."

"What do you mean?"

"You know, for you everything's happy, everything's gonna happen the way you want…it's simply not reality."

"Ehhhh… Reality is what you make it. Anything we want is very real. Look at these crowns. Look at this car. You're going to college… I'm going to college and we are both from the 'hood." I pulled out a wad of money, about $2,500. "I think you need to realize that you live in the fairy tale too!"

Kim shook her head. "Whatever… I'll let you live there because you seem to do okay there."

Later I realized: I do live in a fairy tale. But it's real to me. What I didn't know then was that I was exercising principles of faith without even knowing that such principles exist. I always called things into existence and placed corresponding action behind my words. I was a child, not knowing any better, when Ms. Champion told me what I was going to do; so I received it as a child. By faith. No questioning. No second-guessing. No wondering, "How is that going to happen?" No worrying, "What if it doesn't?"

I activated my faith before I knew I had faith at all. Hmmm…God is a comedian.

I was the first person on my mom's side to graduate from high school. Except for Mike, who graduated from an incarcerated schooling institution. Tila didn't graduate. Andy died. That was the moral of the story for Mom's kids.

Finally, graduation day came. We were at Cobo Hall in downtown Detroit. Doug said, "My brother doin' it man! My brother 'bout to go to college!" It was exciting, but scary for him. After all, "Dad" was leaving. I had to leave him with my aunt hoping that he had enough guidance for the last couple years to push him through. After all, big bro just graduated from high school. That was a big deal for him to witness. He knew the goal and he knew it was possible.

I started Mackenzie High School with about 400 other freshmen. That day, at Cobo Hall, I was graduating with about 115 other seniors. Such was…is…the state of education in Detroit, and in so many urban centers around the country. I don't know where my non-graduating peers went. Interestingly enough, six of us from Mackenzie were going to Michigan. And just like high school, or maybe even a little better, three out of the six—me, my good friend Jessica, and a young woman named Essence—graduated.

I didn't know how sad that was until I became a math teacher in the New York public school system. That experience spurred me to make sure my students would be in the same cohort of graduates that I was in years ago at Cobo Hall.

But more on that later. I still have a number of life lessons to learn… until I reach the other side of the desk. Thanks Ms. Champion. Salute.

# CHAPTER 9

## A Different World
### (Pun and No Pun Intended)

I was leaving the only environment I'd ever known. Up to that point, my sister Che had taken me to North Carolina and Atlanta. I lived in Detroit with my grandparents on my father's side, and experienced the occasional stays with my mother and father in my younger years, where I got questionable guidance, but a firm grasp on the importance of taking care of oneself and one's family.

It was an interesting hodgepodge of mixed messages:

*Whatever you do, you have to support yourself and your children.*

*Do whatever you want to do if it makes you feel good.*

*Strive for excellence in everything you do and don't get caught if it's illegal.*

*If you're going to be a thief, be the best thief you can be.*

*Working all the time to support your family is more important than spending time with family.*

I loved living with my grandparents. My limited experiences outside of that weren't the most pleasant. This new environment was out of my comfort zone, but for me, it was more like an unknown fairy tale. College is a magical place where all kinds of great things are supposed to happen. At least that was the consistent message from television and Ms. Champion among other educators. I guessed I was supposed to be there, but it was nevertheless an unfamiliar place, so I didn't know exactly what to think or how to adapt.

I had one college experience outside of what Ms. Champion provided during my senior year: I went to visit my cousin Anthony at Eastern Michigan University. He was the first person in my world to go to college.

We walked into his dorm on campus and the stench of sweaty socks and clothes hit me in the face when I passed by the guys' rooms. A few black folks, but lots of White kids and that was different. Actually, it was the complete opposite of life as I knew it. And lots of girls, which I could very much appreciate! It was like walking into a mansion full of irresponsible young adults. It was exciting because it seemed very adult-like. But all I could think about was:

*I'm going to make a killing selling weed to all these kids.*

I never saw a classroom during my visit, but that didn't matter to me at the time. I just saw a good time, and an ability to connect with girls and make money. It never occurred to me that college was a place to go where one could attain a profession in order to make a living. It was a place to go because a counselor told me I could do the work; I would make my real money selling weed among other hustles—all of which I might be able to advance at college. Most of the notions I had about college came from movies like *School Daze* by Spike Lee, that focused on Black Greek fraternities and sororities at Historically Black Colleges and Universities (HBCUs). My visit to Eastern consisted of seeing the dorms, going to the parties, and generally seeing people having fun and eating at the student center.

The educational aspect wasn't what drew me. I may have liked some of my teachers, and I definitely appreciated my counselor, but I honestly wasn't that impressed with their lifestyles. They didn't have the "fly" cars, and their lives seemed pretty boring.

My cousin saw me pull out my stash. "You know you can't bring that illegal stuff in here. Your head is in the wrong place. Jesus don't like ugly, and that's ugly."

"Go sit down," I told him. "In order to take care of people including yourself, you have to do certain things in life." My home training was kicking in!

It was a great weekend, it was my first college experience, and it was the only peek I had into what I would be walking into in the fall. Fun times,

106

selling weed, and ace-ing my classes the way I had in high school. What could be wrong with that? I guess things wouldn't be too different than home.

It was another story when my sister Che actually drove me to Ann Arbor. We hit M-14 from the Jeffries Freeway and took M-23 into the campus.

"So have you decided what you're going to do? What are you going to major in?" Che asked me these questions as we approached Ann Arbor. I had no idea what my major would be. My plan, remember, is to sell dope, hustle, and rap. At least until I figure out something that's a bit more fitting. That's really all I knew that would afford me the kind of lifestyle that I admired.

But it's the year 2000 and so I answer, "Computer Science. That's what I really want to do." Computers are the thing, right? Computers are what's in demand.

"That's what I'm talking about," she says. She has no idea that I have no idea. She has no idea what my current aspirations were.

In high school, I didn't take the time to invest in typing skills. I had no problem writing my papers, but I would have this girl named Valencia type my papers for me. I didn't know a Macintosh from a hole in the wall. I'm just saying what I think she wants me to say. And it's working for the moment.

Che's next question was, "Who do you look up to?"

"I'm not sure anymore." Although, I have been paying attention to Kwame Kilpatrick. He's a cool brother. "My man is about to be the mayor of Detroit for real. He's young, and he is educated with the credibility to make big things happen for the city."

After all, he's the same age as I am when I began writing this book: 30. Mayors are powerful. They have money, power, and prestige. They ride around with security guards. They live in mansions. They are automatically important by virtue of their position. They don't have to run from the police, they don't go to prison. And this Kwame is young. He's cool. He acts like us, not stuffy and self-important like the older mayors. He used to be a teacher, too. When we looked at older people who were mayors and teachers, we shrugged our shoulders; but when we looked at Kwame, a teacher soon to be mayor, it was different. You could see by his speech that he was intelligent—he spoke with elegance—but he was very familiar and relatable too. There was power in that. He was really the first young guy of his type that I paid attention to, outside of characters in the movies.

I continued. "You know I think that Kwame guy is a good guy to look up to. Maybe after I graduate from this college thing, people will look at me the same way they look at him. I'll have to figure it out Sis."

When we rode into campus and up to my dorm, I thought: *This looks just like Mayberry.* I saw stores I've never seen in Detroit: Whole Foods, Borders Books, ice cream parlors (ice cream parlors??). Everyone was doing the speed limit. As we proceeded down Washtenaw Avenue prior to turning onto Observatory to go to Mary Markley dormitory, I saw some humongous houses with Greek letters on them.

"Wow! People actually live in these?" I commented to Che. "Yes, but not families. These are frat and sorority houses. Groups of students live there," she explained.

None of this was familiar to me. The Twilight Zone comes to mind as I think about that first trip. So does *The Stepford Wives.* It was all so perfect. At the same time, it's weird, too. I wasn't sure what kind of students lived in this kind of environment. They most likely were a bit different than me.

As we turned onto Observatory Street, the dorm comes into view. We parked directly outside the front door, and I begin to unpack the car and proceed to the dorm. People were beginning to move in and some of them—a lot, in fact—were African American. But these African

Americans didn't look like me. *They're probably not from "Detroit Proper",* I thought.

This was going to be very, very different. I began to observe. I was walking into the dorm with my hat on backwards and tilted so you could see my hairline, a baggy pair of Ice Berg jeans, with the matching Tom and Jerry Ice Berg t-shirt, jewels, Cartier glasses and a crispy white pair of Air Max 95's. A few people had some of the things I was wearing. I was 'hood-rich.

I got a cart and began taking things to my room, situated on the basement floor. I passed the big cement blocks along the wall on the right side of the hall, passing the many dorm doors on the left, and I walked past doors until I approached one with two yellow and blue signs. The yellow sign looked like a paper plate rimmed with curly paper fringes, and had a smiley face in the center and the name "Shawn" written in a circle on the sign. The blue sign held the name of my new best friend, Anthony Bomar. We knew each other from Mackenzie High School and barely spoke to each other then, but he was one of my most familiar links to home, however tenuous that link may have been.

Anthony wasn't there yet, so I walked in the room and claimed my bed. Both of them were twin beds, so the choice didn't really matter.

The dull décor featured a black tiled floor and tan stackable furniture with white walls. Not the best in the world. Kind of smallish. I had seen the dorms at Eastern, so it wasn't a shock. It's just that it became real because it was my new dwelling place.

I began pulling out my shoes first. I had 56 assorted pairs of sneakers, most bought from my weed-selling and other hustles. I placed them neatly under my bed in color-coordinated order. Then I put my prom hat and a late teenage picture of my father on the shelf above my desk. I proceed to hang up all of my clothes. I noticed that some of the students were just hanging up summer clothes, but I brought all of my possessions with me because wherever I went, that's where I lived. And I didn't live with my grandfather anymore.

In the middle of moving, my sister Che, who had helped me, gave me the speech: *I told you I was going to stick around until you graduated and I did. I'm proud of you bro'.* She was heading to Atlanta where she grew up. It was cool having her around while I was in high school.

She kept her word. Respect.

I was by myself for a minute and closed the door. A tear, just one, ran down my cheek. It was at once heavy and sobering, at once exciting and sad, a very different kind of loneliness. I had never been completely by myself.

When I was in high school, I was the Prom King-most-popular-class hair-class cutie known to be smart, and now I'm going to be a freshman in a completely foreign environment. I was cool in middle school, "the man" in high school…but this school was huge and I didn't know if I could maintain the same type of bravado I had literally last week in high school. Will I still be "that guy"? Will people like the way I dress, since it's so different than what I have initially seen here at the dorm? Who will be there for me, the way my grandfather was (even though the last few years were so different than they were when my grandmother was alive), or my grandmother, or even my brothers and sisters? Is there a "Ms. Champion" anywhere on campus who can see my value and tell me, *Shawn, this is the way you should go"?* I felt like I was lost in the forest. I felt kind of lost at home, too; but I had my little brother Doug to take care of, and I had found purpose and centered myself in that role of protector. Then, it never occurred to me that I also needed to be protected. It was a safe role for me, a role to which I had become accustomed, and comfortable. What role would I be in at Michigan?

A shiver came over me. *You still you. This is just a new chapter of life. You good. Chin up.*

"Yo! What up doe?" Anthony Bomar swung the door open and stepped into the doorway with two large duffle bags.

I felt the comfort of home again.

"Come here bro, come in and close the door." He dropped his bags and closed the door behind him. My big brother syndrome began to kick in. Anthony was a track and football star at Mackenzie High School, All-American in everything. But like me, he didn't come from a wealthy family. In fact he didn't come from a "hood rich" family either. He was straight-laced, a by-the-book kinda guy. He didn't have much when it came to possessions, but he was rich with raw talent, humility, and personality. Unfortunately, people respect what they see more often than what's inside a person. If I was going to be hanging out with him, I couldn't have my partner in crime looking like my unequal sidekick. So I gave him a few pieces of clothing I picked up for him. I wanted to make sure he would get my same physical respect that possessions commanded. We were about the same size—clothes and shoes—so Anthony got a mini-image makeover. Anthony got five pairs of shoes, four pairs of jeans, five shirts, three hats and a few jerseys. I began my welcome speech.

"We are two young brothers from the west side of Detroit in college. Now, I don't know much about the folks up here, but I do know you and you know me. With that said, we are brothers and we are our brother's keeper. And from here on out, I'm gon' call you 'Bo'." I didn't know much yet about the iconic coach Bo Schembechler—I knew I wanted "Bo" to be empowered to be great as we pushed one another. My grandfather always told me when you bless someone your relationship with them will also be blessed. With that…"Enjoy the blessin' bro'."

"Yo, these clothes are crazy. And I like 'Bo'. That's cool with me. Respect." The newly-named "Bo" showed his appreciation.

We were ready for the takeover. Anthony-Bo was ready, I was hype because I had someone to hype up—someone to take the place of my real little brother Doug, who had given my life so much meaning. I considered Bo equal, but his humility enabled him to learn from my positive traits as I learned from his humility and other traits. It was good brotherly fit.

---

The students who looked like Bo and I didn't typically come from regular Detroit Public School system schools such as Mackenzie High School. Remember there were six of us from Mackenzie. The others typically came from the more "usual suspect" specialized schools in and around Detroit: the most frequently-named public schools were Cass Tech, Renaissance, and Martin Luther King Jr.—schools that you had to take a test to get in. A lot of African American girls were from Mercy, a Catholic school in the Detroit suburbs. Similarly there were boys from University of Detroit, which was the brother high school to Mercy. Many of them wore their hats to the front. Their clothes were more fitted. They even had University of Michigan paraphernalia on already, and were excited about it! They came with their parents, who were wearing "Proud Michigan Mom" or "Proud Michigan Dad" t-shirts. They were bringing big flats of water bottles and packages of animal crackers for snacks. The parents hugged their children, telling them "call me" and the newly-minted students were saying "Alright mom" and maybe rolling their eyes a bit but they didn't look cynical, just happy. It seemed to be a big event. That was cool.

Meanwhile, Bo and I just got dropped off—me by my sister and him by his mom. He had a pillow, three outfits and some notebooks until I blessed him. I had a ton of shoes and a 32-inch television with speakers. There were no long good-byes for us. We were appreciative of getting a ride, nevertheless.

I showcased my Mackenzie High School diploma on my desk—I wanted people to know where I came from. I put up an old school picture of my dad with one of his hats. I look just like him in that picture—really cool. He wasn't there like the other kids' dads, but at least I had his picture, and the picture was so strong for me it actually invoked his presence. It made the place feel proud and family-influenced.

Now it's time for the real agenda: girls. Freshmen orientation was held in the cafeteria, so we all piled in. Bo and I grabbed one of the circular tables and sat in our seats.

*Yo bro' I can tell you right now which ladies I'm going for and you pick yours.* We didn't waste any time. *Ooh, she's mine. Yeah, that's a good one.* One of the girls I picked looked just like Nia Long. Our "picks" or taste never really clashed; his girls were not my type, and vice-versa.

The head counselor began to speak. "Look to your left. Look to your right. This is the University of Michigan. These are the brightest and best."

I'm really feeling this. *Yep, I'm the brightest and best. That's right!* I still, at this point, have no idea about how prestigious this school really is.

The counselor continued. "Everyone who comes to this University is a leader. You have been selected strategically among the nation's best. Everyone who comes here was among the best in their high school. Approximately, 80% of students who choose the University of Michigan as freshmen graduate within 3-5 years. That means that approximately one of every five students may not make it to the Promised Land...Don't let that be you!"

Every student in the room is tuned into the counselor's every word.

The head counselor continued. "The average student at U of M has a 3.9 GPA and a 31 on the ACT. They are the valedictorians, the student government leaders. They are in the top 10% of their class. They make decisions. They are creative, with diverse talents, and leaders. They are the scholar-athletes. They are YOU."

I looked at Bo with a face that said, *Well, that part isn't me.* Bo had the exact same face as I. Affirmative action was still in play in 2000. I had a 3.54 from a non-prestigious high school, and a 17 on the ACT. Bo had pretty much the same academic standing as well as test score. However, he was a star athlete. I had tremendous leadership on paper and off paper, but also had a bad junior year, which brought my grades down a bit. It wasn't that I couldn't do the work; I just didn't. But I was also class treasurer and a member of the debate team, my high school record was well decorated with extracurricular activities, and my counselor had seen promise. She had seen something in me—maybe the same thing my grandmother had seen. So off I went, to U-M's Summer Bridge Program. And here I was, listening to a counselor telling me that I had an 80% chance of making it at Michigan (probably even less because of my background). Bo and I knew we slid in. We were just now starting to understand the extreme prestige of which we were a part.

I knew more after hearing the counselor than I did moments before when Bo and I were at the tables deciding which girls sparked our interest. I knew at that point that Ms. Champion really pulled some strings to get all six of us in. She had advocated for me, and I knew that she had had to advocate strongly to put me in with these high achievers. I knew I had to make her proud.

And I had nowhere else to go.

---

My angel, however, did have somewhere else to go. While I went to the University of Michigan a week after graduation, she was headed a bit further north, to Michigan State University (MSU) in September, Michigan's chief rival. But that didn't really matter to me. Unfortunately, after the first couple weeks on campus, I knew this long-distance thing was not going to work, and it had nothing to do with the fact that we were going to "rival" schools. My new world was filled with tempting distractions…girls. The last thing I wanted was to be a "dog." I had seen so many men dog women: my brothers, my friends, even my granddad. I was not willing to be "that guy."

After two weeks of being focused on academics, becoming acclimated, and having more than a few conversations with girls in my program, I called Kim to explain. "We're going to have to take a step back," I told her. She did not take it well.

After a long, painful silence: "You are my first *everything*..."

"You're right," I told her. "The truth is I really need to focus, we are young, this is a lot of pressure with you not being around, I've never done anything long distance in my life, and I refuse to cheat on you. I just have to be honest." My attempt was to soften the blow, and I knew it was going to be hard for her; but I figured being honest was better than stringing her along and risking any chance of her being hurt by finding out that I was drifting toward other women.

"I don't think I can talk to you right." I could hear her tears forming.

"I still love you and we can pick things up in the future."

"I just need to be alone."

"Whatever you need, you let me know. I'm always here."

The girls in college were a bit different than the girls I was used to being around. They were all smart, had a variety of strengths, more focused, more laid back, and interestingly strategic with their interest in guys. They were more like Kim. It was like a jigsaw puzzle to figure out if they were interested in a particular boy. In Detroit the girls were aggressive and straightforward. Some were smart and some simply weren't. The majority of the campus girls wouldn't dare "openly" chase a brother. Some were African American, some were Latino, others where Italian, and some were from places I'd never heard of.

I liked the difference.

There weren't many Caucasians in this "bridge" group. It was starting to occur to me that this "bridge" program had people in it that were the brightest and best—only nearly all of them were minorities, like me.

115

The Bridge Program worked for me. It wasn't extremely difficult, but the work was time-consuming just as the upcoming academic year would prove to be. It provided an introduction to the classes I would be taking in the Fall, and not knowing what to expect I just figured it would be an extension of high school. But it was definitely on another level, and I found myself working harder than I ever did in high school because I was intimidated by the college experience, and Michigan in particular. So, I was careful about my time. When some of my peers were procrastinating and enjoying their freedom during the day when they were out of class, I was working. By nightfall, the time many of my fellow Bridge students started, I was already finished.

I noticed a difference. Recall, I had lived with my grandfather for many years and he didn't give me any rules. I made my own rules up as I went along. So the freedom that came with college was not a new, heady freedom the way it was for the students who had stringent rules and regulations at home. When they got here, they thought: "Hey! I can stay up as late as I want to! I can go to the store at midnight! I can eat pizza for breakfast!" For me, that just wasn't a big deal. My grandfather had never come to my room in the morning to tell me it was time to wake up; I'd been used to waking myself up at home. Completing assignments and going to sleep at a somewhat reasonable time without anyone checking on me was a typical day. Instead of having to have someone tell me when to get up and when to sleep, when to eat and when to study, I instead would wake up my brother and set rules and examples for him.

While setting and adhering to my schedule was easy, I did have to learn how to study; no one had ever talked to me about that, at least at the level of detail that I needed. I also had to teach myself how to type. In my English class, they asked us to type a five-page paper. "Five pages... typed?!" At Mackenzie we never had to write more than five paragraphs. I had no idea how I was going to fill what seemed like an interminable number of blank pages. And I typed slow...really slow. Sometimes it took me all night to type a paper that I was already finished hand-writing. I'm a math guy, not an English guy.

116

I had to develop a process. I would hand-write everything first, while everyone else, I noticed, just jumped on the computer and started typing. Their typing skills were superb! The majority of my peers never glanced at the keyboard. Meanwhile, I typed with my index fingers starring at the keyboard and back at the screen between every l-e-t-t-e-r.

# CHAPTER 10

## I'm Different

It was the summer after my first year at Michigan. I was taking Calculus and Conflicts of Religion and working as an accountant at The Domestic Violence Safe House Project. I figured it was best if I stayed in Ann Arbor during the summer instead of heading back to Detroit. It was peaceful and I figured it would be easier to stay out of trouble.

The Religion class was fascinating. One of my writing assignments was on *The Problem of the Existence of God and Evil.* If God is good than how can evil exist? Why do bad things happen? Is there a "greater good?" It was my final paper.

I began with a startling statement. There were some evil people who killed a child and drank his blood. How can anyone possibly find the "greater good" in that? How could God let this happen? It started off as a discussion and turned into a paper. A long time ago, I had decided intellectually that Christianity would be my faith. I did not fully understand everything that meant, and my initial decision was not a decision of the heart, but nevertheless proceeded forward with my thoughts on the topic.

The God of Adam and Abraham is the true God, I stated. I continued with a Bible-based argument: My reading of the Christian scriptures suggests, even demands, a greater good, even in the presence of evil. My argument began with Romans 8:28:

*All things work together for good for those who love God and are called according to His purpose.*

I then went to Romans 10:9

*Whoever shall call on the name of the Lord shall be saved.*

Isaiah 7:15, I argued

*...he knows enough to reject the wrong and choose the right.*

119

tells us that men and women make choices of their own volition, and that they "know enough" to understand the difference between right and wrong. God is good, I argued, but people sometimes choose to do evil things. That child would spend eternity in heaven, so the ultimate outcome is good. God is certainly good, but He has given man free will. In this scenario the free will of man has led to a terrible deed, but the goodness of God will accept the child into eternal paradise. The temporary pain will give way to an eternity of joy and happiness. God is good.

I was leaning towards the Christian faith. In writing the paper, I was more interested in getting a good grade than truly believing what I was trying to prove. But the topic intrigued me. I had done some wrestling of these issues with my roommate Bo, who was raised as a Jehovah's Witness, and I had been taken to different churches sporadically growing up. Neither Bo nor I fully accepted what we had heard. We knew there was something, some entity, more powerful than us; we just didn't know what that was. We would have extensive conversations about the phenomenon of coincidence. Everything that happened seemed to be one big coincidence after another. My roommate and I were a great example. Applied to the same school. Both accepted. Ended up being roommates. Launched our quests for meaning at the same time. So now we had to agree:

*Coincidences are false illusions of 'chance' that are simply evidence of God's existence.*

Pay attention.

Coincidence? No. God.

---

I was the only black kid in my Calculus class. The Russian professor barely spoke English. So he was hard to understand, but I understood mathematical language, so...no problem.

I sported a Detroit fitted hat, brim to the back, my long Cartier chain…I hadn't gotten to my preppy phase yet. My classmates and I scouted the classroom, trying to figure out who we'd want to be in a group with us. I laid back, just waiting to see who might choose me, with my saggy pants and backwards hat. It was kind of like basketball. But it wasn't athletes; we were "matheletes." I just didn't look the part. So I figured I was going to be one of the last round "draft pics." Indeed I was.

But there was this girl, a little chubby and cute…and white. I'll call her Melissa. "Hey. You should come and be with us. Join our team!" I agreed. She was pretty cool, and I appreciated the invitation. I knew that the failure to invite me was due to stereotypes; guys that look like me didn't typically do well in math, at least on television.

Melissa had on a Rolex. Now, two things I know about Rolex's: the second hand moves smoothly, without "tick-tocking," and the glass over the date dial has a magnifying lens. "That's a Presidential Rolex," I thought.

"Melissa: nice watch," I said instead.

"Thanks. My Dad got it for me, for graduation."

Now Mellissa dressed frumpy most of the time. It totally caught me off guard to see her sporting an authentic Presidential Rolex. I couldn't help but wonder what kind of hustle her Dad was involved in. Where I came from if you could afford such toys then you were definitely hustling. My curiosity was piqued.

Melissa invited our study group to her apartment. Upon entry we had to remove our shoes. Her carpet was plush and there was marble everywhere… not a typical student apartment. "This is dope," I said to anyone listening and no one in particular.

I noticed a magazine on her coffee table that was hoisted in a cradle. It clearly displayed the cover of a man in a suit smiling. The magazine was *Forbes*.

121

"Melissa, what is this 'For-bess'?" I asked.

"Oh, that's *Forbes*," she answered from her bedroom.

"Who's this guy on the cover?"

"Oh, that's my Dad," she answered as if it were no big deal.

"Cool."

I asked her about her dad and she told me about the companies he owned and the things he had done. I can't remember his name to this day. At the time, I knew it was something pretty significant, but I had no idea what *Forbes* was. I had no idea that this world even existed. For me, this was just another piece of the puzzle. I was slowly finding out that life was full of opportunities that were available to me.

Now I knew why she had a Presidential Rolex, one that did not "tick-tock."

---

While taking a Conflicts of Religion class, I found myself having in-depth conversations with my roommate. Who is God? How do we fit into his overall plan for mankind?

In class we were studying Judaism, Christianity, Buddhism, and Islam.

I was in Angell Hall in class with a wide variety of students. Some classmates believed and followed different walks of faith. There was a Gothic guy with black pants outlined with safety pins, black hair swooshed to the side held with thick gel and an armful of bracelets. He wore an assortment of skull and bones t-shirts and rode a skateboard. He was an atheist. Then there was a girl that looked like a saint. She wore skirts past her knee, flat shoes, freckles, long red hair, and she was quiet. Kind of like Mother Theresa. She was Catholic. Then there was me with my baggy jeans and my tilted brim fitted hat. I was trying to figure things out.

One day I happened to look up. I saw an angelic girl. Asian-looking, long dark silky hair, round face, beautiful smile, arched eyebrows, pursed lips. She was walking outside my classroom. On one of my breaks I walked outside, hoping against hope that she would walk by again.

I didn't see her in the hallway. I stalled and walked to the bathroom, but there was no sign of her. Coincidently (you know how I feel about coincidence), I saw her as I passed the door next to my classroom. She sat near the window. She was intently looking at in the direction of the chalk board. I stood there; she turned towards me and caught me staring! I snapped back, acting like I hadn't been looking so hard, smiled, and quickly walked back to my classroom. After that, I'd catch her walking past my classroom while I was sitting in class. Somehow, I couldn't bring myself to speak to her. It was easy with other girls. But not the Angel.

I had a friend named Mark, a poet and an English major. We were talking and walking though campus near the Diag. Mark started talking to someone while I was distracted by people-watching and the warm sun.

I happened to look at who he was speaking to. Whoa! He was talking to the Angel.

After they finished talking, I asked Mark: "Who was that?"

"That's Liz," said Mark.

"Dude. She's gorgeous. Is that your friend...lady friend?" I had to feel him out.

"Naw. We're cool, but not like that," said Mark. "She's in Bridge Program this year."

Recall, "Bridge" was the transition program at U-M primarily for urban students—mostly underrepresented minority students before the 2006 statewide ballot initiative known as Proposition 2 changed the way that

123

U-M could configure its admittance policies—to help them make the transition to college and ensure their academic success. I had been in Bridge the year before.

"I'm gonna have to tutor or something over at Bridge this year," I said. I was doing well in Calculus and quite frankly all of my classes throughout my first year. I almost had a 4.0 my first semester if it wasn't for the B+ in English. "C'mon, let's see if we can help some people out dawg."

Anything to meet the Angel.

We went to the Mary Markley dormitory, and Mark was greeting all the students. "Man, you must know everybody!" I said to him. Then I casually asked, "Hey, let's get to the point bro… where's Liz?"

"She's right here."

He already knew my mission and placed me directly across the hall from her room. We were visiting another girl that he knew from hanging around the dorm.

Liz wasn't in her room. So we chilled across the hall.

"AAARRGH!!" A scream came from across the hall.

I ran out, and it was the Angel, screaming, running out of her room.

"It's a bug in my room!"

*Super Shawn* to the rescue. I rushed in, moved furniture around, found the bug, and killed it… all in about 45 seconds.

"Oh my Gosh, thank you so much! I am so afraid of bugs." (*This must be God*, I think.)

"What's your name? Where you from" I asked.

"Elizabeth. But you can call me Liz. I'm from The Bay area in California. And you?"

124

"OK Liz. I'm Shawn, I'm from Detroit, Michigan, and it's cool to meet you. What you workin' on?"

"Math. This stuff is so hard."

"Really… Well, I'm a boss at math. I'll tutor you, if you would like?"

This time was different for me. Freshman year I had my fun dealing with a host of different girls. I'd gotten some of my 'fun' out, At this point I simply wanted one girl to keep my attention…not to mention that she was different. I decided to move very, very slowly. I was going to treat her as a friend and see how that worked. Plus, I was still working on myself. I liked to do fun, crazy things like head over to the parking lot roof top of a dorm and roll down the ramps in wheelchairs.

When Liz went home for the summer to California, we talked every day on the phone. Turns out my Angel, Liz, was a Christian. My meeting with her came at a most opportune time, and she really got me into deep spiritual discussions. We had some amazing conversations.

"There's lots of suffering in the Bible," she shared with me one day.

"Really. What are you thinkin' bout?"

"Think about it. Cain killed Abel. David was chased by King Saul, David killed Bathsheba's husband. Jesus was hung on a cross. Why"

It was almost like a math problem. All these people were precursors of Jesus, and their deaths had meaning in the context of His coming. It began to make sense to me. I thought initially that she was from the cast of Clueless, but…no. She was really smart and thoughtful.

Plus, she wasn't rich. She was of Mexican descent, from a one-bedroom apartment with three siblings, her mom and dad. She was a first-generation college student, just like me. I identified with her so much; we really hit it off. I was able to help her in math, and she helped me with spiritual growth. We had so many touchpoints, it was unbelievable.

Coincidence? No. God.

I was on my way to Accounting class, and the weather was gloomy. All of a sudden, I see people running, panicking and screaming "Oh my God!" It was a strange but exciting sight. I picked up my pace on the way to class.

I entered the classroom filled with somber faces. One girl was crying.

"What's going on?" I asked.

"There's been an attack on the United States. We don't know what's going on, but the Twin Towers have been hit." A dad of one of the students—Kelsey—worked in the Twin Towers.

"What's the Twin Towers?" I asked.

"You know, New York City. The Twin Towers."

I had no idea what they were talking about. All I knew was there had been an attack on the United States. And I kept hearing: Twin Towers. New York.

Kelsey's dad was an investment banker. And none of us knew what was going on. Where could we go? Would they hit Michigan? No one knew anything.

I found it interesting that Kelsey kept crying. She wasn't the same after hearing the news that her dad died. I just didn't have the same experience. When my dad died, I was OK. When hers died, she was apparently lost.

I knew that I was in a special place, a place where I would meet students completely different from me.

On the way back to my dorm, I kept hearing these unfamiliar words: Twin Towers. Pentagon. I knew the Pentagon was in Washington D.C. and directly correlated with the U.S. government and the President. I knew the shape of the five-sided building, but I had no clue of what happened inside.

Then I sat down to watch television. It was there that I learned a little more about these things. I felt like I was just getting my feet wet with a wider world. Interesting. It seems that even those that are walking the right path are still subject to disastrous lives when fools take control.

You can take the boy out of the 'hood, but elements of the 'hood will still remain in the boy. After 9/11, studying was still cool but I understood that there was a particular dark world that I previously had known nothing about. Not sure why, but I began taking mini-breaks from school. I made sure not to miss the small-sized discussion classes, but I would skip some of the large lecture classes where attendance wasn't taken and I could easily get the notes later. I needed to make money. I would leave on some Saturdays, and come back on Tuesdays.

I was going to Detroit. I had connections with distributors of illegal substances, 26 foot U-Haul trucks full of marijuana coming from across the country…at least that's what my contacts told me. They would back the trucks into the driveway with millions of dollars of weed that had to be broken up into pounds and placed into garbage bags for local distributors. Off the trucks there were bundles that were packaged and compressed into large bricks bound in plastic and slathered in Vaseline. When we opened the bundles, the weed just blossomed out. It was like a sweat shop from New Jack City, with mostly ladies doing the hard work of packaging the weed for sale. They had to do their work topless so no one would suspect they were wearing a wire or stealing any of the product. I was working right alongside with them.

By the time I finished, my fingers and hair were coated in green "lather." I was a walking "blunt." I'd get paid about $4,000 just for the work, then take a pound back to school to sell.

When I got back to school, I'd take a vigorous shower, then sleep and go back to class…just like a regular student. I did this about three times between September and November.

I could easily justify my actions. The reasoning went something like this: Melissa's dad is on the cover of *Forbes*. He has business. I have business too. The best of both worlds. Street lords and CEOs. I could do both and *really* get paid! People had stuff. I wanted stuff too. These kids at school got money 'cause their parents got money. They really don't have their own money. But I got money and I'm getting an education. I'm talking to my angel Liz and can buy her nice things. I'm learning about God. So it's all good. Right?

---

November 19, 2001. That date is burned in my mind. Recall, I have a hook-up with weed. Now, I have a hook-up with jewelry thieves too.

"I got a couple jewelry spots in Ann Arbor that you could hit. You get the jewelry, and I got people who can buy it." I had a network of hustlers with major cash who knew what to do with "hot" jewelry.

My homeboy, OJ—he sported a Cadillac DTS—came up to Ann Arbor. I asked my colleague in crime, "Money Mel" to come up and work with him. I didn't really trust OJ completely, and I wanted to make sure one of my guys was in on the job. OJ had a runner, Reggie, who was going to help too. OJ had the car. Mel would drive. Then they'd come back to me with the merchandise. I'd pay Mel from my cut. OJ would pay Mel for driving. Once I brokered the sales with my "connects" I would be paid with clean hands.

I gave them my list of jewelry stores when they arrived. We had already cased the spots to get the lay of the land. My homeboy from the 'hood and I rode around in an '85 Cutlass Supreme throughout Ann Arbor a few weeks back. That's not necessarily the whip to drive in the suburbs if you want to have a low profile. My homeboy Roscoe walked into Louis Jewelers, acting like a customer, just looking around and asking questions. He was in there for no more than ten minutes, then came back out to the car and we drove off.

The cops stopped us. Of course.

"Officer, I'm a student at the University of Michigan," I said politely and somewhat proudly.

"Let me see your ID."

I pulled out my yellow block "M" card. "Sir, I'm a sophomore. My friend just wanted to check out some jewelry, and so we checked it out. There is nothing going on here."

The (white) officer looked at his (white) partner as if to say, "Let these kids go." Then, to me and Mel: "See that's the problem. I'm so sorry. I gotta be honest with you: the people in the jewelry store called us. They were afraid you were going to do something. You may not want to go back in there. They saw the kind of car you were driving, they saw that one of you stayed in the car, they racially profiled you, and they just thought you were casing the place."

I poured it on thick. "Officer, I was just reading my book for class."

"I'm so sorry," the officer repeated. "I get so tired of these people and how they look at you guys," he continued. "Look...you go ahead and make sure that you prove these people wrong about who you are. Have a good day gentlemen."

We were definitely not going back to that store to do the "work." I gave OJ the addresses of the other stores, but they had trouble finding the locations. Mel called me, "Bro', you know we're not from Ann Arbor. We can't find these spots."

I was a bit pissed they couldn't figure it out. "Aight."

Something told me not to go with them. But I failed to listen to that "still small voice."

I got in OJ's gold Cadillac DTS with the black tinted windows and 20-inch rims. Not exactly the kind of fuel-efficient, hybrid car driven by the typical Ann Arbor resident. Definitely an attention-getting car in this neighborhood. But we're 'hood boys. Nothing but the best for us.

We went to Zeigfried on Main Street. "Zeigfried is crazy loaded bros," I told them. Then, the strategy:

"Don't take nothing while I'm in the car," I told them. This is just so you know where the spots are located. Go in, then come out and take me to class. Then handle your business and we can finish our business."

"OK," said Reggie. "This is what I'll do. I'll just go in and ask a few questions to set the stage bro', then tell them I'll be back with some money. That way, when I come back, it won't be no issue."

We parked about a block down the street, near a coffee shop. Reggie was wearing a button-down shirt, tie, and some slacks, a watch with diamonds that belonged to OJ so the jewelers wouldn't suspect anything. He walked into Zeigfried and noticed all the jewelry was under glass. The strategy was to take a razor blade and cut the gum right between the two pieces of glass where they connect, then quickly grab the goods.

"You know what?" Reggie said to the salesperson. "Let me see this ring right here. She's gonna be so excited!"

"Poppin' the question, huh?" smiled the jeweler. "You think you're ready for that?"

"Absolutely," answers Reggie. I'm going to be the best husband and father you've ever met in your life."

Instead of presenting Reggie with the ring that he requested, the trusting jeweler brought the entire case from under the glass to show Reggie. This was out of the ordinary to present an entire case of platinum diamond rings. The jeweler bought his story completely.

Reggie looked up and said, "Oh my gosh, what about that one over there?" The jeweler turned around to get another sample. When he turned back, Reggie was gone...with the case of diamond platinum rings!

"Hey, come back here!" Reggie fell and swiftly got up with the case of diamonds in tow. "Hey, hey, hey!"

The people in the coffee shop were staring at the car, pointing at the 20-inch rims. They couldn't see us because of the dark window tint. We were laughing at their naiveté. "They look like some groupies."

Then, Money Mel spotted Reggie running toward us. "Oh s—t. Reggie running and somebody's chasing him, mad as hell!" Money Mel started the car, and I flung the driver side rear door open. Reggie jumped in with a case of diamond platinum rings!

"F--- class," I said. "Head to my dorm!"

"Look nigga, we straight!" Reggie was elated. "We got...how many? One, two, three...

He had stolen fourteen diamond rings.

"Dawg, this is nuts! We 'bout to get it in! We just need to make it back," I said.

As we were driving down the street, I saw them out of the right side of the window. "Oh s--t," says OJ "The boys comin'."

We saw the first police car, then a second, then a third, then a fourth. We bent left towards the College of Engineering on North Campus. The cop car to our right came behind us, the one to the left followed suit. All told, there were ten police cars... too many for OJ's DTS to handle.

"Nigga, I'm sleep," says OJ. "I don't know nothin'. I'm sleep and I'm 16."

"Aight," I say. "Yo, I was just going to class."

Mel chimes in: "I was just driving. Reggie, you got to take this s—t. The only one they saw was you."

"F--- it," says Reggie. He stuffs all the diamond rings in his sock. "F--- it, I'll take it. It's all good."

We assure Reggie. "We got you. Don't even trip."

We came to a stop. We were across from Pierpont Commons on North Campus. Police officers rushed the car with guns out. They tapped on the driver side window with their guns drawn.

OJ says, "Can I help you officer?" Money Mel didn't say anything.

"There's two more in the back!"

The police snatched us all out and searched us. I saw the Michigan blue bus ride by, and it was turning. The students were pressed up against the glass windows, looking at me and my crew. I hid my face with my hoodie and looked down, but I couldn't hide. I looked at OJ. He must have been nervous because he was biting his fingers.

"Yo, you good bro'?" I asked OJ.

"They not about to get me," he replied. "My story is that I'm 16, I was sleep. That's all."

When we got to the police station, they locked us in different rooms and had us handcuffed to pipes on the walls. OJ aggressively rubbed his fingertips and they began to blister and turn pink. I wondered, "What the hell is he doing?"

Once we were separated, I heard one of the officers say, "I think I know one of these guys." That officer came into my holding room. It turned out to be the officer from a few weeks ago that let me go.

He looked at me with a mixture of sadness and disgust. "I can't f--ing believe you," he said. "You were supposed to let them see what you could do, and this is what you do?" He looked at me, hung his head. "I believed in you kid... I really did." With a sigh of extreme disappointment he walked out. There were no words.

I felt like I had let down my entire race. This officer had believed in this little kid with a Michigan ID. It was almost like he was my father. I wanted to tell the whole truth, but I couldn't turn my back on the whole crew too.

Our truth was: Reggie was going to have to take the rap. I was going to go with OJ's story that he was sleep, and Money Mel's story that he was just driving the car. Yep, that's it. I didn't know what was going on either. I was simply heading to class.

Although we were in different holding rooms we could hear the conversation in the atrium while each of us was being finger printed. I heard OJ talking to an officer.

"What's your name kid?"

"My name is Chris Dodson."

"How old are you?

"I'm 16 sir."

His name definitely wasn't Chris and he was every bit of 20 years old.

"Show me your hands," said the officer. OJ showed the officer his chewed up, raw hands.

"Damn! How'd you mess up your fingers?" asked the officer.

OJ lied again. He said it so innocently. "Playing football. Tackled in the street, sir."

I thought, "What a con! The boy is good at what he does."

133

The officer let him go.

It made perfect sense why he intentionally destroyed his fingers. They couldn't get accurate fingerprints that would reveal his ridiculous record. OJ seemed to be the smartest criminal among all of us. He had the most experience dealing with the law.

The rest of us told our real age. One by one the officers questioned us. My officer came in and said, "Looks like they're pinning it all on you."

I smelled his lie as soon as he came through the door with a smirk on his face. I knew it couldn't be OJ. He was "sleep," and his story required that he didn't know anything that was going on. Money Mel was "just driving," and his story required the same feigned ignorance. That left just one person: Reggie. He was going to pin the college boy as the mastermind. Unless this was the officer's ploy to get me to talk.

I decided to go with the agreed-upon story. Stick with the script.

They shipped me, Reggie, and Money Mel out to the Washtenaw County jail. They put the three of us in a holding cell with a few other guys, then closed the gate. Clang!

In the cell was a concrete wall, about six feet long and waist-high. Behind it was a toilet. No door. No privacy. The rest of the cell was dirty and unkempt. Not a place I wanted to sit down anywhere.

One of the guys already in the cell scrutinized me. "First time, huh?"

I looked him dead in his eyes and responded, "Last time." He said something about me being a pretty boy. I saw Money Mel begin to position himself to take the guy out. I didn't answer. We were already in enough trouble.

Then a kid came in. He was about 20. "What up doe niggas, what's good? S--t, this b--ch is cleaner than a m----- f-----. I mean this is ka-lean, damn!"

What?

He continued. Nigga, I just came from Wayne County Jail. They got roaches big as baby feet up in there! This is ka-lean!

About five minutes later, an old white guy, bald with a dingy red beard came in wearing a t-shirt, black boots and torn pants. The leather had rubbed off the boot tips, revealing the steel underneath. He started making weird noises. Money Mel and I looked at each other. We nodded. Once again we had each other's back.

The old guy went back to the toilet. He pulled out, and everybody looked away. Then he started urinating and continuously grunting… He reached into the toilet.

What the…?!

He swished his hand around in his own urine, then took some toilet paper and started hitting himself on the top of the head with it. The urine splattered everywhere!

"Officer! Officer! I called, thinking they'd have to answer this one. "This crazy m----- f----- splashing piss!"

The officer was unmoved. "That's your business, none of ours," was the reply. Then he started laughing.

The 20-year-old got upset. "F--- this. Hey! Officer! Would somebody remove this pervert? This guy is f---ing nasty! Oh s--t, it's piss juice on my damn neck! You better get this m----- f----- or I'm gone kick his a--!"

The officers came in to get me. They took me into a room and I had to take off all my clothes and bend over. They searched my "body cavity" with a flashlight and determined that I was clean. Then they brought Mel, then Reggie. They put all of us together again, and chained our feet and hands together, and the cords chained hands to feet. Here we were, walking like hunchbacks, shuffling along. Orange one-piece jumpsuits.

135

"You're going to J-Block," they told us. I didn't know exactly what that meant. I didn't know it at the time, but J-Block was different from the other lettered blocks. We went through some steel doors into another entrance to a larger room with cell blocks on two levels shaped like an L. I entered into the first cell on the left, lower level. Money Mel was on the second floor above me. I didn't know—and didn't care—where they put Reggie. I kept hearing the officers say something about "23-hour lockdown." I didn't know what it was, but apparently it was exclusive to J-Block.

How the hell did I get here? Yesterday, I was in college, sitting in class. Today…

This was my first time in a jail cell. I was numb and reality had not settled in. I had visited my brothers. Now, like them, I was on the other side of the wall. I laid down and went to sleep. Trying to forget. Hoping that I would wake up in a different reality.

I was awakened by a billy club dragged across the solid cell doors. "It's morning chow time sunshine!" said the guard. I wasn't hungry. But I did want to check on Mel.

I looked out the door and saw a tall and heavyset white guy, bald with tattoos, with a swastika on his head.

"You have 30 minutes to shower and chow boys!" said an officer.

I shook my head, hearing him explain our confinement and the 23-hour lockdown. Apparently, J-Block was where they put the ruthless murderers and rapists that commit the most heinous crimes.

I decided not to take a shower or eat. Mel didn't come out either.

"You got 30 minutes," we were told. Thirty minutes of "recreation or showering" outside of our cells, then back to confinement. I recalled hearing about 23-hour lockdown from my brothers. Those are the restrictions they place on people in the hole. This was a pretty good introduction to the jail system.

I was clearly in the wrong cellblock with the wrong cats. If anything I considered myself slick instead of ruthless. I was just a college student with a few side hustles keeping a few dollars in my pocket. I hadn't killed anyone. This must be some kind of funny joke the officers were playing; I just didn't find it funny.

Shortly after our 30 minutes of "recreation" was over everyone entered their cells and oddly there was loud screaming. The culprit was above me on the second level on the opposite side of the L-shaped cells. All I could see was stuff splattering against his window, and I heard strange noises coming from his cell.

"What the hell is going on here?" barked the guard.

"He's doing it again!" said another inmate.

"You mean he's tossing s—t again…"

The guy was relieving himself and throwing it against the window!

I couldn't do anything but laugh at this disgusting guy. I was accustomed to people talking loudly in study rooms and getting excited about new information or simply solving a math problem. Now I'm in small rooms with locked doors and my peers are tossing s—t instead of sharing ideas.

Through the slit in my door I could see the small 13-inch television on the guard's desk. I was able to make out the news.

"Jewelry heist, downtown Ann Arbor!" says the announcer.

Dang.

"Four young men, African American, robbed the Zeigfried Jewelry Store. It was a heist!"

They said it as if I went in the store and held people up with guns. Then they showed all of our mugshots.

137

*Oh s--t,* I think. *I'm in trouble now. This is crazy. I'm about to get kicked out of school. What will my teachers think? I'm supposed to be the hope of the 'hood!*

I sat there on my cot, silent. I placed both hands on my head and stared at the ceiling. I had to think. I jumped down to the floor and did 30 push-ups to get my mind flowing. On the ledge, I spotted a book. I would have been in class right now. I might as well read something.

So I picked up the book. It didn't have a cover. What is this?

It began:

"In the beginning."

This is the Bible. But it didn't read like the Bibles I had seen. It was written in everyday English. What? Somebody rewrote the Bible?

I liked the way this one read. I read the first five chapters, then went on to read half of Genesis.

I thought about the paper I wrote: "The Greater Good." Things do happen for a reason.

I decided to pray. I put the Bible back on the ledge, and got on my knees on the side of the cot.

"Lord, I know I don't talk to you much, outside of what Grandad taught me when I was a kid, but if You're really real, I need You now more than ever. I'm supposed to be the smart guy that my grandmother always said I am. I'm not supposed to fall into the same statistical trap that many of my loved ones have. Help me break the mold, God! I don't mean wrong. I'm learning about You. I got good people around me. If You give me a chance, You ain't gotta worry about me no more. Man. I'll do whatever You want me to do. I'll dedicate my life to making sure people don't end up in the same situation as me right now. You won't even catch me jaywalking."

This is not supposed to be my life.

I fell asleep. It was 1:00 pm.

---

At 3:13pm, I was awakened by a voice:

"247896... 247896... Hey, what's 247896 name?"

"His name is Blanchard."

"Hey Blanchard."

I looked at my wrist. That's my number.

"That's me." I felt like I hit the lottery.

"You're coming with us."

They called out another number. It was Money Mel's number. Neither of us knew what was going on.

"Did you see that s--t?" Mel and I said to each other when we found ourselves in the same room. We starting talking and comparing notes.

"We're taking you to B-Block. You guys were misplaced."

They call my number again. "2-7-8-4-9-6. You're coming with us. You're lawyer's here."

*Me?* Yep, that's me. Cool.

They took me to a room and my lawyer walks in. He was about 6'3". African American. Big guy with alligator Gucci loafers.

"How are you sir?" I asked politely.

"My name is Ray Richards. How you doin' good brother? Your brother sent me."

Thank God. Terry had sent one of his attorneys to navigate my situation. "What the hell happened? Your brother's been telling me good things about you. What happened?"

"It's a long story," I broke the whole story down to him. "Just get me the hell outta here."

"No worries. We're about to get you out in just a minute."

Then: "You must be a pretty popular guy."

"What do you mean?"

"You got girls and their parents calling for you. Professors calling for you. Man, people want you to go home, man."

I closed my eyes and thanked God.

"I know some good people sir."

We went before the in house judge and I was released. No bail required!

Mom met me, along with my brother Doug, both of them smiling and happy to see me.

Mom looked at me as if to say, "You're not exempt." She was relieved, but slightly happy that I wasn't the perfect kid without sin.

"Yeah," she said, "you too. We all been in here now. All my boys been locked up. I thought you was the only one. Thought you was gon' have the clean streak." Then she laughed with her mouth closed, cynical and taunting. It wasn't quite motherly.

Money Mel's mom was there with a bucket of KFC. Mel had to make bail; he had a felony already. He had stolen shoes from Sports Authority; since they cost more than $100, it was considered a felony.

I hadn't showered or eaten in three days… I definitely grab some chicken.

The case wasn't over. I was given a court date, then taken back to my dorm room. Mom dropped me off and left, which was OK—I didn't really want to talk to anybody.

I went to class the next day and called, of course, the Angel. Someone had already let her know what happened. She had been blowing my phone up.

"Wrong place wrong time," I explained to her.

"But what happened?"

I told her everything. I told her what I prayed in the jail cell. I told her I was going to take that prayer seriously.

I stopped cold turkey. No more Detroit runs. No more jewelry "connects." No more selling weed or any other illegal activity. Those three days were enough for me. I couldn't fathom how people became repeat offenders or violated probation. I went right back to work on school. No games.

Remember, I had been working as an accountant at the Domestic Violence Safe House. I just knew I was going to lose my job. I told my mom about it. She called the Safe House. "My baby was at the wrong place at the wrong time with these thugs…"

I kept my job. I found out later that professors had called, offering to bail me out. That's what all the calls had been about.

I immediately resumed my legitimate life. But I had to make the court dates.

"Do you want to plead to anything?"

I pled "no contest." That means I would let my lawyers handle everything.

They sent Reggie upstate to prison. Fortunately for Money Mel he had my lawyer too.

141

I went to court for the next year. Finally, Ray Richards said: "Look. They want to get you in a program. That's if you plead guilty, they'll put you in a program called the Holmes Youthful Trainee Act aka HYTA. HYTA is available for criminal offenders ages 17-23. The result of taking the plea is that the court doesn't enter a judgment of conviction, your record would be sealed and the case would be dismissed upon compliance. You have no priors, so that's in your favor. Once you finish probation, they'll expunge it from your record."

I'll take it. It's a good deal; after all, I actually was the mastermind. I had let so many people down, both dead and alive, and even that kind police officer that believed in me. Thank God for the wake-up call and the second chance.

I went to my probation officer and did a drug test every week. That was easy; I wasn't into doing drugs; I'd had a bad experience with drinking when I was 16, and you only have to tell me once. Over time, checking in with my probation officer to drop a urine sample changed from once a week to twice a month, then once a month.

The probation officer hated me. First, he asked me what happened. "Wrong place wrong time," I told him. "You young punks, you guys come in here...you do dumb s—t and think somebody's supposed to forgive you. This is ridiculous. You say whatever you want to say. You'll just get in trouble again just like the rest of them, young punk."

"Sir, I just came to drop and leave," I told him.

He was real hard. I'm sure he had some experiences and history that made him think the way he did. I left the office and prayed for the kind police officer. I didn't want to be any officer's excuse for mistreating any other Black man.

I had to make a decision to intentionally change. God had set me up. I could have been sentenced to a couple years as a conspirator. However, favor took over immediately after my prayer. I knew that it was Him.

I was a believer from that point on.

142

Two weeks later, I went to get baptized at my Aunt Corky's church in Inkster. She would talk about Jesus until she went to sleep, wake up on the prayer line, bake cakes for the church, bring candy for the kids, watch the Word Network daily, listen to the gospel station in the car, had a Bible in every room in her house, and best of all she would love every person she came into contact with irrespective of whether they earned it. She was a faith-filled woman so I decided to go to her church. I wanted to make a public service announcement about my salvation.

We sat in the pews of the small church on Middlebelt Rd near the Detroit-Wayne County Metropolitan Airport. It was the typical Baptist church with exposed wooden beams. Aunt Corky had one of her "Sunday best" dresses with ruffles and rhinestones, a stylish brown wig, a big pink hat. She fanned herself with a cardboard church fan with a thin wooden handle. Her relationship with God is apparent. Funny, I once thought she was absolutely crazy for all this constant Jesus-ey talk, prayer, and churchgoing. But my thoughts soon turned to admiration. This woman was committed on another level! She really lived what she believed.

That day, the message was about faith and consistency—duly appropriate given my thoughts given what I saw in my aunt. I looked over at her and she grinned from ear to ear. This was the first time I had ever come to her about going to church. Previously, I had consistently found a way to dodge her offer to attend.

"You must stick to the path, carry the cross, and die to thyself daily! Can I get an Amen?"

"Amen," the church responds in unison.

"Let's read Genesis 37:23. You see Joseph's own family threw him away. The same people that were supposed to oversee his life! He was jailed yet he stayed faithful! Hallelujah, praise the Lord! He stayed faithful and consistent and eventually became the overseer of the land of Egypt! I ask you this… What are you supposed to oversee? Who hasn't been

143

there for you? Have you gotten off track? Do you want to get back on? God is always faithful and consistent… Tap into his power…today."

I went to the altar call. The church stood and clapped. My aunt cried. They were pleased to see a young man come forward. The pastor said a prayer over me and I went into the back room to prepare for baptism.

*Are you saved young man?*

*Yes, I am.*

*How do you know?*

*According to Romans 10:9 - If you declare with your mouth, "Jesus is Lord," and believe in your heart that God raised him from the dead, you will be saved. I believe this and know it's real. I was saved before I walked into the church. Baptism is my official proclamation to God that I give my life to him.*

*Amen brother. You're wise. Welcome to the family.*

I left the church that day knowing that there was a long road ahead. *I'm far from perfect*, I thought, *but I'm in progress*. I could see better than ever. All these happenings that I once thought were coincidence was truly God communicating with me. God winks.

I heard the message that day. *My past and my future will be something like Joseph's*, I think.

## PHASE 2
# CONSCIOUS MENTORSHIP

**INFORMAL MENTORSHIP**

**FORMAL MENTORSHIP**

1. NETWORK - FRIENDTORS
2. SOCIAL MEDIA
3. MAGAZINES
4. BOOKS
5. BIBLE
6. CHURCH
7. MUSIC
8. ART
9. HOBBIES
10. MOVIES
11. TELEVISION SHOWS
12. MOTIVIATIONAL SPEAKERS
13. NEWS MEDIUMS
14. FAVORITE WEBSITES
15. SOCIAL GROUPS

**SPONSORS**

**DIRECTORS**

**EXAMPLES**

# CHAPTER 11

## My Ideal Self

I didn't tell many people about what happened, but it turned out I didn't have to; apparently quite a few people saw my face on the 5 o'clock news. I told, of course, Liz, a good friend, and my suitemate, but no one else on campus. Surprisingly, no one mentioned it. I think people thought it was kinda cool in a criminal, demented kinda way; it just solidified my 'hood credentials being from Detroit proper. With a backstory like mine, this kind of behavior is expected, statistically.

I called Liz on the way back to my dorm and as always she was welcoming and sweet. I walked up to the Bates II dorm door and she was waiting for me, she was as elegant and graceful as I had always known her to be. After a light hug, she said in my ear, softly: "You know you can't do that Shawn."

"I know," I told her. Her voice almost made me forget I was being tried as a felon. "So what do YOU think I should do?" Not that I didn't know; I just saw her as my protector for a season. She was there to protect me from myself. She represented what I could be if I tried hard enough. She was beautiful enough for the big screen, but her inner beauty was even greater. She loved the Lord, she was a praying sister, she loved her family, and she was a true friend. The most loyal person I had ever met.

When I came back to school from my short stint in jail, it was the strangest thing: no one ever talked to me about what happened. At least they didn't volunteer any thoughts in my presence. No one ever asked questions. It was always up to me to bring it up, and only if I wanted to…which wasn't very often.

I came back to some news: my roommate, Bo, was getting married! I had met his soon-to-be wife, Jennifer, the summer before while I was taking Calculus, at a house Bo and I sub-leased from a group of female students. We'd both been interested in the same pretty girl: Jennifer. I actually saw her first. Recall, Bo and I typically had different tastes. Apparently, not that time. "Bro', that's me," I told him, in the familiar non-compete language. "Bro', let me get her," Bo said. I acquiesced. After a few "couple trips," and after he met her parents—nearly four months after my jail experience—they were married. Things were changing. He was figuring out life, and so was I. He was getting married. I was learning how to be a gentleman, and how to stop that "second life" of mine that I vowed to leave alone.

This was a journey I would have to take alone.

---

Ms. Z. That's what we called our "Writing in the 21st Century" instructor. Ms. Z was slight of build with a full head of gray hair and a ton of energy. She looked 85, but her daily bike-riding and overall healthy lifestyle gave her a youthful appeal, along with her sweet-sounding, Mary Poppins voice.

It was second semester of my sophomore year and I walked into Ms. Z's class to meet a fellow student named John. John was about a year older than me, well-dressed, a little heavy, but most importantly—cool. John had a key ring on the executive style table that we all sat around. It had a fairly prestigious car brand linked to it:

Lexus.

I had seen people in high school with Lexus and Mercedes keys, but then you'd go outside and you guessed it…No car. They just had that nice key ring. So I assumed this was another cool black guy with a dream or at best maybe his dad has the actual car. After class, John, Liz, and I were walking and talking and John veered off, saying "Alright bro', see you later."

*Beep-beep.*

148

Those keys were definitely connected to an actual Lexus. But not just any Lexus. Oh, he had the hardtop drop, the new Lexus. I figured he was another rich kid, probably with a father on the cover of *Forbes*.

A few weeks later: the same scenario.

*Beep-beep.*

This time, it was a DTS Cadillac. Now that car's a bit more familiar to me. As a matter of fact, I don't even care for the DTS anymore; I think you know why! A lot of the 'hood guys had the DTS, including OJ, the guy I got into trouble with. But John also drove a hard top drop Lexus, so he couldn't be too 'hood. Does this kid have two luxury cars?

The end of the semester was near. And once again, John had another set of keys.

*Beep-beep.*

John was opening his door to 3rd luxury car. This time, it was a Mercedes S600. Whoa! Now that's a $120,000 car! I had to say something.

"Man, I saw you with the Lexus, the DTS, and now the S600. What the heck do you do?"

"My dad owns a lot of restaurants," said John matter-of-factly as he sat in his car with the door open. "He's in the franchise business and owns a dozen Burger Kings." This was the first actual black guy I'd seen who obviously had money but was not doing anything illegal. Revelation: Black people can own something without going to the black market. John was even helping to run one of his Dad's restaurants.

What? This is Burger King money? "'Have it your way' money?" You can drive around like a drug lord owning Burger Kings? That was the point where I knew I could step my game up instead of mystically thinking that only the white guys and athletes had all the fun. It could be done. And most impressively it was being done!

This was new to me. I'd seen people work at the plant and have pretty nice cars, but they didn't really own anything except maybe their home after 2,000 years of payments, or maybe a car or two. Business owners, in my mind, were old people with lots of resources and toys they've accumulated over the years. It takes a lifetime to become wealthy from business, right? By that time it appeared that they were too old to enjoy their wealth. John's father didn't have much gray hair, he wasn't old at all. He was just "older."

I was hungry for knowledge and practical understanding. I was even more convinced that one day I could be on the cover of *Forbes*.

John's father, he said, was his backbone. He had someone in the home to study, which made his business sense practical. I studied something else. I studied my family members like Mike, Terry, and my mother. Whether they actually dealt with the black market or not, they were all entrepreneurs, CEOs, with managerial skills and a keen understanding of economic principles. They were "Really Good, Bad Examples." I may not have known what to do, but I had a handle on what I shouldn't do. The knowledge that I had learned from them was like eating chicken wings. You have to eat the meat and spit out the bones of life or choke from taking everything literally. Discernment was a key element in this practice. Even my own schemes were done a bit differently than what I was taught growing up. Funny, I thought I had it all figured out. My original idea of "spitting out the bones" placed me in the Washtenaw County Jail. However, I had all the legit knowledge I needed to excel within my grasp.

John though, I thought, didn't have to sift *any* bones out.

During this time of reevaluating my ideal self I began to create a healthy universe, surrounding myself with the world and life I wanted and could imagine. I studied television and movie characters: Will Smith as Mike Lowrey in *Bad Boys* with his dope condo, his Porsche. He was a rich playboy and a cop! So I kinda wanted to be like "Mike." Then I saw him in *Hitch* and he was the perfect gentleman, very charismatic but definitely not a playboy. He also found pleasure in helping people. Hitch didn't have the Porsche though. *I know!* I thought. *I'll be a mixture of Hitch and "Bad Boy" Mike Lowrey.*

Then there was *Boomerang.* Eddie Murphy played Marcus Graham, who suavely strolled into an elaborate office dressed to impress with expensive suits. Everyone valued his intelligence. He had a brain. Dressed like a black James Bond. And was cool.

*OK,* I thought. Mike Lowrey was a trust fund baby with money, but just wanted to help people. This is where I spit out the "trust fund" bones because that certainly wasn't my reality. Hitch was smooth with the ladies and a super-gentleman. Women loved him. But he only cared about one. I liked that. Additionally, he was an entrepreneur who found his niche with his own product of love. I'll have to figure out my own product…

It was settled! The plan was to become a James Bond-Mike Lowrey-Kwame (then-Detroit Mayor Kwame Kilpatrick—more on him later)-Hitch-Marcus Graham. I sold my jewelry to completely release my attachment to my former self. This was a practical form of eating the meat and spitting out the bones. I decided to focus on God, and continuously work on "Shawn." I understood that my personality was largely a product of my environment whether I chose to accept my environment or decided to use my "Really Good Bad Examples" to be something different. What was that difference? I never clearly articulated what it was. Thus, my personality evolved into a fluid concept as I found myself collecting personas and sifting through my favorite aspects as I worked to craft my ideal self.

Noticing that the answers were all around me, I began to look for practical examples of my ideal self. Ironically, a lot of it existed within the people that I was around on a daily basis. Bo was purely kindhearted and possessed an innate ability to make others comfortable. Mark was friendly and trustworthy to the point where he was able to make anyone become psychologically naked or vulnerable before him, Ron was a gentleman, Liz was spiritual, and John had the business mindset. I turned my friends into "friendtors" (a merger of

151

friend and mentor). I spent a considerable amount of time with each of them and to feed my soul and spirit with great examples of human beings.

Not to mention, I created a healthy universe to purify my mindset: I subscribed to magazines such as *Forbes*, *The Robb Report*, and *GQ*. I watched movies that embodied the characters that I admired. I listened to R&B, Neo-Soul, Classical, and Gospel music and minimized my consumption of rap. I intentionally surrounded myself with "friendtors." I joined social groups and a church with diverse like-minded individuals.

Some of those things I needed to discard were connected to my own family. I couldn't be like my former idols anymore. I no longer looked to them as my role models.

I had a job as an accountant, but decided I needed to work more. I applied to be a Peer Advisor, a Course Assistant, a mathematics tutor, and a mentor to obtain multiple sources of income, while consistently expanding my mind and network of positive folks. I wanted to do legitimate work. I wanted to become what I didn't have. I didn't have a go-to tutor. I didn't have someone who could tell me what Michigan was about. I decided to become that person. No one would keep the secrets of success from anyone in my circumference. I'm telling everyone whatever they need to know! So, I decided who I was.

A charismatic do-gooder that's about my business. That's me.

# CHAPTER 12

## My First Mentee

Summer of 2003 was my first summer as a Bridge Program peer advisor, I drove back to Detroit every week to check on Doug. He had been placed in the Boys and Girls Juvenile Detention Center at the beginning of the year, and was in and out of juvenile facilities since I left for college. Fortunately for him, he had the possibility of coming home at the end of the summer. He was living with my spiritual aunt, Corky. It seemed that no one had been able to really get a handle on his behavior. After all, Doug's father had been in prison virtually all of his life. And our mother, well…you know our mother. Overall Doug had a lot of autonomy, autonomy that he snatched forcefully from most authority figures. At this point he was 16 and he was already a seasoned drug dealer and smoked weed like a chimney.

At the release hearing, the judge said, "He needs to be supervised by an authority figure that he will adhere to. Someone with enough time to pour into this bright young man before he gets himself into too much mischief. Clearly, he is a leader, according to the nature of the offenses on his record. He has quite the personality and he has always been much more respectful than many of the young men that I see in this court room."

I stood, "Your Honor, he can stay with me," I said to the judge. "Doug does need to be with a man. I was his overseer in the past while I was merely a young man in high school. It wasn't a walk in the park, but I had him on the right track. I can try my best to make sure that he's focused and back on the right track again."

It worked.

Doug came home from juvenile and I enrolled him in Huron High School around the corner from my place at the Highlands Apartments on North Campus in Ann Arbor. By this time—it's been two years since my hiccup with the law during my sophomore year—I was a

153

totally different person. I made my "friendtors" useful, I had an array of mentors, and cultivated a healthy universe that enabled me to purchase two cars from working 3-4 meaningful jobs. Collectively I worked 40-50 hours a week and was enrolled as a full time Economical Mathematics major. I was living intentionally and growing spiritually. Don't get me wrong: I was far from perfect, but I was in progress. I still found pleasure dressing in fancy clothes. I still liked nice things. But now I earned everything I possessed and I owned it legally—and managed to save money too. But life was busy: working at the accounting office after class, tutoring in the evening and on the weekends, mentoring, attending parent-teacher conferences, making sure Doug completed his school work, studying for my own coursework, and completing my homework at night. I made sure Doug was taken care of and I was also taking care of my live-in girlfriend too. So I was playing the role of a college student, a father, and a husband: three roles I've never seen done or at least done well...

Doug was enjoying his new life. I gave him one of my cars and he picked up a job at the Subway Restaurant up the street. In addition to working, he was exposed to what college life was about—something he's never seen first-hand before. I took him to student-led comedy shows, football games, step shows, interesting guest lectures, and study sessions with friends. I showed him the fun side and demonstrated the hard work side.

A month after Doug began living with me in Ann Arbor, we were walking around campus through the Diag, a large open area in the middle University of Michigan's Central Campus. He noticed the multicultural community of Black, White, Asian, American Indian, and Hispanic students. He saw varying degrees of class based on the cars, bags, cell phones, and shoes the students wore. Nothing was homogeneous, at least not physically. What was homogeneous was the motivated mindset of everyone irrespective of their physical makeup or cluster. They were focused, but still able to have fun and enjoy different kinds of recreation and expression.

"It's kind of like Mayberry," he told me. "But I like it."

154

Wherever Doug goes, he is a leader. But that can be a good thing or a bad thing.

One day, Doug came home with an Apple® laptop.

"Where'd you get the laptop?" I asked.

"Mike Jones gave it to me for some favors I did for him."

That didn't sound kosher to me. "OK, I want to meet this Mike Jones."

Now Mike was a suburban kid who claims "Detroit" as home so he could be perceived as "real." He was black, but not tough, urban, or from any environment that grows layers of tough skin. He was simply perpetrating a tough persona.

I couldn't wait to meet Mike. I had to watch Doug's affiliations because unlike many teenagers in Ann Arbor, my little bro' was the real deal. He wasn't slick or sneaky; everything he did was "in your face" and transparent. He started young, learned from black market bosses, and didn't need any new ideas or remnants of old illegal ideas. This whole laptop situation was iffy and placed Mike in a box of a slick guy or wannabe slick guy. Time would tell.

During my first conversation with Mike I noticed that he was definitely a wannabe slick guy. *Boy,* I thought, *stop and go watch the wind blow... you're not from anywhere real. You live in Ann Arbor so just go ahead and attend your good school with your AP classes and all of your upwardly mobile friends and have a seat. If you stop trying to play tough guy and be what your environment wills for you to do, you can be in the same boat that I'm in: the college boat.* I decided I needed to keep my eye on this guy and a close eye at that or I could see how he could persuade Doug to be sucked into our old ways.

I had another opportunity to learn more about Mike a few weeks later, when my brother threw a party.

I didn't know he was throwing a party until I heard the noise downstairs in my apartment building. I was in the middle of studying at my dining room table with my headphones on. Very rarely do I hear

155

loud music in my building, so I got up and walked downstairs to check it out. The party turned out to be in the basement and the apartment belonged to "Chuck," a skinny, pale white guy who would be considered what some call "Goth." Short for Gothic, a way of dressing that features multiple piercings, jet black hair, spikes on shoes and blow-out bell bottoms…lots and lots of black, including black makeup. Chuck was about 27, and my brother had no business doing anything with this older, kind-of strange guy who also happens to be a "weed head."

While approaching Chuck's apartment, the first person I saw was Mike Jones, right outside the doorway.

"What up doe? What are you doing down here?" Mike didn't live in the building.

"We're just chilling with Chuck and some friends," was Mike's answer.

"With Chuck?" I was wary about asking how they were connected.

"Yeah," says Mike. "He's our boy."

In this situation my suspicion leads me to believe, "He's our boy" is code for "The only thing we really have in common is drugs." After all, Mike (and Doug) don't like "Goth" girls or listen to "Goth" music. They're hip-hop guys. I'm all for diversity and everything, but these two (Mike and Doug) are not trying to build "community."

I decided not to escalate…yet. "Alright bro'," I told Mike, "take it easy. Stay out of trouble kid." I walked in the open doorway and saw Doug near the stereo shuffling through CD's. He turned around and said, "What up doe bro'? You must have heard the music bangin'. We're keeping it light and chill at the crib today. You feel me." He smirked. I was just glad that Doug was in the building where I could keep an eye on him.

I went back upstairs to my place on the 3rd floor. I sat back at my table to finish reading a chapter in my Macroeconomics book. I reached for

156

my headphones and suddenly I heard a loud crash. Boom! Plink-Plink-Plink! It came from downstairs and shocked by the noise, I darted towards the door. Next thing I know, I heard footsteps, running, and loud voices yelling and laughing. Then a lot more broken glass. To my surprise, the window that extended from the 1st floor to the 3rd floor ceiling was shattered. I stood on the 3rd floor platform in the stairwell and peered out of what used to be the window. I saw about eight bodies running for cover away from the building. Mike was last, laughing, and shaking his hand briskly, as if he had just punched the window out himself.

"What the hell is wrong with you, boy?" Fake Thug Mike looked up at me from the first floor and scurried away with the rest of the crowd.

Doug was clearly angry with Mike and everyone at the party. Agitated he walked out the front door of the building: "Get the f--k on with that punk pussy s--t!" he said. "F---ing up s--t at my crib!" He was fussing and cussing…and then he saw me. The look on his face was reminiscent of the six-year-old boy that crapped on the expensive clothes while Mom was in the dressing room.

When he saw me, he closed his eyes and lowered his head.

"Come up here bro'," I told him gently. Doug couldn't even look at me. He placed both hands over his eyes.

"Doug! What the hell, bro'?!"

Doug started to explain. "We were just having a party and someone had a little too much alcohol and people got out of hand, big bro'."

"Bro, don't you know this guy Chuck is 27? What kind of 27 year old hangs out with high-schoolers. He's six years older me! What were you doing hanging out with him anyway?"

I have some choice words for 'Fake Thug' Mike that I share with my little bro' as well.

Doug: "Chuck cool bro', he let us have the crib for a party." As for "fake thug"… I have some choice words for him too! Fa-real!"

Go in the crib bro'. We'll talk when I get back.

I angrily marched down to Chuck's place determined to make sure these parties and the random relationship ended here.

"Chuck, you know I could have reported this. Anything to do with you and my brother, I'm not having it. Do you understand that?"

"Yessir, you're the big man," said Chuck. I wasn't sure what he meant by the "big man." Not until a couple days later, it was almost dark outside and he knocked on my apartment door.

I opened it. "How can I help you Chuck?"

"I know you're the big guy, you're the "big man" and everything and I didn't want to bother you," says Chuck, "because, like, you move it big. But could you just, like, get me a little bit or get Doug to give me a little whenever he gets home? I'm loyal and trust worthy… I promise I'm good for it. I can get you back on Friday."

It's all clear now. I knew what he was asking, but I played along. "A little what?" I needed to know what Doug was doing specifically.

"Sorry man you probably have all kinds of different supply. I just want a little dub, weed. I don't deal with all that other kind of stuff! It's too hard for me."

"That's all you need is a dub sack? Cool. You can take it up with Doug. He's in his room taking a nap. I'll get him up for you. Come on in." At that point, I was acting as undercover police officer in my own place and I wanted to catch Doug red handed—well, not to turn him in but I wanted him to know that I was aware of his hustle.

"Doug, yo Doug!" I yelled down the hallway, "Chuck wanna see you."

He sniffled and yawned from resting "Huh? Chuck? Ah, yeah, OK, alright." He scrambled in his room for a minute, then opened his bedroom door and came into the living room where Chuck and I were with a music CD in his hand. "What's up Chuck?" He doesn't know I'm aware of the bag of weed he's holding on the other side of the CD. "Chuck, I "DUBBBED" that CD for you man," Doug said, winking at Chuck. He and Chuck fist pound and he passes Chuck the CD with the weed that I'm not supposed to notice. "This is the real stuff man, quit playing that heavy metal." Then, looking at me, Doug dismisses Chuck with a throwaway line, "Playing that BS. Later Chuck...I'll catch you later." Then Doug casually went back to his room and closed the door.

I looked at Chuck clinching my teeth.

"You have me confused. School is the only acceptable product in my place. I don't want to see you anywhere near my brother again!"

"Sorry," Chuck replies, "I won't deal wit' him."

"Don't call my brother, don't text or email my brother, no parties with my brother. I mean that."

"I don't want no problems from the "Big Man.""

"And stop calling me "Big Man." Get the hell on and leave the weed on the table, thank you."

I know that I have a past. But that lifestyle is over and I resent being thought of another way than my current day status. It irks my soul. I was sure that Chuck assumed that because I had two cars, a decent apartment, and nice clothes that I must be doing something illegal. His mind went towards moving large quantities of some kind of product. For me, that's stereotyping and honestly I stereotyped him too for being Gothic and hanging with young black guys. I thought he was a crackhead or taking something harder than weed. I guess we all start with our assessments based on past experiences.

159

I was pissed but maintained my calm demeanor. Now it was time to deal with Doug. I walked down the hallway to his room in the back.

"What's up bro'?" I said to Doug casually. He answered in kind. "Chillin' bro, just a little tired and about to knock out this homework."

"What was on that CD you gave Chuck?" I asked as I went into the bathroom to get something.

"Oh, it's just some stuff I did like two weeks ago, some Jay-Z, some Nas, some AZ...you know, put him on the classics man. Same kinda stuff you put me on bro'."

I entered Doug's room with something behind my back: a plunger. "So you and Chuck been real cool, huh?"

"Yeah, I been exposing him to real stuff. He stuck on that dark life. You feel me...hahaha."

"Is there anything else you want to tell me?"

Maybe Doug didn't understand my question.

"Naw, Chuck cool. I mean he ain't gay or nothin'," he says, laughing.

While he was laughing I took the plunger, swung, and broke it across his rib cage. I bruised his ribs and threw three blows to his chest, frustrated. He curled over and yelled "What the hell is wrong with you bro'?!" I yelled back, "You!"

My brother was slim, 5'9" and I was stronger and much bigger. He wouldn't dare hit me back. Not because he was afraid. Doug didn't fear anything. He knew he was wrong and his role was little brother. I felt bad for hurting him, but he kept lying to me and I couldn't have that. He would not end up like some of our older brothers on my watch. I would see to that.

---

Soon after, Doug and I went to visit grandad to see how he was doing. We knocked on the front door, but no one came.

"Granddad... Yo, Good Buddy, You up? You in there?"

Granddad's room was directly to the left of the front door. I walked over to his window on the front porch. I leaned toward the glass placing my hands above my eyes to minimize the glare from the sun on the glass. I pressed against the glass to see if there was any movement in his bedroom. Squinting my eyes I could vaguely see a figure under the covers. Maybe he was sleep.

*Tap Tap Tap...* 'Granddad? I'm at the front door, good buddy. It's me, Shawn, and Doug."

Granddad slowly moved the covers revealing his face, sat up, and waved. He stood, staggered, and sat back on the bed. He shook his head from side to side then sheepishly yelled for his granddaughter, Janirah, to open the door for him. She was eight year old and playing upstairs. She ran to open the door. Something wasn't right. Granddad never needed assistance with anything—not opening a door and definitely not standing up—nor had he ever been sheepish before.

Entering his room Grandad smiled, but didn't stand to give me his normal handshake and hug. He just sat there smiling. His shirt was off as usual and he had on some underwear. There was nothing new here, but his thigh was oddly swollen. There was a lump the size of a nerf football protruding from his skin. It had been five months since the last time I saw him, and he never mentioned he was sick.

Granddad had cancer. Stage Four.

I had come to visit Grandad to check on him because he was being tried in Federal court for money laundering. It was something about the Gold Mercedes S500 and my brother. This was no small dilemma to blow off.

161

My brother Terry was on trial in Federal court for multiple offenses: the murder of an ex-Detroit Police officer, drug trafficking, witness tampering, felon in possession of a fire arm, and money laundering. I was a character witness for him during his trial. I only knew my brother to be a great guy. I know he wasn't perfect, but these charges seemed unreal. When kids saw him in the neighborhood and the ice crème truck came, they ran towards him screaming in excitement because they just knew that they would be double fisting ice crème sandwiches and Italian ices. He would send busloads of kids to amusement parks. During Thanksgiving he gave away turkeys to needy families with his friends. He was a man that loved being a father figure to many.

And I am his blood brother as an honor student at the University of Michigan, raising our younger brother, working three jobs, and admiring the philanthropy and love my brother gives to so many. And so I told the Federal judge my thoughts and experiences with my older brother. It was the only way that I could assist my brother. Just being myself and being honest about my truth.

At the end of the five week trial the jury deliberated for three hours and found him guilty on all counts. At 35 years old he was convicted and sentenced to life without parole for the murder of the ex-police officer and drug conspiracy, 20 years for money laundering, and 10 years each for firearm violations, and witness tampering.

He didn't leave the courtroom silent.

"I ain't dangerous," he said, "I'm a man. I'm going to rely on the Lord and the appeals court to look out for me."

My brother has 11 kids and according to this verdict he's going to miss out on a lot of high school graduations.

I watched him as the officers escorted him out of the court room. Terry and I locked eyes, gave a head nod, no smile. It was Tuesday, December 14th, 2004.

Granddad never made it to the end of trial and therefore was never sentenced. He died from the cancer that spread throughout his body. I'm sure stress played a role.

Granddad and Terry were added to the flock of influential people in my life and Doug's life that left, whether purposefully or not. My grandmother, my father, my brother Mike and his twin, Grandma Virginia, and now Granddad and my brother Terry. Now, for the first time, even though Granddad had never really hovered over me like a parent, and I only saw Terry sporadically, I felt like I had no covering. The feeling weighed on me like a heavy blanket. I couldn't depend on anyone if I wanted to. The irony of it all is the fact that other people actually depended on me.

I could wallow in my own lack for only so long. After all, finals were around the corner and Doug was affected too. He was still a teenager. He spoke at Granddad's funeral and everyone smile, laughed, and was moved by his heartfelt words as he paid his last respects to M.C. Higgins.

"I never had a man in my life outside of my brothers. Both of my brothers respected this man and he loved me too. Rest in peace Good Buddy. You'll always be a father figure to me."

Doug has a way of being impactful at such times. All I wanted from Doug was for him to graduate high school. Through the ups and downs of being shot at from point-blank range, going back to juvenile and even breaking out of a juvenile facilities, high speed chases from the police, and everything else, he did it—just as his principal said during her special speech to him. As his big brother and mentor I prayed it was the end of his roller coaster journey. Unfortunately, it was just the beginning.

He was my first mentee.

---

I graduated from the University of Michigan in 2005 with a degree in mathematics and economics and I was primed to start my teaching career and master's degree in New York City. I delayed my departure to New York for exactly one year because someone else was actually going to graduate in 2006: my little brother, Doug, now officially a high school senior.

The graduation was a long time coming and when we got to that day, I was happy on so many levels. *My brother is happy*, I thought. *He's stuntin' wearing a white pinstripe suit with black gators. This is his big day!*

But most importantly, Doug made it through and against some pretty insurmountable odds.

On June 2, 2006, our family walked into the Allen Park Municipal Auditorium and took our seats. Mom had the biggest smile on her face and sat to my left. My sister Tila and her three children sat next to her: A'rmani, Shayla, and Jeril. We all had the same smile that was plastered on my Mom's face. Excitement. Relief. Hope.

Halfway into the ceremony the principal paid special homage to a special young man.

"There is one young man who just never gave up. Despite the ups, downs, and everything in between, despite all the obstacles he went through he made up his mind and said, 'I'm going to graduate.' Let's give a round of applause for Douglas Little!"

The crowd went wild. Mom stood there with tissue and manicured hands wet with tears from wiping her melting makeup. She couldn't contain herself and could only clap. Slowly. No words.

Meanwhile, I was beyond excited! "That's my bro', I see you boy! Let's get it! You already know! We can do all things young bro'!"

Doug walked across the stage with his hands in the air then posed in a "B-Boy" stance, arms crossed, with a huge grin. He continued walking and shook the hands of every teacher and administrator, thanking them

164

individually for believing in him. Then he threw his diploma up in the air and caught it, and yelled "Yeah Boy! This is my hat!" and walked off the stage, head high, proud. Ready.

"Where my bro' at?" Doug says as we gathered outside to meet him. "Right here bro'!" I said. "We're going to get your paperwork done for Wayne State. They have a program that's just right for you. It's similar to the Bridge Program at the University of Michigan. I've already talked to the Director of the program and they are looking forward to connecting with you! You're all set bro'!

"Big bro', this is crazy man… I really did it! I've seen you do it for years, but me…Dougie Fresh…Mannnnn! I'm ready for the next level bro', I see the blue print."
A tear ran down his cheek. A tear ran down my cheek.

"I told you I was just waiting for you to go ahead and cross the stage, and then I'm out. You did it baby! Words can't express how proud I am! This is better than my own graduation from college."

We laughed, fist pounded, and hugged.

It was a great day.

The next day, I was on a plane. New York bound.

# CREATING CONSCIOUSNESS

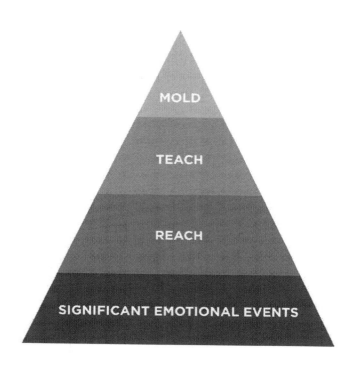

# CHAPTER 13

## The Other Side of the Desk

Our school was on Eagle Avenue right off the 6 Bus Line. I caught the bus from 155th and St. Nicholas in Manhattan and crossed the Macomb's Dam Bridge, passing Yankee Stadium on the way to school. There was a three-story brick elementary school building, P.S. 140, in the front of Holcombe L. Rucker School of Community Research (HLR). Our high school, HLR, was located in the annex behind P.S. 140. The annex was royal blue with a burgundy horizontal stripe that surrounded the trailer. It had only one hallway and formerly was a kindergarten building. HLR was a new school and the grand opening was in 2006—the year I came to New York. Kids traveled from all over the Bronx, Harlem and even Brooklyn to attend. They were drawn by the name, but they didn't know they would have a single-hallway high school and share their gym with an elementary school. At least for the first year of operation.

Rucker Park is a famous park in Harlem on 155th and 8th Avenue where legendary athletes are known to have played. The founder, Holcombe L. Rucker, created the park to leverage education and athleticism for young people using the "each one teach one" model. Kids were drawn to the school because of the name; likely so they assumed it was a big basketball school. We certainly weren't big in our first year. We didn't even have a basketball team, but the Park founder's name and legacy was directly associated with the school because his grandson, Sharif Rucker, was the school's founding principal.

Principal Rucker was a cool brother that was absolutely passionate about changing the lives of young people through education. He was from Brooklyn and always was an honest hustler who sold juices, candy, and newspapers as a kid in some of the roughest neighborhoods. He had vision. He was young, 31, a member of Alpha Phi Alpha Fraternity, Incorporated, with a background in higher education, and you would never catch him without a tie. He represented what we wanted our youth to become. So did I.

It was the first day of school and I created a four-step process to mold my students into excellence. I prepped and practiced my approach and mastered my curriculum. One false step at the beginning of the school year could make or break the entire academic year for any educator. My process was:

*Vulnerability* – Get to know them and let them know you.

*Reach* – Display care and genuinely connect with their core.

*Teach* – Pour in their open mind.

*Mold* – Through their trust and respect of your knowledge, help shape their decisions.

This was my game plan, developed in my short years of experience and based on my observations on how others shaped me.

It was the first day of school, September of 2006. I shook all students' hands as they entered the room—similar to Coach Carter. Once my first period class was inside the classroom I closed the door, walked to the front of the class, and told them a story about me and my brothers.

*Good morning scholars. Yes, I said "scholars." Know that I will be addressing you exactly as what you are. I am Mr. Blanchard from Detroit, Michigan and I will be here with you all the way through your high school graduation. With that said, it is a pleasure to be here with you today. We have a journey together and I've studied long and hard to be here with you. All of my life experience and knowledge has been crafted by God himself to make sure that you will be able to receive everything that I have for you. Let's begin today with some introductions. I'll begin. Oh, and the theme of this talk is simply, "Why."*

*Ya see, I have a number of brothers. I love them all dearly and they mean the world to me. As a matter of fact one of my favorite brothers is Mike. I Love this guy. He taught me a lot about how to hustle in life and make ends meet at an early age. When I was in the 9th grade just like you all are now, Mike was shot in a drug transaction. He was shot and killed over the poison that he sold. It poisoned his life. He was a twin and his twin was already dead.*

*I have more brothers.*

*I have my oldest brother, Terry. Now Terry is one of my favorite brothers. He was who I wanted to be when I became a man. I mean the knowledge, power, finesse, finances, and love that he demonstrated was unlike any man that I had ever seen. He's a handsome brother too! I love this guy! As matter of fact he's even in newspapers! On the cover. Pass this around please. I know this is math class, but whoever feels comfortable enough to read the title please read it for me.*

"I'll read it Mista," said one of my students. The headline read: "King Pin's High Life to End Behind Bars: T. Stuck had many roles: Drug Boss, Killer, Rapper."

The cover photo was an image from 1996 of my brother standing tall with his hands in the air wearing a full length orange mink, orange mink hat, light orange custom suit, orange big block 'gator shoes, and jewels, with his arms open wide and three cars parked behind him: A gold S500 Mercedes, a black Lexus Truck, and a white on white '96 Impala.

"Whoa… This is your brother Mista?" One student said incredulously.

*Indeed it is. And he is much more of a caring father and good brother than the headlines care to depict. Don't let headlines deceive you. However, understand that he is serving life in prison with no parole and 11 beautiful children can only see him in jail.*

*Ya see, I also have a younger brother, Doug. Now this brother is one of my favorite brothers. We didn't have our fathers around growing up and my mother is a very interesting lady. Let's just leave that there. So, I had to step up as a teenager and raise my younger brother. It was rough… He was in and out of juvenile facilities and the smartest kid everywhere he went. He's really smart! I'm so proud of him and as a matter of fact he just graduated from high school three months ago!*

*Let's give a round of applause for that…*

171

My students' hands began clapping frantically. "That's awesome Mista! Wow! That's whassup!"

*Unfortunately, he is currently in the Wayne County jail in Detroit Michigan for a second degree murder charge.*

My eyes slightly watered and I had to quickly compose myself.

*Ya see, many things can happen in a matter of months. I thought I was finished with my brother because I was there for him until he graduated high school and every step of the way beforehand. How quickly I forgot that I needed help beyond high school too. That's a story for another day. The very next day after he graduated I was on a plane to New York City to start my master's degree course work and train to make sure that I was well equipped to teach you everything that I know about mathematics and life in general.*

*Ya see, this is about mathematics, but this is also personal.*

I made eye contact with a few young men in the room and looked into their souls. They felt my true self and it was apparent that some of them had experienced some of the same things I was describing.

*This is my "Why." I...I am here to make you great. I am here on behalf of my brothers and everything that I have learned to pour into you. A few good people poured into me. Now it's my turn to pour and our journey together begins here. Know that I care, I'm passionate about your growth and our journey. With that said, I love everyone in this room. Let the learning of mathematics and life begin, scholars!*

I couldn't tell who the "Alpha" kids were. I just knew that every mouth was open, and that you could hear a pin drop. It was powerful.

A couple of days later, Miss Roman, the secretary, interrupted my math class. "You have a phone call that you need to take," she announced.

"OK guys, we're on page 58. Continue your work and I'll be back."

"OK, no problem Mr. B," they all said, practically with one voice. They were already with me.

172

"Remember: we're scholars," I reminded them. I didn't want any issues while I took that phone call.

In Vietnam, they might have called that brainwashing. But brainwashing can be used for good or evil. I prefer to call it "indoctrination." After all, everyone gets indoctrinated with something. If you're going to be indoctrinated, let it be with a message that pushes you toward success.

I walked down the hall to the office. "What's going on?" I asked.

It was a parent. "Mr. Blanchard, I just had to call and thank you so much."

"No problem," I answered. "Who is this?"

"This is Teddy's mom."

"OK. What's going on?" My interest was piqued and frankly, I was relieved that it wasn't a message about somebody being shot or sick or dying. I'd grown accustomed to interesting phone calls over time.

"I just want to tell you that whatever you're doing to him, you got him energized. I have never seen this boy do homework EVER. He comes home right away and get his homework done, and he keeps talking about Mr. Blanchard, Mr. Blanchard. I don't know what you're doing, but whatever it is keep doing it 'cause that's what he need."

"Thank you," I said, then hung up the phone, smiled to myself, and headed back to class.

"I told you, you wanted to take that call," Ms. Roman chimed in with a smile as I left the office.

I never told Teddy that his mom called. When I walked back in the class, he was the first person who looked up at me. He waved his hand. "Hey Mr. B, everything good?"

"Everything is definitely good, Teddy. What are you doin'?"

"I'm working."

"That's my scholar," I said. "Keep it up."

"Yep," he smiled.

It was that smile that let me know something that excited me and still excites me today: *I have influence.* I was making an impact on Teddy's life. I didn't know Teddy's complete family background or any significant emotional events that may have taken place in his life. Regardless, he resonated with my vulnerability and care for his well-being and upward mobility. That connection enabled him to open his mind to learn and furthermore to be molded to make some decisions a bit more wise than he might have otherwise. I was affirmed that I was destined to influence others, particularly young people.

At the end of the day, I was leaving the classroom and passed by the office. Miss Ronan said: "You know, that wasn't the only phone call you got today. Taj Love? His mom called too. She said: 'I don't know what the hell Mr. Blanchard is doing, but Taj ain't never done no damn math problem. Tell him whatever he doing to keep on doing it.'"

Miss Ronan continued. "And you know Taj comes from Brooklyn." We're in the South Bronx and he has to come a long way to get here.

This is only the third day of school, and progress is already happening.

I was warned that this was the honeymoon period until the students became comfortable. If that was true than it was up to me to make sure it was a honeymoon that they remembered.

I had two 25-student sections for math—Sections One and Two. Section Three I had for financial literacy. There were four sections, but I never saw Section Four during the first semester.

Each section had their own personality. Section One was full of high achievers and alpha males and females. They were intelligent and active. I enjoyed having them during the first period when they were the most focused.

174

Section Two was laid back and easy to manage. They were eager to learn and reserved.

Section Three and Four were both full of students who had interesting stories. Being from Detroit, I could certainly empathize with many of their life circumstances. However, some of our kids didn't have older brothers, a grandmother, or anyone that paid them any attention. That's where we came in as educators. We provided them with care from the moment they hit the door in Holcombe L. Rucker High School.

Section Four was like my "stepchild." I rarely had a chance to interact with them. I didn't share my first day of school conversation with them as I did with the other sections.

My sections often boasted about our classroom antics and camaraderie. "We ain't never seen nobody like him," they would tell their parents. He from the 'hood, he's a young guy, he smart and cool!"

My classroom culture was: *We're here to work. We're smart. We're scholars. And that's cool.*

Jimmy was a Dominican kid with a curly Afro assigned to section 4. I'd seen him in the hallway and he was known to be obnoxious in class. He was in the hallway during passing time as I posted outside of my door to greet scholars as they came in. Jimmy walked closely behind a young lady and reached for her butt. "JIMMY!" I yelled from across the hall. "Come here young brother." He rolled his eyes and walked over reluctantly.

"Yes, Mista?"

"I don't want to see you reaching to touch a young lady again or we are going to have problems. If you do it I will be calling your house."

"Okay, Mista."

With a smirk he skipped to his next class down the hall.

175

The very next period I was watching Jimmy like a hawk. No games…
He certainly wasn't going to grope any innocent young lady on my
watch. Sure thing, he was at it again! "JIMMY! Boy get yo' butt over
here! Now, I told you that I was going to call your house if I catch you
in the act. Give me your phone number.

"Mista, I don't know my phone number. We just moved."

"Is that right? Well, I want your phone number first period tomorrow
or I will be going home with you after school."

Mista that's "OD"! (Code for overdose or doing "too much.")

"OD it is my brother. Your hands are OD so get that number to me in
the morning so we can both calm all the 'OD' activity down."

"Okay Mista. My bad and I'll see you tomorrow."

He walked away and kept his composure for the duration of the school
day.

There were a number of scholars that came early to eat breakfast.
Jimmy was one of them. The very next day first period began and I
didn't see Jimmy anywhere. He skipped out on the breakfast crew.
During second period I went into the bathroom and caught him in
there attempting to stall until passing time was over.

"My good buddy Jimmy. I need that phone number."

"Mista, I don't have it. We don't have a phone number."

"Is that right? Okay, well that makes things easy. I will see you after
class and we can go to your house together."

I watched Jimmy every period in our single hallway school making sure
he didn't attempt to leave early. During the last period I saw him hastily
grabbing his coat from his locker and darting towards the exit. I ran
over to him trying not to slide in my dress shoes as he tried to get away.

176

I ran across the gravel directly outside the door and grabbed him at the gate.

"Let me go Mista or…"

"Or what? Young brother, you already know what we discussed. Now let's go back inside to get my jacket and I'm coming with you."

Jimmy pushed, tugged, screamed, and attempted to kick me while I restrained him. My tucked shirt came out and my tie was thrown on the gravel. The security guard came and grabbed Jimmy to take him inside the building to the office. He went kicking and screaming.

I figured his guardian must be strict and he knows what's going to happen when he shows up at home with a teacher from school.

In the counselor's office the security guard continued to restrain Jimmy as he cried and eventually calmed down. After an hour of more obnoxious behavior Jimmy broke down and began to cry.

He was homeless. There was no phone number. There was no home.

Jimmy rode the train and slept at random friends' homes. He was the oldest of 14 siblings and his mother decided to let him go on to be a man on his own. He came early and stayed late to eat breakfast and to take snacks after school to make sure he had food for the day. School was his safety net.

Lathan (not his real name) was also in Section Four, a dark-skinned, heavy set kid. About 5'3". Mischievous. Called himself a "Blood." But I could tell he was soft.

"You know wha' I'm sayin', Blood! Dead a-- Blood."

Our school was funded by the Bill and Melinda Gates Foundation, which enabled us to purchase smart boards, new books, new TI-82 calculators, and brand new laptops that we placed in a lockable push cart. One day, some laptops came up missing. One, then two, three, and four.

We couldn't figure it out.

A sweet kid told Mr. Rucker. "Lathan been taking those. I saw him."

Mr. Rucker called me to his office and said, "We have got to get those laptops back."

"Cool," I said. "We can go right up to his crib, if you want... You know I'm down."

"Precisely," said Rucker. "That is exactly what we're going to do."

We looked up Lathan's address. It was an apartment building in the Bronx. The building was old and worn as well as the fixtures. The buzzer had red and green wires hanging and the apartment numbers were scribbled into the brown doors with sharpie markers. The buzzer buttons were worn down from many, many fingers buzzing to come up.

We pushed Number 6.

"Who this? Who there?"

"This is Principal Rucker. Holcomb Rucker High School?"

"Come on up."

We walked up the steps. The stench hit us. It smelled like week old trash and dead animals. Maybe a dead rat. Yeah, something of that nature.

New York is like a box of chocolates. You never know what you're going to get.

We walked up a spiral staircase to the sixth floor, then made a left and went down the hallway. The elevator was broken.

As we walked, I looked at Rucker and the English teacher Mr. Geottleman. Rucker looked back at me.

"Alright...you ready to do this?"

"Of course. Let's do it," I answered.

We knocked on the door. The mother (I think) slightly opened the door, chain still on. "Who is this?"

"We are Lathan's teachers and principal," said Mr. Rucker.

She unlatched the chain and opened the door.

The apartment was literally unwalkable. There were boxes and crates and books everywhere, along with a stained mattress on the living room floor. The light was dim, coming only from the kitchen. We could see into the kitchen, where there was an open pot with flies hovering around it. A faint whiff of food put me in mind of Hamburger Helper.

I looked at Rucker and Geottleman and they looked at me.

"Have a seat."

Rucker sat on the crate. So did Geottleman. I decided to stand up. I saw a few creatures scurrying across the floor. And they weren't ants.

"How can I help y'all?" said the woman who we thought might be Lathan's mom.

"Some laptops came up missing, and someone gave an anonymous tip that Lathan was a prime suspect," Rucker explained.

"Lathan, get yo' a-- out here!" the maybe-mom yelled.

"Huh?"

"Get yo' a-- out here!"

"OK. Here I come."

It was about 6:45 p.m. The bed creaked and we heard Lathan shuffling down the hall to the living room. When he came to the opening he saw the three of us.

"Oh s—t." Lathan ran back to his room.

"You gone yell s—t, you get yo' dumb a-- back," says maybe-mom.

Lathan came back, sheepishly. "Yes? How can I help you misters?"

Rucker began, "Lathan, we noticed that there were some laptops missing at the school. Someone tipped us off that you were a culprit. We all like you a lot, and we figured that if you had the laptops, you would give them back"

I explained. "You're a good kid. Principal Rucker has agreed that we could work some things out and make sure you don't get expelled…if you decide to give up the computers."

Principal Rucker interceded. "We want you to be the best you can be, but we can't have you doing anything like this. Can you tell us about these computers. Do you have them?"

Lathan averted his eyes. We all looked at each other.

"Um…no." Lathan replied.

"Lathan, understand; we have a witness that said they saw you take them," I said.

Geottleman chimed in. "Lathan, you know we have cameras at the school."

"No y'all don't," was Lathan's weak-voiced, head-down reply.

"Yes. Right in front of the hallway. Where the cart is, after school? We saw you put it in your book bag."

"Okay… I know, I kn-kn-know where they at."

"Could you get them for us?"

Stuttering: "I-I-I didn't m-m-m-mean to take 'em."

"Could you get them for us?"

Lathan goes back to his room. He comes back with four laptops.

"Am I gon' get in trouble?"

"A'hm gon' whup your m-----f------ a--!" screams his maybe-mother. But she's not maybe anymore. Any woman in the 'hood who talks like this to a young black man is surely the mother.

"I'm not gon' get in trouble, right? Could you say I'm good? They told me to take 'em."

The guys—the "they" Lathan was speaking about—were Bloods. Bloods is a gang that originated in California. But the meaning of the group has changed over the years, and Lathan has unfortunately found himself as the low man on the totem pole of this dubious organization (and trust me, it is an organization). The low man on the totem pole has to do the dirty work, and has to take the consequences from the authorities. They were planning to sell them, but hadn't picked them up yet.

Lathan gave us the names. We took the laptops.

"I'm gon' whup his a--, and thank you very much. I will make sure that the only "Blood" around here is the blood that shoots out his a-- while I'm whoopin' it!" The acting "mother" was actually Lathan's aunt and guardian. "Keep doin' what you're doin' at the school," she said, and— looking back at Lathan—reiterates in her own colorful way what she is going to do to his backside.

"Please don't whup his a-- too bad," I implored. "We like his a-- in one piece. Lathan, we'll see you tomorrow." We chuckled as we went back to the car.

"You see?" said Mr. Rucker. "There is so much more to do at the school than teaching math."

I gave an "Amen."

There were a number of students at HLR with similar "issues." Some have been kicked out of other schools and placed accordingly. The New York City education placement system is…let's just say it's interesting.

The P.S. system in New York is a lottery system. Parents indicate their first, second and third choice schools for their children and that is how the schools are populated. Schools that still have empty slots after that process are provided with students whose parents registered late, and those are typically the kids with the most "issues." It is from this mixed bag of students that "Ty" was placed at HLR.

Good ol' Ty. He had just been released from Rikers Island. He was about 17. In the 9th grade.

Ty came to the school with braids and a chipped front tooth. He always wore True Religion jeans and a red shirt. He had a five-point star tattooed on the back of his hand which was a clear indicator of his gang affiliation. He also had a sleeve on both arms (a fully tattooed arm is known as a "sleeve") which consisted of praying hands, a joker card, a scroll with Asian lettering, and the birth and death dates of someone that was tattooed near his left wrist. He always wore a red hoodie to school, but he wasn't supposed to wear it in the building. Judging from his origins and his swagger, we knew Ty's makeup. He was a Blood. Much more serious than Lathan.

Ty was placed in my Section One math class.

I realized that the hard-to-reach youth really respected my back story and evolution. If I told a scholar my story, it was almost automatic that they were more eager to listen, pay attention, and try their personal best. If they didn't know my story, almost invariably they would "act out."

Ty didn't know my story. And of course upon entry into my classroom he began to scope things out. He tested the water.

"You cool, man. I f--ks wichu."

"Brother watch your mouth," I said to him right away. There was a reason why I addressed him with respect. In the 'hood, the one thing that young men demand is respect. They will respond to your direction if you show at least a modicum of that respect. They are accustomed to a lack of respect or lack of faith in their ability, whether it comes from home or with the authorities. If you give a nod to the idea that you see their humanity, it can be a lifeboat, while failing to show that bare minimum of respect can almost be like a shipwreck for them. I preface my critique with the word "brother" to show that I see him; a man whom to others may be a menace, or invisible, or even worse. But to me, Ty is a "brother." I needed to let him know that.

Ty's response lets me know he recognizes my salute. "Aiiight."

I took a mental note that there was certainly a need for a sidebar conversation with him. Never let them go unchecked. But for now, that is enough…

…for exactly about one minute, that is. "Math is good s--t kids. Y'all keep doin' y'all work little kids, this is good. As the students were filing out of class, he clapped and 'cheered' them on. "This is good work, kids, Have a good day, kids."

He was positioning himself as the authority over me. That cannot happen in a class and definitely wasn't about to happen here. If a student is allowed to exercise his/her dominance the entire class will fall apart. That is a universal school truth, regardless of race, class, or geography.

The students looked at me as if to say, *You gonna let him do that?*

"Excuse me sir," I say to Ty. "Stay back and talk to me. The rest of you enjoy your day!"

"Alright, y'all go ahead. I'm gon' to talk to Mr. Blan-chard." Ty continues to clap until the last student is out of the classroom.

"How you doin' brother?" I started out.

"I'm good, bra-tha," Ty says mockingly.

"I'm interested in where you come from," I begin to explain. "As you can see, the culture in my class is a particular culture where young people that I refer to as scholars come to learn. And that's what it's going to be here. So right now, this is a sizing up, a bit of a dick-measuring contest if you will."

I need to use that language to let him know, in elegant-street style, that his approach, his challenge to me cloaked in comedy and seeming good-nature, will not go unnoticed. Or unchallenged.

"I'm not sure where you coming from, brother. What school you come from?"

Ty sat up, cocked his neck. "I'm comin' from Rikers, know what I mean?" He rose his head up sharply and quickly. In a move that is sometimes a greeting and sometimes a warning. In this case, it was a warning. But the young fella had yet to realize he was exactly that to me… A little fella.

"That's good. They have math class there?"

"They had that s—t, but I didn't f--- with it."

"OK. OK. Well where are you from?"

"I'm from New York." He starts to get antsy. "Where you coming from, 'cause I got class." He continues to clap his hands slowly while only the two of us were in the class and the halls were clear. His way of maintaining control.

"You know what? This calls for a bit of a backstory about me now that I know a bit about your backstory."

"What's this, interrogation? Ty replies, irritated. "This ain't Rikers man."

"Listen. My man, I'm from Detroit."

"Word? Dee-troit? That's a country town, man. That's country folks. That's some down South s—t. I have some n-----s up in Rikers that are from Dee-troit. Country niggas.

Yeah, I'm from Detroit bro'. I'm from the 'hood. I got quite a few brothers there bro'. A few been down that route. A few of them dead. A couple in prison. I've even been caught in the system myself.

I pulled out the newspaper with my brother Terry on the front cover. "Let me show you something.  You know who this is?"

Ty sat up. I had his attention. "Aw man. Kingpin. Damn!" Then he started reading the article. "Yo...my man's a f---ing boss! He goin' down too? He got mad time! Yo this is crazy son! This paper a few years old. Who is this?"

I let him know. This is one of the many reasons why I'm here. "That's my brother."

"Oh s—t!"

Now I had him. He put out his fist. "Son. You a real nigga my man. You got realness in you. Peace. You must really recognize real, huh?"

"Man, I come from a very interesting background. I may dress like Fonzworth Bentley, but...I am from the 'hood, good brother.

"All due respect. I respect your path, man. Respect."

"Let me tell you something. I do what I do because I care. I see young guys like you, and I place my energy towards making sure you don't get on this path. I have a younger brother that I raised who just graduated from high school this year. This summer he had a situation that has him facing a Murder 2 charge. Young. Nineteen years old with the possibility of missing a large part of his youth.

"But I'm here with you right now. I ain't trying to let you go back to Rikers. I ain't trying to let you do any of that. So I tell you what: Here is a notebook, a pencil, and my very own pen. You are going to come in here tomorrow, and you are going to do work."

He nodded his head and repeated twice. "All due respect. I got you, sir."

We bumped hands. "I'll see you tomorrow."

"Thanks for the pep talk Mr. Blanchard. My bad for disrupting your flow."

I wrote him a pass. "I need you to be chill all day. I'm going to ask you at the end of the day how your day went."

"Aiiight. I'm gonna be peace today. Much respect. I ain't never seen a teacher that was real like that."

At the end of the day, I saw Ty again. "I did some work. I kept it pretty peace today. But I'll see you tomorrow in math class."

"Excellent. When you come to class tomorrow, I need to you to put your notebook to use."

The next day, Ty came to class, notebook in hand—the one I gave him. And the pencil. He came in on time. "Do I have an assigned seat?"

"Yes sir, right here."

Ty sat down where I indicated. The class looked on, intrigued.

Ty raised his hand. "I'll do number 2."

He was correct. Then he began to explain. It was an order of operations problem. Daily I placed three questions on the board and gave students five minutes. Once time was up they had to go to the board to explain.

Ty began his explanation. "Yeah, you know, it's PEMDAS, 'Please Excuse My Dear Aunt Sally" and first you got to make sure that you multiply before you add, then after you multiply you can add these, and the answer is 17."

The class was looking at each other. They all had gotten 17 too.

"Good," I replied.

It was clear that Ty already knew how to do the work. This was just the first time that he displayed his intelligence.

At the end of class, Ty said "Thanks, Mr. B. Love the math class. Peace." Then he went into the hallway, hands folded.

"School's over for me. School is over." But to the other students in the hall, he admonished, "Go to class." The students were kind of intimidated.

Ty did this every day. After my class, he would go in the hallway. Or he might leave. He got suspended quite a bit. But he always came to math class.

Although he was intimidating he was not without challenge from his peers. There was a female equivalent to Ty named Delise who dished Ty some choice words. "You so beyond ugly Boy, with yo' missing teeth and nappy lint ball braids on yo head!"

Without hesitation, Ty cuffed the back of her head with his hand and smacked her face down on a wooden lunch room table. Hard! "Respect. You gotta respect me."

Ty was a Blood, like Lathan. Just a bit higher on the ladder. Students in school and even adults outside of school respected him.

It was proven when Lathan and some of his boys decided to fight Ty. They had a beef with him and confronted him after school.

"You gotta respect us too, man!" they told him.

187

"Oh yeah? I'll tell you who do this Blood s——t fareal."

He pulled out his gun. "I do this. Now I'm gonna give you b---ches a chance to get the f--- on."

Which they did. Quickly. Word got back to everyone that Ty was toting a gun. They got the message: Don't mess with Ty.

Soon after he was expelled despite his mathematical ability.

Ricardo was interesting. He came, like Ty, later in the school year. He moved from Florida, leaving a mother who didn't believe she could control him. Therefore he was sent to his father in NYC. Ricardo was 5'10", heavy handed, orange-tinted skin and yellow-tinted eyes. He was always fidgeting. Never could sit still. Ricardo was placed into my first period math class before Ty was expelled.

Ricardo asked a lot of questions.

"How you doing brother, nice to meet you."

He responded in kind. "Nice to meet you too." He was respectful.

He glanced at the math book I handed him with uncertainty. I specifically placed him in a group of students who were hard-working. He appeared as if he needed the extra support; Ricardo could go either way. I couldn't help, but noticed Ricardo consistently gazed out of the window, daydreaming. I would catch him doing anything but the work. And he just loved to ask me questions. Only one problem; they were questions that had nothing to do with the work at hand.

"Hey Mr. B," he would yell out, "you got a lot of them ties?"

"Yeah Ricardo, and you got a lot of math problems so let's get to them."

Or: "Mr. B, where you live? You live in Manhattan don't you?"

"I do live in Manhattan, but I want you to live now in this math book. Keep going." I'd always try to bring him back around to the assignment at hand.

I could tell he admired me. He asked me how tall I was and I told him 6'1".

"I bet you play basketball."

"Yes I do." It was out of hand, but I had to find a way to engage him. So I decided to turn the tables and ask him a question myself.

"Hey Ricardo. Who is YOUR favorite basketball player?"

That was easy. "Aw, Kobe Bryant," he said.

"You like basketball?"

"Yeah, basketball is dope."

"Well, you know basketball players have to be pretty smart so you need to do this work if you want to be good, even at basketball."

"Ok, ok I feel you. Let me do this work."

In the other classes, Ricardo just couldn't get focused. He was barely focused in mine. He might hit a kid in the back of the head. He would fight, or ask too many distracting questions. Rambunctious.

As the days wore on, Ricardo became increasingly antsy and unfocused. I was able to control him, but again he was out of control in other classes. He didn't like being controlled and tried to skip my class because it left him powerless. Finally, his father was summoned to a meeting with the school counselor after a fight that Ricardo initiated.

"Ricardo! You are in school to do your work! Stop playing around in school!"

Smack! Ricardo's face became plum from the smacks and anger.

189

Then Ricardo: "You're not gonna f---ing hit me no more!" He reached for his father's throat and choke slammed his dad to the ground, inhaled, hocked a loogie…and spat on him twice. Right in the face.

"You're not gonna f--- with me no more! Who's the boss now?"

Ricardo walked out of the counselor's office, leaving his books on the floor. The counselor was clearly scared. The security guard took Ricardo outside.

I helped the father, globs of mucus on his face and shirt, as he picked himself up from the floor. Planted on his face was a mixture of embarrassment, disappointment, and fear. He wiped his son's mucus out of his eye, and began to stutter. His voice trembled as he apologized for his son's disrespectful episode.

"I apologize for my son's behavior. I'll take care of him when we get home. I'm not sure how much longer he will be living in New York City at this point."

Ha! I knew that was coming. And coming fast! Who would be the authority at home now?

After the incident Ricardo was enrolled at HLR for roughly a week. His dad shipped him back to Florida.

Per usual I had a long day exerting tons of energy, and had one more class until the day was over. I decided to sit down and pray. Teddy strolled in.

"Oh. Sorry."

"That's OK Teddy," I said. "Come on in."

He looked at me with his eyebrows cocked, quizzically. "Mr. B: you a man a God?"

"Yes," I told him. "Yes I am."

"I knew it! I knew you had to be. I'm a man of God too. I ain't perfect yet, you know what I'm sayin', but I try. I do. But Mr. B, you perfect! How did you become perfect?"

"Young brother, I'm far from a perfect man. There was only one of those."

"I can't tell," he replied. You cool, everybody like you, you be fresh, you know, and the kids don't act up in yo' class. They already know what's up. I do the work too. Mannnn, I do extra work 'cause, you know, that my worst subject, but you make me understand. But you a man of God, huh? I'm gonna be a good man of God, I'm working on my man of God stuff." Teddy spoke in run-on sentence-style. His ideas seemed to run faster than his comprehension of the actual ideas.

"We'll have to go to church together one day," I told him.

"Aw that'd be cool, man. Let me know."

I looked down at his shoes, they were tattered. "What size shoe do you wear?"

"Don't talk about my feet nah, I got big football feet Mr. B., I wear an 11."

Teddy was 5'4" and stocky with a size 11 shoe. He played football. Of course not at HLR, because we didn't have an athletic department during our first year of operation. He played for a recreation league.

"We wear the same size my man… I have a couple pair of untouched crispy sneakers for you."

Teddy was excited. I invited him to my town house. As an educator we weren't supposed to invite students to our homes, but most good educators bend the rules for students. I didn't care. Taking a deeper dive into the lives of students and displaying care has its honorable rewards. It's a risk, but I don't know any other way to reach them. The bureaucracy of life builds barriers to growth and their natural need to be nurtured: From home, to school, the television, the street corner, to

191

the so-called trustworthy law, they are de-humanized, invisible, and simultaneously feared and ignored. Maybe if they see the way I live, I speculated, some of that will rub off on them and they can either get out or stay out of trouble. Even as a first year teacher renting a town house with a couple friends in New York, that was living the American Dream in the majority of my students' eyes.

"This is cool," said Teddy as he glared at the columns of shoe boxes in my closet. "All these shoes yours?"

That was my cue. I handed him a couple pair. With a huge smile on his face, he said "I'm gonna bag these!"

Now Enrico was another character. He was Latino, 5'7", and cursed a lot. Similar to Ty, he entered the class being disruptive and cursing on his first day.

"Watch your mouth, young man," I told him.

"Aiiight. Then under his breath: "What the f--- is this?

"Young brother!" I repeated, a little more intensely than before.

"Yeah, ok. Then under his breath, "This is some bulls—t."

"Come here brotha'." I took him out into the hallway. "Listen: nobody in my class talks the way you are talking, and nobody's going to start. Including you."

Ty walked past. "Hey. Respect that man."

Enrico blew him off.

"Have a good day Ty," I said.

"I got ya back Mr. B. Peace."

After exchanging a few words, noticing the respect from his Alpha male peers, and the culture of the environment, Enrico calmed down. At least for a couple of weeks.

It was a Tuesday. A thunderous noise and shattering glass rang outside my classroom. I ran from the front of my class to the door and peered into the hallway. Enrico had punched the glass window near the stair well with his fist, blood gushed from the gash between his knuckles and the three-inch hairline cut across the palm of his hand. He was alone and cursing at the top of his lungs, this time in Spanish. Fortunately for him we had a school nurse and medic on duty that were able to quickly stitch his wound. He was suspended for his "random" aggressive behavior and deliberately destroying school property. By the time the nurse finished with him school was out and he stopped by my classroom.

"What's up Mr. B" said Enrico. "I just stopped in to ask you for that extra homework you were talking about?"

As if nothing happened and his hand didn't have a huge gauge covering his writing hand.

"Here it is right here. So what's up? You okay? Come kick it with me?

"I'm chillin'."

"What you got up today?" I asked.

"Trying to figure out what I'm gonna do."

"What do you mean?"

"Well," Enrico explained, "I'm gonna either buy these Jordans and be real fresh, 'cause you know, they were trying to clown my sneakers callin' em "bum biscuits"...Fact is, that's why I bust the window 'cause I was pissed off."

Enrico's gang affiliation was Crip.

"So, I just hit a lick and I know that you know the game, I got about $120 and these Jordan's cost $150. I gotta find another lick to come up on $30 cash."

"What kind of hustle you into?"

He looked at me with the side eye.

"Ummmm… You cool so… I stole a TV. My Crip fam put me on all kind of hustle missions. That's how I eat."

"Literally eat, or is that just a figure of speech?"

"Naw Mr. B, dead a--, my bad, I mean straight up, that's really how I eat. I don't want them ragging on my shoes, so I thought I'd go ahead and hit another little lick and get these Jordans so I can be fresh when I come back to school, and I'll just steal something to eat. It won't be the first time, you feel me."

He laughed with expectation of me joining in. I didn't.

"Tell you what, why don't we get something to eat right now?"

"Naw Mr. B, I don't want to spend any money. I told you what I'm doing wit' my money."

"Don't worry about it, I'll get the food. We can eat here."

"Say no more!"

"Go ahead and get started on the extra credit work."

I ran across the street from HLR to the Chinese food restaurant and picked up some sweet and sour chicken and vegetable fried rice for Enrico and me. Then I stopped at the generic ATM machine that charges every debit card $3.00 for a transaction. I never liked using this one because the buttons were filthy.

"Thanks Mr. B! This is my favorite chicken! I'm going to eat half of this, save the rest for later, and come up on these Jordan's today… Watch! And this math ain't that bad but showing the work with my unbandaged left hand is a little tricky. You're going to have a little struggle checking my work, but you'll be aight! LOL!   He continued to

194

complete his work dropping rice and sweet and sour sauce on his assignment.

"Look like you're going to have more rice on the math paper than in your mouth! LOL!"

"My bad," he chuckled. "I appreciate this a lot. You a cool dude Mr. B."

"I don't know what kind of hustle you planned on doing to get the Jordans," I said to Enrico. I didn't want him to steal or whatever scheme he was going to pull to make sure the students weren't making fun of him. "But I tell you what," I said as I pulled out $160 in 20 dollar bills that I withdrew from the dingy ATM machine. "Buy your Jordans with this—I put the money on the table and slid it towards him—and eat for the week with the money you already have."

He looked at the money, then at me. "Go ahead, young brotha', it's yours." Enrico slowly reached and grabbed the money, keeping his eyes on me. Once he took the cash he clinched it with his good hand and stared at the money in his clinched fist in his lap. He abruptly stood and headed into the hallway.

He stayed out there for a short while. I let him handle whatever he needed to while I continued designing polynomial lesson plans.

After two minutes or so he strolled back into my class room, eyes red. "Man, nobody's ever done nothing like this for me." He paused and looked at his bandaged fist. "Nobody ever give a f--k about me man." Sniffling he rubbed his nose with his good hand. "Thank you so much. I gotta go." He collected the extra credit work that was scattered all over the table into a neat pile. "I'm gonna bring all this work back tomorrow. I promise!"

"I want to see those J's on your feet when you come for in-school suspension tomorrow."

When I saw Enrico the next day, he raised his pants leg with his good hand. "Hey Mr. B."

195

"That's whassup!" I shot back at him.

During lunch Enrico turned in two weeks' worth of extra credit work. He also had sweet and sour chicken with vegetable rice delivered to the school for lunch.

"It's on me today."

---

One of the coolest kids in the school was my man Jelson. His personality was really laid back. He kept a clean low Caesar haircut and always dressed well. Despite the fact that we had a dress code, his shoes, jackets, and accessories were always a bit beyond his peers. He was a bit older, about 16, and a handsome young fella. Dominican kid. Slim. Always had a hat. "Yo, you be fresh, man," he would always tell me. He was one of the kids with an IEP—that's an "Individual Education Plan." He wasn't very sharp and it appeared that he didn't have much guidance at home. Frankly, I think all he needed was a good mentor that had the time to give him more attention than a teacher and his home could offer. The kid was a stellar gentleman and a ladies' man. He actually had a girlfriend that didn't attend HLR, but he sure was drunk with whatever she served him. She had enormous influence over him. I figure he was looking for a reason to exist. He found it in her. That is until he told his girlfriend, "If you leave me, I'll kill myself."

She did. He did. He shot himself in the head.

At the end of the school year, I was burned out. Jelson put the icing on the cake. I would be remiss if I didn't make mention of the many scholars that were moving up the education ladder at HLR. That's what kept us going, including Mr. Rucker. He went all "Lean on Me" on the student body near the end of the first school year and kicked a number of trouble making kids out of the school by keeping a paper trail of their insubordination: Ty, Ricardo, Enrico—all gone.

I managed to stay busy and sane while completing my first year master's degree course work, overseeing student government, teaching financial literacy, teaching math, instructing gym, leading advisory, coordinating town hall meetings, tutoring after hours, recruiting teachers for HLR, recruiting inspiring educators to the New York City Teaching Fellow's program for the city of New York, and serving as a "Soul Winner" on the weekends with my church.

I had a ton of love and energy that was fueled by my past experiences. I needed to release my bottled energy that propelled me to reach the other side of the desk. I wanted to save as many young people as I could. Besides my personal experiences I had an enormous chip on my shoulder.

After years of helping my brother Doug and getting him through high school he had finally crossed over to living in a dorm with a roommate. Only it was called prison. He had a bunky and was sentenced to 12-20 years for second degree murder.

# CHAPTER 14

## We Are All Students to Some Teacher

What to do?

I was well overdue for a break so I decided to take the summer off from my master's degree course work and I was definitely not going to teach summer school. In fact I wasn't going to step foot in the South Bronx until the school year began. To recharge my sprit I attended church every Saturday. My pastor, Dr. Creflo Dollar, taught in New York on Saturdays and Atlanta on Sundays. I was considering getting involved in with another ministry outside of Soul Winning called the Vision Keepers. This ministry was comprised of Pastor Dollar's personal assistants. They were the "men in suits" during service, but the "men that voluntarily served" prior to and after service. They were young and sharp ranging from early twenties to late forties. It was a brotherhood in nature and the members seemingly worked harder than anyone else in the church. They came early and stayed late, had a focus that I appreciated, and a bond that was grounded in selfless love and a relationship with God.

One particular brother, Keith Campbell, caught my attention due to his impeccable style of dress. In my 24 years of living I had never personally witnessed a black man dress as effortlessly or as stylish, and was as well-groomed as fictitious television characters. This was an element of fashion that only James Bond could achieve. I noticed his gentlemen's attire and conduct consistently for more than six months. I proclaimed him to be a style "guru." I recall the Saturday evening of our first formal conversation. He wore a light-weight, spring-colored plaid suit jacket, a subtle gold pocket square, spread collar shirt, tan tie with a tie bar, khaki color pants with no break in the length, topping it off with a pair of cognac double monk strap shoes and no socks. At the time I couldn't articulate his fashion décor. I simply knew it fit perfectly as if it was specifically made for him. With that said, it was the perfect time for me to ask the gentleman and style expert some questions.

"Excuse me brotha'," I said, "Salute to you for being a man of impeccable style and spiritual character. I've watched your movements and I must pay you homage for your consistency. From one man to another I appreciate you. Do you mind if I ask you a couple questions?"

With a firm handshake, "I'm Shawn Blanchard, respect." I went on to ask:

"Why does your suit fit differently? How much does it cost to achieve this James Bond look?"

"I buy my clothes custom or I just get them off the rack and have them tailored," Keith answered. "A couple of the major places to get a suit taken is the waist of the jacket, and the circumference and length of the arms. From there you can accessorize according to your taste. As far as the price is concerned, it's fairly inexpensive with a decent tailor. To do what I just mentioned to a suit jacket it can cost anywhere between $40 and $200. "

I wasn't sure what the heck he was talking about exactly, but he had my attention. "Where you from, anyway?"

"I'm from St. Louis."

"Oh, I'm from Detroit."

I decided to add Keith to my growing list of mentors. He was ten years older than me and seemed to have made a really good transition from his former life in St. Louis. Every time I saw my brother Keith, class was in session whether he was deliberately teaching or not.

I was inspired to join the Vision Keepers (VK) Ministry. To become a member, you had to display your dedication by having a heart to serve and take a supplementary course. If a man is going to represent the church, he had to have a thorough understanding of the Word of God.

The church rotated between Madison Square Garden Theatre and the Manhattan Center on 34th between 8th and 9th Avenue—no actual church building yet. Our duties included but were not limited to setting up the reception tables, books, instruments, banners, stage, handling offering, prayer, and making sure the congregation was greeted and taken care of accordingly in love. We did that every week, and had Bible study every Wednesday. We worked 12-15 hour days on those Saturdays in shifts. It was completely voluntary and we all enjoyed serving and building a brotherhood of spiritual substance.

Every VK was a man of substance moving in the spirit of excellence: financial analysts, business owners, photographers, entrepreneurs, or a man working towards greatness. However, no one had a problem doing manual labor. That was intriguing yet one of the many reasons why I loved it. We were all there to serve. It was essentially the first time I had been a part of a group of men that was solely about pure love and service. Powerful: to see men from all walks of life, all ethnicities, and creeds deeply involved in service. Completely selfless.

---

When school began in the fall, I dropped a number of extracurricular activities that I was leading or participating in during year one. If I continued at my first year pace I would be burnt out before the end of year two. That meant gym, student government, hosting assemblies, and recruiting for the New Your City Teaching Fellows program was all coming to an abrupt halt. It was already a handful addressing the emotional devastation that our students faced on a daily basis while trying to teach math. Over the summer I read a number of motivational books that were suggested by some of my mentors such as *Think and Grow Rich* and a host of magazines such as the *Robb Report*, and *Black Enterprise*, and the common theme I found was that the most successful people took breaks on the weekends. The idea of restoration is very powerful, and it intrigued me. I picked it up and found ways to restore myself from a harsh week's work every single weekend.

The year was 2007. I taught a class called "Advisory." The theme of the class was leveraging life lessons and the greatness in mentors. It was Mr. Rucker's idea to have a period during the school day where students could talk in a counseling fashion without the pressure of school to build a familial culture: A lot of the Bill Gates-funded schools provided the course, but left it up to the schools to be creative with the implementation. So the teachers had a bit of autonomy on the delivery of the concept.

I decided to discuss individuals that made a mark in my life that inevitably cultivated my thinking.

"I want to be a politician," I told my scholars. "Like Barack Obama." I brought in his book, *The Audacity of Hope* and let them peruse through it and other writings, just to expose them to the fact that there was another way to live. "Like Kwame Kilpatrick."

During the fall of the 2007 school year I recall sharing: "You see this brother Obama? Mark my words: he is going to be president one day."

What I admired about Obama is that he was always cool, calm, and collected. He led without barking. Suave. The coolest politician ever, other than Bill Clinton and J.F.K.

For me, Obama was the Mike Lowrey/Marcus Graham of politics. Kwame Kilpatrick, Detroit's mayor, on the other hand was the "Hip Hop Mayor." He still maintained kind of an edge. Barack was a bit more subdued. I liked that. Honestly, I'd had enough of learning what an "edge" can get you.

I watched Obama's debates and found him to be resilient. It was an intellectual resilience and kinda comical too. He was so sure of himself, but not in an "in your face" way. He might debate with people who spoke more eloquently than him, like Alan Keyes, who pontificated elegantly in contrast to Obama's more simple prose. Yet Senator Obama's words meant something. They were genuine. Powerful. Real. Made an impact.

I learned from him to listen first and when you do decide to speak make it impactful instead of pompous.

---

*From Gs to Gents* was a reality show. Fonzworth Bentley was the star. He became famous for serving as P Diddy's assistant, holding his umbrella and actually taught him how to dress in gentleman attire. Fonzworth took "'hood" guys and turned them into gentlemen by taking them through a series of courses and missions. I particularly admired the way he dressed, and was in the midst of a refining process to develop my own understanding of style. This man and the scope of his reality show was the über version of what I was doing at the school! He was so deliberate in his approach. He had a strategy that caught my attention—and it looked like the strategy actually worked for grown men!

Fonzworth would take the "gentlemen in process" out to dinner and bring in celebrities who would give them "missions." One week, it was to take a woman out on a date: three guys to one woman. They had to act like gentlemen—not something they were used to. They had to show manners, not say anything out of line, etc.

Wouldn't it be great if I could do this for my young male scholars? I thought. I began brainstorming "courses and missions" that could have an impactful effect on their lives—missions that would move them into manhood by teaching them what was important, in an "on-the-job" life training of sorts.

When I got back to school, I gathered several of my fellow educators. One of them was Ryan Glass. He was white, one of the Teaching Fellows, born in South Africa. So he was "African American," if you will. He taught math. Graduate of New York University and also attended Northwestern, an actor turned teacher.

African American. That's what he would tell his scholars. Every year, scholars had to recite a series of "random facts" about themselves as part of an icebreaker. Ryan Glass's random fact was always: "I am

203

actually more African American than you! For those of you that consider yourself African American." That always got their attention.

"I was born in South Africa," Glass would explain. "Have you been to Africa? Didn't think so!"

The scholars liked him.

Then there was special education specialist, Kofi Dawson. He was a member of Alpha Phi Alpha and graduated from Clark Atlanta University. He was dark brown, slim with a long facial hair that was kept and lined with precision, low Caesar, and looked like a soccer player.

The kids thought he was cool.

Anthony Bryant, music teacher who led the music ministry at the famous Abyssinian Church in Harlem, was an eloquent speaker, and a Morehouse Man. He was stocky and about 5'7".

Adrian Brooks transferred to Adelphi College on Long Island from a community college, then got a master's degree and became an English teacher. He had taken a non-traditional route, and displayed how the four-year college plan was not for everyone. He wore dreadlocks and looked like Theo Huxtable.

All of us were in our mid-twenties and excited about educating youth. We were different yet we had a solid team.

During lunch time the five of us met in my classroom to brainstorm about creating an organization to serve the Alpha male community in our school. We figured if we could steer them in the right direction we could control the school's culture. Learning from experience we didn't want to see any more Jelsons take their lives, Tys in and out of juvenile, Ricardos fighting their own parents, Enricos breaking glass with bare hands due to stress, or naive wanna-be gangstas like Lathan. Honestly, my thoughts were deeply rooted dating back to my brother Mike being gunned down in a drug transaction, my brother Terry being shot and sentenced to life with 11 beautiful children, and my very first mentee, Doug, being sentenced to 12-20 years. We had work to do! A number of the hard-to-reach young men were expelled from Mr. Rucker's *Lean on Me* approach to cleansing the school culture, but honestly all of our students had varying degrees of issues that needed to be addressed. Some were simply more manageable than others.

"I think I have a way to do this," I explained during our lunch meeting. "We can take the same approach as Fonzworth Bentley's *From G's to Gents*. Let's make our lessons impressionable and exciting. They can go on scavenger hunts in teams around the city and meet us at a college once they complete their task! Or we could have them do "speed dating" just to meet role models and prospective mentors from an array of professions they don't even know exist! Low key…we may learn something too!"

We all laughed, but it was true. We were all young men ourselves. Constantly evolving and leaving bread crumbs for our scholars.

Everyone agreed.

Kofi chimed in stroking his beard, "What should we call it? Majestic Men? Royal Men?"

We agreed on "Men of Majesty." We thought it was just the right touch of regal and edge that would capture the attention of our chosen male scholars. Believe me, for many of our students we were certainly speaking the word "scholars" into existence. Men of Majesty would be an identity, a "gang" of sorts, but one that would help them toward a more successful and purposeful life than they might have otherwise.

"We need a crest," Ryan Glass retorted. He was always creative.

Our crest was awesome: two Lions flanked a shield, inside the shield were four compartments: books, a dove, bars of gold, and a sword.

We collectively made a list of our guiding principles.

Our seven pillars:

205

Servanthood

Leadership

Scholarship

Self-Control

Humility

Integrity

Spirituality

Anthony drafted the rhythmic Majestic Pledge:

*I am a man of majesty.*
*I show forth majesty in all that I think, say, and do.*
*I am crowned with humility and scholarship.*
*I am robed with servanthood and leadership.*
*My scepter is integrity.*
*I am girded with self-control and spirituality is my sword.*
*I embody royalty and act justly therein.*
*I am a king enthroned in majesty.*
*I am a majestic man.*

Each founder organically fell into our roles. Anthony came up with the spiritually grounded pledge. Ryan designed the crest and ceremonies. Kofi formatted the group in the likeness of a fraternity. I designed the missions and Adrian assisted everyone.

We decided on the colors: Purple and Gold. They represent royalty.

It was a great partnership.

We had to find a way to creatively invite the young men we thought would benefit most from the extensive interaction with dedicated male mentors. We created scrolls and burned the edges for a look of authenticity.

The scrolls said:

"You have been invited to Majesty. Meet us in room 113 at 3:30 p.m. today."

We made a decision to select the "Alpha" males. To parallel Jesus's methods, we invited only 12 young men.

The hierarchal progression:

*Young Master* ➡ *Master* ➡ *Knight* ➡ *Majestic Man*

Upon accepting our offer to join our esteemed organization each member would begin as a "Young Master" and progressively matriculate until they reached the status of a Majestic Man. As the leaders of the organization we gave ourselves the title "Head Masters."

With the *From G's to Gents* foundation and our diverse talents and resources we were sure to create change in the lives of our members. I was anxious to begin the process.

It was Wednesday, October 8th, 2008. Ryan, Kofi, Anthony, Adrian, and I made sure that each young man received an invitation scroll throughout the school day. We divided the 12 into groups of threes— we grouped them so that none of the young men in each group were too acquainted with one another.

By 3:30 pm, all young gents were in one of the four assigned locations according to their scrolls while the final preparations for the transition room were being set.

We were in uniform: black suits, black shirts, black shoes, purple ties.

We planned accordingly to share the same spiel with the young men in each room that housed the small group of prospects before taking them to the transition room:

*Gentlemen, you will be given the opportunity of a lifetime today. This opportunity will place you on a path to excellence that can change the trajectory of your future.*

*As you eat pizza and drink your beverages fill out the 5 questions on the paper that is in front of you. Shortly we will begin.*

## The 5 Questions

✓ What is an excellent life?

✓ Do you believe your life will be excellent?

✓ Who do you know that is or has been enrolled in college in your family?

✓ Name three of your role models and explain why.

✓ Would you like assistance to become excellent?

Everyone followed instructions and proceeded to answer the questions in each of the four prospect rooms.

In each room, we said:

*Gentlemen, if you would like to be excellent than you will have to learn trust. You are all strong minded and it is up to you to discern who you will trust in life. If you would like to go on a journey of excellence, line up in a single file line and you will begin learning trust with the "Trust Walk." You will be blindfolded and you will follow with your own understanding. All in favor form a line.*

The lines were formed.

We began the "Trust Walk." Each young man, blindfolded, put his hand on the shoulder of the person in front of him, and they began to walk. The halls were empty. Silently they followed the direction of the person in front of them. The first in line was the lead.

We transformed my classroom, Room 113, into a sanctuary. We closed all the shades and covered the windows with black plastic bags. Purple sand covered the floor. Huge candles were placed on each of the room's seven tables that formed a circle, with a 12 slot candle holder in the middle. It was pitch black dark, and smoke wafted up from the

208

floor—not from fire, as some of the young men thought, but from dry ice we had placed strategically around the room. The empty 12 chairs were placed in a horizontal line awaiting the prospects to have a seat.

The Head Masters that brought the blindfolded prospects to the door gave a special rhythmic knock to be admitted to the room. Knock…Knock-Knock…Knock

As they took the final steps of the "Trust Walk," the 12 young men were lead into a dark room to their appointed seats and met with a single voice whispering, "You will need to be silent during this transition," the voice echoed. "Do not utter a word. Remain silent until you are told that you can speak."

Once all 12 were in place, we had a complete 60 seconds of silence in darkness. The silence was deafening, especially for a group of teenagers raised in our now too-noisy culture, with hostile reality TV, overwhelming social media, deafening music, and a demanding culture that leaves no option other than fill up all your empty space with fast paced, loud activity.

The young men had no clue why they were chosen or what was going on.

Ryan Glass had a didgeridoo. That's what he called it… The didgeridoo is a long horn from Australia that makes an eerie, grainy, low sound, almost like what you might hear on a boat. He began blowing. Mmmmm…Oooooomm until it faded into silence.

Silent. Still in blindfolds. We began.

*You have been chosen. There are many among you, but you have been chosen. You have been called into Majesty. What you are about to see here, you will not repeat. You will not utter a word to anyone, because only you have been chosen.*

Kofi and I silently yet wildly gestured back and forth, making sure that all of our colleagues and partners in crime were in place. It was not a time for laughter and the seriousness on the faces of the blindfolded prospects chilled the mood.

"Gentlemen, remove your blindfolds!" barked Ryan.

Slowly they took them off, then began looking around the room. They were looking quizzical. They saw five "men in black" with purple ties standing in front of them. They saw 11 other young men seated to their left and right.

Ryan continued. "Welcome. We are Majestic men, and there exists a secret society among us known as Men of Majesty. We have seven pillars which comprise our principles."

I lit the first candle.

"Leadership."

Adrian lit the second candle.

"Scholarship."

Kofi lit the third candle.

"Integrity."

Ryan lit the rest of the candles.

"Humility. Integrity. Spirituality."

Charles Bryant recited the Majestic Pledge:

> *I am a man of majesty.*
> *I show forth majesty in all that I think, say, and do.*
> *I am crowned with humility and scholarship.*
> *I am robed with servanthood and leadership.*
> *My scepter is integrity.*
> *I am girded with self-control and spirituality is my sword.*
> *I embody royalty and act justly therein.*

210

*I am a king enthroned in majesty.*
*I am a majestic man.*

Charles continued, "Gentlemen, our society is a society of excellence. Filled with a host of strong men with multiple degrees and spectacular skill sets. Filled with caring hearts and compassionate minds and the ability to leverage their gifts to live from the fruit of their labor and righteously serve. If you go on this journey with us, that will be your life too. Your life, in fact, will forever be changed. However, this is not an easy road and it requires your dedication to excellence, your dedication to the process, your dedication to Majesty on your way to becoming a Majestic Man. If you choose to accept the call, come forth one by one and light one of the twelve candles before you. The first among you will spark the flame with a match. The rest of you will continue to light your candle with fire from one of your would-be brother's candles,"

One by one each young man stood and with pride they lit their candle and went back to their seats.

Yes.

Yes.

Yes.

Yes.

Yes.

Yes.

Yes.

Yes.

Yes.

Yes.

Yes.

Yes

Criminal records, gang members, lack of guidance—the most intriguing 12 among the Alpha males in the school.

"Welcome gentlemen. You are now brothers and termed *Young Masters* of *Men of Majesty*. This is your Crest. Each element of the crest represents one of our 7 pillars.

Servanthood = The Sword

Leadership = The Crown

Scholarship = The Books

Self-Control = The Shield

Humility = The Bars of Gold

Integrity = The Lions

Spirituality = The Dove

"Your first mission is to understand and recite the Seven Pillars and the meaning of them within our crest. You will also need to know something specific about at least six of your eleven new brothers. You can work with your brothers if you like, or by yourself. It's up to you."

Upon 100% acceptance the new Young Masters were released and given another burnt-edge scroll on which the riddle of their first mission was written.

*Rushing greatness is like rushing the process of grass growing... Strong roots (foundation) will always enable you to grow faster, but you will always grow at the pace of merely fast growing grass.*

*Location: Meet on the corner of 81st and 7th Ave.*

For every minute they were late they earned the pleasure of ten pushups, only they didn't know that until they arrived.

Being boys they simultaneously loved it and hated it.

It was 10am on Saturday, and we were meeting on 81st and 7th Avenue off the C train, north of the Natural History Museum and across the street from Central Park.

Everyone came in twos or threes, but there was no sign of Roland. Roland was one of our sophomore members. He was 5'5", about 125 pounds on a good day, his skin color was a shade lighter than a paper bag, and his face was hairless with strong facial features. He went through a host of transitions with his mother battling cancer, his father was serving ten years in prison after being involved in a drug raid, and his family was having issues with suitable housing. His mom left New York and headed to Virginia after her other son (Mel) was shot and killed over a girl. She wanted to provide a better life for Roland as a high school freshman. In turn, he flunked every single class in the 9th grade. She decided to move back to NYC, setting up in the South Bronx, and stumbled upon HLR.

We waited until 10:10 a.m. to make sure we didn't miss Roland coming up from the subway station. Only half of our young men had cell phones and Roland wasn't one of them. We also had to make sure that he had enough fare to get back on the train. We began to walk across the street to enter Central Park and heard a young man yelling "Bro's! Bro's! Wait for me!" Roland darted across the street with Louis Vuitton sneakers, a Louis Vuitton t-shirt, a pair of True Religion jeans, shades and a leather bomber. The epitome of "'hood rich."

Apparently, somebody didn't take the dress code on the scroll seriously.

He slapped fives with his bro's and Head Masters. After the kicks and giggles all Head Masters stared intently at Roland.

"What? What I do?"

"You were late. As a Young Master you are to make sure that you are prompt and regal in all things you do," I said. Head Master Ryan Glass, how many minutes late was Young Master Roland Gainer?

"Eleven minutes Head Master Blanchard."

Gentlemen, for every minute you are late you will have to do ten push-ups. Young Master Roland Gainer was 11 minutes late today. How many push-ups does he have today gentlemen?

In unison they announced, "110 push-ups sir!"

"Awww Man… One hundred and ten push-ups? Man y'all going ham! Aight, aight I got this."

Roland jumped to the ground and began doing push-ups as everyone watched. He was strong and didn't have much to push up, anyway. He began struggling at around 70 and made it to 83 until his frail arms gave out.

"Whew, got my LV shirt sweaty… I can't do no more man…"

"You can't be late anymore either," chimed HM Kofi, stroking his beard.

Young Master Thadeus jumped to his side, "I'll do the other 37! It's 37 right?"

"It's 27," Roland corrected him.

He did 27. With ease.

"Man, if I would have known that, I would have helped him out!" chimed Young Master Kareem.

I stood there with my arms folded, silent, with a smirk. Clearly a portion of our first lesson was accomplished.

"That was lesson number one today. It's all about brotherhood gentlemen. If one falls you all fall. If one struggles you all struggle. As a unit you are your brother's keeper. We told you as you left the initial ceremony that you can help one another if you choose. That is a life lesson and in all things. There are lessons being taught every single day. Only some actually learn from these lessons. Be that one."

We proceeded to enter the park and continued with a series of brotherhood exercises and information drills. The concept of being as strong as the weakest link was understood from the strength that resided within Roland, Kareem, and Thadeus. They pulled up the rear and slack from their brothers. It was becoming evident who the leaders would be. Despite the tardiness, and the dress code, Roland knew the pillars, the crest, and half of the pledge fluidly (the pledge wasn't assigned). Kareem knew everything and so did Thadeus; they lacked the same fluidity as Roland, but they knew it all. We ate after a long morning of brotherhood training. As a bonding tool it was then that we instituted our majestic handshake. Two slaps, a grip, and bowing to the King in front of us. They owned it. We all owned it.

Thadeus also had humble living conditions and a humble personality. He was 6'0 tall, slim, with a dark brown complexion and slits in his eyebrows. He had a pretty boy demeanor and always carried himself as a gentleman. He didn't have a man present at home, but he surely had it with us.

Kareem was from Harlem, a pure leader. He looked somewhat like Thadeus, but didn't have a "pretty boy" swagger. He was more of a man-child. His shoulders were broad and he could be a bully if he felt like it. He was heavy handed, strong, and built like an ox. Good thing he took his aggression out on the court, if he fell into the wrong crowd. He could do tons of damage.

215

Many of our members lived in the South Bronx and rarely strayed from their community, despite the richness in diversity a few train stops away in Manhattan, Brooklyn, and the other neighboring boroughs and neighborhoods in New York City. There are roughly 100 colleges and universities in NYC and some of our members didn't personally know anyone in their family that attended a post-secondary institution. You guessed it! Exposure overload was one of our goals to keeping their mind moving beyond their community.

Now: a number of aspects in our initial approach to our good deed of creating this organization was founded by the passion to serve and provide a chance to dig deeper into the psychology of young alpha males. We were virtually breaking every single school regulation. From field trips without permission slips, to buying gifts and food for our members, to inviting them to our homes for missions to meet distinguished friends of ours. Thankfully Mr. Rucker understood our hearts and the fruit from such efforts, he provided the guidance of how to conduct this kind of change legally to keep his protégé and rock star educators safe from legal issues.

We met almost every weekend for the entire 2008-2009 school year with the exception of some holidays and testing periods. Approximately four months into the program we began to perform missions twice a month instead of every weekend. With five Head Masters we managed to rotate and keep the organization moving forward on our own dime.

Trust me, it was not easy. Eventually we changed a number of our methods. Instead of tapping Alpha males we let them apply given its growing intrigue and the limited cool knowledge others had about the organization. Our members that left the school were transitioned to honorary membership status because our mission entailed that we had a close eye on day-to-day intimate interaction. In return the school culture was positively impacted.

The 2009-10 school year was in full swing and Men of Majesty had new members under our new regime. Through our application process we had a number of extremely dedicated new members that wanted the guidance and brotherhood they witnessed from the outside. Roland, Kareem, and Thadeus had now achieved "Master" status with a host of new Young Masters that they mentored into the brotherhood.

During one of our weekly Wednesday meetings in November, we began discussing potential missions for the Holiday season. We decided to enable our members to have a hand in creating some of the missions now that we had some senior members that understood our mission thoroughly.

"We should help a family," said Chad.

Chad was one of our newest members who transferred to HLR for his senior year. His nick name was Trigga, because he strikingly resembled Trey Songz. He was extraordinarily intelligent, excelled in every course and exams, had impressive recall, and even became the first male President at HLR. Of course he was coerced to be a potential candidate. He accepted the challenge and his Men of Majesty brothers campaigned hard for him. It seemed fitting that he wanted to assist a needy family because his family struggled to make ends meet. He reminded me of myself because he helped his family through different modes of making money. Also, if he did it right, he could catapult his family through using his intelligence in college and beyond.

"How about we get a Christmas list from some families with kids in a shelter and give them what's on their list?"

"Great idea Mr. President! But we should probably keep it to one family to make a big impact," said Thadeus.

"Let's do a family in a shelter." said Kareem while twirling a basketball on one finger.

Yeah, let's hook up a family in major need," said Roland. "We need to find a family that's MESSED UP."

217

Head Master Kofi Dawson said, "OK. I have the perfect place! I'll go to the Hernandez Shelter, select a few families, and gather their specs to let you all decide which family you want to aid."

Roland: "How are we going to raise money? Y'all not paying for it! Y'all already pay too much money on stuff for us! If you are feeling generous you can spend all that money on our Christmas list! Hahahaha."

All members gave Roland the side eye as he laughed alone.

"Bro's... I was just playing man... Dang, tough crowd! Umm, okay about what you said Head Master Kofi Dawson, that sounds good to me. So, how are we raising money?"

Chad said: "Let's ask around for money. People do it all the time on the train, in the streets and on every corner in NYC. We just need some kind of gimmick. Like dancing, singing, or whatever our skill set is."

Thadeus: "I have the perfect idea!"

We took Thadeus's advice and bought bread, lunch meat, condiments, cheese, bags of chips, juice cartons and brown paper bags. Our sign read:

*Preparing food for the homeless. Please give.*

So our guys were literally panhandling at Columbus Circle in Manhattan. It was the perfect location with tons of traffic. It was just cold enough for us to see our breath, but there was no snow on the ground. No dancing or singing was necessary. Our gimmick was simply giving.

"Ladies and gentlemen, ladies and gentlemen: Right now our assembly line is making sandwiches to provide food for the homeless and raise money for a needy family for Christmas! Please give to the cause!"

To our surprise, people gave generously! Chad received a $100 dollar bill from a tourist. Roland was given $50 from a former homeless couple, others simply dropped dollars in the bucket directly in front of our sandwich table. In total there were 15 members making sandwiches and raising money.

After preparing the food we fed over 200 homeless people and raised $542.65 that day.

The Head Masters raised an additional one thousand dollars. The family that we chose consisted of a single mother with diabetes who was recently laid off from work and had three young children. The youngest boy had autism.

Watching our members purchase gifts, budget the money, and balance the needs vs. the wants was rewarding. They all expressed experiencing a feeling they'd never had. Ironically, a couple of our members were currently living in shelters and needed the same kind of assistance. Conversations of why more people in the world didn't do the same thing were raised. At the end of the day we couldn't speak for other people, but we were comforted by the overwhelming joy that comes from being a blessing.

# CHAPTER 15

## Substitute Dad: Round Two

The Director of the Comprehensive Studies Program at the University of Michigan, Dr. Nick Collins, referred me to Dr. Patricia Gurin, a celebrated professor of Psychology and Women's Studies at U-M, to mentor her grandson Bryan Dameron. That's how I initially met him. I became the role model that he needed during his critical middle school years. He was in the 7th grade then. Time has passed, and now Bryan was in the 11th grade.

I moved to New York when Bryan hit high school, but the time I was able to spend with him before I left enabled us to build a close knit brotherly rapport. During his beginning stages of high school, Bryan and I continued to communicate with one another and he even came to NYC for a college tour during his first year of high school. Every now and then Pat would call me and say, "Hey, would you talk to Bryan? He needs a bit of your energy." We would periodically have these kinds of casual, spur-of-the-moment check-ins. I would also sometimes just give Bryan a call to see how life was progressing and talk a bit more in depth about things that only brothers might talk about: Girls, peer pressure, girls, school, girls, and family. You get the point. We talked a lot about the elements of life that piqued his teenage interest.

With Bryan and me becoming so close I became an integral part of the family. One day, I received a phone call that truly displayed how integral I had become to Bryan's family.

"How are you?" Pat asked. I gave her the usual update topics. Our math department was in the top 5% with respect to closing the achievement gap, a number of "Aha" moments and transformations were taking place with Men of Majesty, and my personal growth as a Vision Keeper was always consistently developing.

"Shawn that's wonderful! You are so consistent in your pursuit to make the lives of young people better! I admire your ability to connect with the psychology of young people that tend to be difficult to reach." Pat knew that when Bryan was around me, he straightened up and acted out of his better self. Pat also knew that this same transition takes place in many people for as long as she has known me. She admires that trait.

"What's going on with Bryan? I haven't actually spent time with him personally since the D.C. college tour."

"That's actually why I'm calling," she said. "You're accustomed with dealing with impressionable urban young men, Bryan in particular.

"Bryan's been caught selling marijuana," she blurted.

Oh. Really… Bryan???

Bryan's mom, Jennifer Gurin, was Mexican. Pat and Jerry Gurin are both Caucasian professors who adopted her when she was a baby. Jennifer had a child with an African American man from the projects in Ann Arbor. Bryan was 5'8", golden brown, with jet black thick, curly hair. He was slightly chubby and could be heavy if he didn't watch his intake and monitor his level of physical activity.

Bryan lived in two worlds: one family has two grandparents in academia and a mother that's an accountant. The grandfather is Jewish, from the Bronx while the grandmother is a Caucasian woman from Indiana. Both teach at the University of Michigan. His mother happens to be Mexican. The other family, his father Lee Dameron's side, is characterized by individuals—including his father—who work blue collar jobs if they are fortunate. Bryan's dad initially went to community college on a basketball scholarship, but that didn't work out. He works in construction and honestly Bryan's father is not a "bad" influence. He definitely wants the best for his son. He's simply still figuring out life himself.

The cousins on his dad's side were eager to have reckless fun smoking weed, entertaining as many ladies as possible, and not taking school seriously. The peer pressure can be overwhelming. They called Bryan "white boy" because he talked "too proper" for their taste of cool. Bryan found himself making adjustments by speaking more slang and broken English to fit in with this side of his family.

As it turns out, it was true: Bryan was selling weed in school. He attended Pioneer High School in Ann Arbor. And just like Bryan's dual family worlds, Pioneer has two worlds. There was the world where the parents have completed college and are working in middle- to high-income careers. They take vacations and send their kids to artistic music and dance classes. This group of youth was encouraged to be creative, and were taught creativity by way of the classroom. They attended Harvard, Yale, Michigan. The other "world" is composed of the kids that lived where Bryan's dad's family lives. They don't do as well in school as the other kids. Life teaches them to be creative. The parents in this world encourage kids to learn to work and make a living. Often these two worlds don't intersect or even understand one another often. They are separate silos.

Bryan was wedged between these worlds. He was bred to think academically and have space for creativity by his upper middle class mother's family, but yearned to the "cool" in his father's blue collar family. He often "played dumb" to fit in. He was in the honors classes but didn't really want to be there once he reached high school. School simply wasn't as cool as selling petty drugs, interacting with girls who would give them the time of day, and getting high like the celebrities in the music videos.

A hall monitor said that he witnessed Bryan dealing some capsules. The clear plastic capsules were filled with marijuana. He saw Bryan exchange a handful of capsules for money. He then told Bryan's dad. Lee was completely against his son living that kind of lifestyle. He may not practice 100% of everything he preaches, but he 100% believes in his son's ability and bright future.

In response to Lee hearing about Bryan's illegal activity he immediately contacted Bryan's grandparents. They had no clue about Bryan's involvement with marijuana. Bryan was smoking weed, selling weed, and "borrowing" his grandparent's car to go out at night and party with his "friends". They were dumbfounded. "Who is this kid? What is going on?" They reacted the way that individuals in academia, who are sheltered from what young people—and not just those in the projects, but young people from all backgrounds—are getting into these days.

"We've given all these recent acts of rebellion some consideration and we have come up with a few ideas, but we aren't sure about any of them." Pat stated. "What should we do? Boarding school? Scared straight?

"Or maybe he should come out and stay with you…"

Whoa…Stay with me?

"It would just be like another version of Men of Majesty. I've noticed your abilities and it may be the best situation for him. We'll take care of him financially, so we wouldn't ask you to take that on. We would be asking you to simply be *you* with Bryan included."

I didn't think boarding school or Scared Straight were the right programs for Bryan.

"Just sleep on it, and tell us what you think is best," she said.

It was 9:00 p.m.

I made some peppermint tea, went into my room and played my thinking music. Sounds, clouds, and horns. I stared at the wall for three hours. It was 12:15am. Was this the same kid I built bike ramps with?

I was a 27-year-old bachelor and educator living in New York City. A very exciting city to live in. My former professor and mentor wants me to take a 16-year-old and, literally, raise him?

I have done this with my brother before. But my little brother is serving 12-20 years in prison right now. I had him with me when he was 16 too. I even fractured his rib when he didn't respond according to my guidelines. So, I wasn't exactly successful. What could I do differently with Bryan?

Hindsight is 20/20. I had grown leaps and bounds since then. I'd had much more practice and success with young people during my experience as an educator and mentor in New York. I have a more spiritual focus. I have taken those "pieces" of people I have admired—real and fictional—and internalized their "hero" qualities. Maybe with this extra wisdom, I can pull this off.

Boarding school is too impersonal. Men of Majesty is too temporary.

I had Doug for two weeks before he started "wild'n out." How can I extend that time such that it becomes permanent for Bryan? I had to come up with a better plan. But I also had a multitude of resources for ammunition.

It's going to be Men of Majesty on steroids!

Talking to myself, staring at the ceiling with sounds of clouds in the background, I thought: "Two years with Bryan. OK. I can do this..."

I used the Socrates Method on myself:

Q: What went wrong with Doug?

A: His friends.

That won't happen with Bryan.

I know: I'll have my Men of Majesty guys watch him. I'll choose his friends for him without him even noticing. They will model what I've been doing with them. Hmmm... Kofi Dawson. Yeah. He's the Alpha with the beard, the cool guy. Bryan will like him. He'll spend time with Bryan after school. Another good example for him to look up to.

I'll introduce him to my Vision Keeper brothers, too. We meet on Saturdays. There's dozens of them. They impact me, and that's a difficult task. He will definitely fall in line there. Reinforcement.

225

I smiled and twirled my metal ink pen through my fingers. Bryan will have nowhere to run. He'll be surrounded by role models 24/7.

And he needs money. So: I'll hire him. He will be my teaching assistant. He'll report to me, so I'll know he's actually working. That way, he will see that I have money, and I have it legitimately. You want to shop? Cool. You want to work? Cool. Then work for me. Maybe he'll be attracted to these groups and decide to join them. Maybe he'll decide to serve in the church.

I'm a fitness guru too, so we'll work on getting healthier…together…daily.

So here it is: I'll be his spiritual advisor. I'll be his trainer. We'll do P90X. I'll be his teacher, his advisor, his headmaster, his employer, his super brother-pops, and role model.

I will have to be everything to Bryan. I really think this can work this time.

I've been here before. My failure with Doug has taught me a lot and set me up for success with Bryan. I was born for this. And just in case he wants to wonder in that direction, I'll have him talk to Doug weekly from prison to hear about the mess that he has gotten into. That will certainly discourage the negative while pushing the positive.

I made my decision and slept on it. It was comforting knowing that I had been here before. My shortcomings would equip me with tools for the win. I didn't care about the time invested. I knew what it took to do this, and I loved Bryan like a brother.

I considered it my moral obligation and duty to help Bryan formulate the idea of the "Man" he wants to be. I must saturate him, surround him with achievers. That's the only way I can make it attractive.

With Doug it was different. He spent lots of time with me, but when he went back to be with his friends, the lifestyles were so different that I was the one who looked like an alien.

226

Everywhere Bryan looks, he will see success. The headmasters, me, the school principals, the Vision Keepers, Men of Majesty, will all be the "new normal." I won't look like an alien as I did with my brother, because excellence will be the standard everywhere he turns. The one who sells dope and gets high will be the odd ball, instead of the other way around. To Bryan, I will be the rule instead of the exception. Everywhere he looks, he will see people like me. In turn, his ignorance will be the exception and not the rule.

Kind of like propaganda. Kind of like brainwashing. Actually, it is brainwashing.

I woke up the next day and called Dr. Gurin. "You know what? I'll do it."

Pat Gurin literally screamed in my ear!

The grandparents and Bryan's mother called his father. "Bryan is going to New York to live with Shawn. Shawn is going to change his life, just like he's doing with his 'Men of Majesty.' That's the program he's created with a group of stellar educators posed to transform young misguided or unguided boys into gentlemen who have responsibility and character. And it's going to work with Bryan too. Just wait."

"Let me have a conversation with Bryan," said his dad. He also believed in me, and respected what I had already done for his son and was in full support of the move to New York.

Lee rounded up Bryan and his cousins. He wanted to be the bearer of great news, in his mind, to Bryan.

"You're not about to be like us," Dad Dameron begins. "You're not about to be like me," he said, making his point even more emphatically. "I didn't make the cut with the education track. You're smarter than me. There's no way in hell you are going to trample the Dameron name into the ground. You are going to be the answer. I can't even show you what you're supposed to be. But from what I hear and know about Shawn, he's a good brother. And you're moving to New York."

227

I wasn't there, but I was told Bryan's eyes turned red. He got up from his seat and began to tussle with his father in front of family. But he is no match for his dad. This was not a Riccardo scenario! LOL!

"Think you not going to New York if you want to. You outta here son."

That conversation took place February 1st, 2010.

On February 3rd I was at LaGuardia Airport in Queens, waiting for Bryan at baggage claim. Needless to say, they didn't waste any time. I didn't even talk to him on the phone before he arrived.

Bryan landed and called me on his cell. "What's up bro'?"

"I landed man."

"Meet me at baggage claim." I noted a hint of shakiness in his voice.

I had on deep brown leather oxford boots—John Varvatos. Denim tattered jeans and a v-neck sweater, thick burgundy knitted scarf, a skullcap, leather gloves, and a peacoat. Hugo Boss.

I looked up as Bryan was riding down the escalator. He was sporting a goatee, and he was a bit taller—I hadn't seen him in almost two years, since I took him on the DC college tour. He has cut his hair low (he took my advice), jet black and smooth as a Rottweiler's coat. He wore Timberland shoes, untied of course. And an oversized short-sleeved orange Polo shirt, must be a 2x...and though he's growing, he's still only about 5'6". His jeans draped over his boots and he wore a khaki-colored coat with fur around the edges of the collar. The coat was unzipped...cool kid, even in the cold. At least that's what he thought.

"What's up bro?" We dapped, and I gave him a Metro card.

"What's this?" he asked.

"That is your NYC passport, your visa to all transportation in the city," I told him. "Bus, train, you name it."

228

"Bus?" he asked quizzically. He's from the Midwest and that's not the most popular form of transportation in Metropolitan Detroit.

"Yeah, that's how it's done in New York," I explained. He was going to have a lot to get used to.

We grabbed his two huge bags with roller wheels and walked over to the bus stop. We swiped our cards and headed to the back and sat in two adjacent open seats. Bryan was preternaturally quiet. I understood: he's been exposed. He figured I'd start acting more like a parent. He thought the brotherly relationship would be ruptured.

I wanted to quickly disabuse him of his apprehensions. "Bro'," I began, "Let me tell you something: whatever took place in Ann Arbor—scrap that. It's not going to happen here and I won't harp on it. We're going to start from the beginning. You managed to get yourself in a dump truck of trouble, but you're here now. We're going to build you into an upwardly mobile monster. You're about to kill the game."

I continued, "You know I already know what happened. I know everything. But that's behind you. So, sweet…how you feeling?"

Bryan's face brightened. "Feelin' good now. I thought I was about to get a verbal thrashing from the bro'."

"Nah man. That's already been done. We have work to do. Everything's good. Welcome to New York!"

"Now you're going to have to pick up the pace here," I began explaining. New York is not Ann Arbor. You'll have to be a lot more aware of your surroundings. It's a concrete jungle here, and you're about to turn into an animal real quick."

Bryan smiled and chuckled. "Alright."

We continued talking and passed over the Queen's Bridge into Harlem. Our bus passed the famous/infamous 125th and Lennox Avenue. We went down 125th and the Apollo appeared on the left hand side of the bus. Bryan smiled and looked around at his surroundings. I could see him visibly relax for the first time. He felt safe.

We got off at St. Nicholas and took the C train to 155th, walking to 159th where my apartment was. I had moved further uptown to Washington Heights from my town house on 138th and Frederick Douglass. Still, whenever anyone asked where I lived, my answer was still: Harlem. It's a place that stays in your blood and I couldn't get it out of mine. Sort of like when people live in a Detroit suburb but claim Detroit as home when people out of the state ask.

There is much to do. I had to complete the temporary guardianship paperwork and Bryan literally has to be in school the next day. His mother prepared all of the proper paperwork and faxed all necessary documents. Remember: it's early February and he's been upended, so we don't want to lose any time getting him in and acclimated to his new life, especially with respect to school.

February 4th: Bryan wore his Rucker uniform: khaki pants and a powder blue Polo shirt. He still has on his Timberlands. I had already prepped the members of Men of Majesty to watch out for him.

"Hey Mr. B!" yelled the students in their standard greeting for me. Then they looked at Bryan. "Whoa! It's your brother! Hey, Mr. B brother!" they say almost in unison.

Now Bryan is not the shyest guy but he was somewhat taken aback. He responds, with swagger, "Yo. What's up."

In come the Men of Majesty: Chad, Thadeus, Roland, Kareem. They meet me in the classroom

"This is my bro', Bryan," I told them.

"Alright! What's good son?" they ask Bryan. They slap fives with each other.

The kids start piling in, whispering not quite out of Bryan's ear reach. "That the brother," they are saying to each other. "That's Mr. B's brother."

Bryan was kind of puzzled. "What is this? They seem happy to see me bro'…"

"I told them you were coming," I explain. He doesn't know the culture yet.

At lunchtime, Bryan approaches me. "Bro': question."

"Yeah, what up doe?"

"How does everyone like you bro'? The dudes say you so cool. The girls say "Oh, you Mr. B's brother?" and I told this one girl, "Yeah, and I'm the closest thing you're going to get to Mr. B.""

He was already showing his charisma with the girls on my accord. But he's happy, so it's cool.

"Did you get her number?" I asked.

"Got it right here," he answered.

"OK, do your thing. Just make sure you're a gentleman. You represent more than yourself here. You also represent me. Side note… No ladies are allowed over to my place from the school. I can't have young ladies at my place from this school. That's a line I can't cross."

"I don't want to get you into any trouble bro. I'll just get girls from elsewhere! LOL!"

"Funny man." I was relieved that he was getting acclimated with ease.

"This one girl, she's kind of hard to deal with. Her name is Naja. She's been acting crazy, mean-mugging me, didn't want to give me my book in class. Just straight up difficult! She look like a girl you don't want to mess with too. Plus people were listening to everything she said in class

231

and she's oversized. I didn't want to say nothing crazy to her. So I fell back. I'm not going to mess with her brodie. I'm the new guy and don't want to kill my vibe in the first week. No need to make any enemies, ya know."

My advice to him was simple. "Kill her with kindness."

"What?"

"That's what I do," I explained.

"Alright," he answered. "That's the key huh?"

We were on our way home, and Bryan talked to me about his day. He enjoyed it and felt welcomed already.

Roland approached me on the 2 train platform. "Man, Mr. B., we thought your little brother was gonna be one of those strange kids," he said, "but Bryan is pretty cool. He's not even lame! B, we'll see you tomorrow!"

Bryan was adjusting well to a different kind of culture shock on multiple levels. Since they were in a Title I School, our students were eligible for free lunch on the federal government's tab. That was definitely not the case at Pioneer. So it's the 'hood here in the Bronx—but with a difference. Here, the smart kids were the rock stars. There were no minority "silos," because the entire school is composed of students of color. Some are academically sound, some are trying to get better, and the rest, pretty much, are inspired by the first two groups of people. We work long and hard to maintain a culture of excellence. At Rucker, we were turning stereotypes upside down on a daily basis. It was far from Mayberry, it was a work in progress.

It was in that context that Bryan arrived on the scene.

While at home Bryan was doing his homework. "Hey Bro', just like old times."

"Yeah. That's what's up," I say back to him.

232

Buzzz… Buzz…My cellphone rings.

"Hello."

"This is a pre-paid call from, "Doug", an inmate at Oaks Correctional Facility. If you would like to accept this call, please press "0"."

I pressed "0" to accept.

"Yo yo, yo yo! What up doe bro'?! I got the food package, books, the money, and the pictures you sent! The pictures go crazy bro'! Thanks a million," said Doug.

Excellent bro', and all is well, just sitting here getting work done with young Bryan.

"Big bro', can Bryan hear me right now?"

"Yessir. He sure can."

"Hey Doug, I can hear you bro!" Bryan calls out. What's good?"

"Young Bryan! What the hell is wrong with you li'l bro'? You want to be in this box eating ramen noodles and slop? It's a gang of cats in here that would eat you alive young bro'. This is a different world and it's not for young smart guys like you. I was raised in the 'hood, thus, I understand this life because I was raised by real bosses. Shawn and I didn't have the kind of roles models that you have. Take advantage young buck! You see how excited I am about some pictures…You're out there and you can look at all the pictures you want to in real life while I daydream about it in here. Don't be hard headed like me! Big bro' told me what to do all the time. Most of the time I listened, but the things I didn't listen to made life difficult. I mean from choosing bad friends to smoking weed like a chimney, just know that you're with my big bro' and he got the answers if you're willing to listen."

The automated voice chimed in, "You have one minute."

"Hey big bro', this about to cut off. I love you bro'. Tell Mom and everyone I said I love 'em if you talk to 'em before me. Be sure to listen to everything you're told young bro'! Big bro' keep me posted on his progress. He over there taking my place… He better make Round 2 easy for you! Love you bro'!

"I love you too bro'."

"I gotchu Dougie Fresh. I'm listening to you loud and clear bro'," replied Bryan.

"Yeah you better because…"

*Auto response:* "Your time is over. Bye Bye."

Bryan's mouth was wide open.

"Bro, I never hear a prison call in real life. That sounded like something from the movies."

The last time Bryan saw Doug was when we were taking pictures as Doug went off to prom.

My goal was to expose Bryan and Doug played his part well in making sure he was an integral piece of the process just as we discussed a few days prior. He called at the perfect time. I didn't expect Bryan to completely change overnight, but I expected to see some signs of the fruit of change based upon the multiple entry points of growth and the multitude of mentors that he would be around. He likes the kids and admires that they respect me, which builds additional peer pressure to follow my lead. Doug was the buffer on the rough side of life. He also likes Kofi, Men of Majesty, and the school culture as a whole.

The ladies? Ehhhh… Bryan's coming from a culture that calls young women "hoes" and "b--ches." He knows absolutely nothing about being a gentleman. I have to introduce him to this lifestyle.

It was settled. Everywhere I went, Bryan would go too. If I went on a date, I'd have a third wheel.

By this time, I had a new girlfriend. Bryan doesn't know yet, but he was about to find out.

"Where are we going?"

"Dinner with my lady friend," I answered.

"What do you mean, 'lady friend?'" he asks.

"Well, she's really my girlfriend, but that's a term of endearment that I use to identify a special lady that I like. It's fitting knowing that she isn't a random girl. She's a beautiful lady."

I was constantly introducing him to new terminology about women, terminology he hasn't heard before. Ladyfriend vs. Girlfriend.

We went to a Thai restaurant between 38th and 39th Streets on 9th Avenue near Madison Square Garden. We're standing outside the restaurant, waiting for her, and up drives a Yellow cab. I opened the door and she gracefully steps out. We hug.

Bryan's eyes: wide open.

I opened the restaurant door for my "Lady Friend" and Bryan. He gave me dap and bit his knuckles as he passed me holding the door. The waiter escorted us to our table and I pulled out her chair. She never stopped smiling.

"Baby, I'm so excited about my new song."

"New song?" asked Bryan. "You like music?"

"Yeah I like music," said my lady, understated.

"Bro'. She actually has a Grammy."

Bryan's eyes re-widen. "Whoa! You got a Grammy?"

"Shawn, don't tell all my business," she admonishes.

"Well, you're good at what you do," I retort.

Bryan was picking up everything. He was paying attention to every piece of everything as if he was going to go home and practice in the mirror.

I ordered the drunken noodle, mild with no peanuts and pineapple fried rice with extra vegetables. When the food came, Bryan quickly grabbed the plate with the most food.

"Whoa there… I see somebody's hungry. Slow down bro', let the lady go first." I told him. "It's all you after her. The best is always for you over me."

I don't think he even heard that.

We left the restaurant. I said my good byes to my lady. We only had time for a quick bite before she headed out for a few shows. Bryan and I walked back to the train. He shook his head, still in disbelief.

"Bro'. She has a Grammy, bro'? And she like you bro'? She bad! And I could tell she like you too. She was smiling and kept looking in your eyes, bro'. I know that look all day! I know how women do it. Trust me, I know how they do it!" *Rubbing his hands together.*

"Oh yeah?"

"Oh yeah, I know how they do it!"

"As long as you know how to treat a lady, you'll always be alright with the ladies," I begin to explain.

"Know how to treat 'em, huh? Bro', but how do you get a woman with Grammys?"

Then, he looked down at my boots. "Man…I ain't feeling them boots. Why would you wear those? Who said those boots were fresh? She actually complimented you on 'em too… I just don't get it."

236

"And another thing," he continued. "Sometimes I notice that you don't really match. I notice that. Why do you do that?"

I laughed. We're talking about style here. I explained, "I like the boots broham," I explained. They were "rubber duckies." Marc Jacobs boots, all black with the blue gum sole. To Bryan, dudes don't wear those kind of boots. To me, this was just another lesson.

You see, I simply like the boots. I don't care whether other people wear them…or not. I am an individual. I like what I like. I don't need permission or validation from anyone.

"And the whole matchy-matchy thing?" I told him. You don't have to do that. You can complement or color block. It's totally fine, mixing different earth-tones and colors.

That means it's perfectly OK to wear brown and green.

The next day, we went to church and Bryan had a chance to meet the Vision Keepers. I introduced Bryan to my man Alaska, Haitian, who's an A&R at Sony and managing an artist that he recently signed to Rock Nation; Raleigh from Chicago, the photographer; Keith, where I adopted a lot of my style tips—he's a celebrity hair stylist: to Karim, the investment banker from Chase, who's Jamaican. Then there was Josh, the Puerto Rican who was a "soul-winner." We were a melting pot of ethnic cultures…similar in many ways to Bryan's family make-up.

And they all dress differently, as individuals. Nothing homogeneous.

Again, Bryan was taking it all in. "Hey Shawn: What do you mean by 'complement'? 'Cause these guys look fresh like you do. I think they all got the complement thing. They do it before they throw on their suits, then when they change into the suits they do the same thing with their ties and pocket squares."

"Oh I'm fresh now, huh?"

"Well you know, they're all different…like you. Nobody wears baggy clothes either, like you. Somehow you can still tell everyone has their own way of doing it."

"Right," I answered. "These are all individuals. Like I am. And like you are. You gotta be you bro'."

"Yeah," Bryan says…thoughtfully, smoothing his chin with his thumb and forefinger. "I like…'complement'."

"We'll go shopping soon," I told him. "Switch some things up a bit."

Bryan was really intrigued with the camaraderie among Men of Majesty at school. He witnessed the guys check in with me daily as soon as I arrived. He saw them going to my room to Ryan Glass's room, to Kofi Dawson's room, to Adrian Brooks's room, all the current headmasters. At lunchtime, daily you could find them in one of our rooms at some point, eating with us and chatting about life. The relationships were undeniably healthy and exactly what each member needed.

All of the headmasters were in their 20s, with master's degrees. For the first time, education, and individuality, and manners, and cordial behavior…they're all the norm. All of his 'trying to be cool' and 'proving' to the guys back home that he was "'hood" doesn't work here. If he engages in that behavior here, he's the alien. Not to mention he would look foolish because it simply isn't his truth.

Each member liked it too. They never experienced such comradeship and trust with an educator, but they embraced it. Bryan wanted a piece of that experience too. It helped to know that the members were on the basketball team, class President, alpha male socialites. At the same time they put their best foot forward to do well at school. Even if one fell behind, they didn't need a teacher to get on their case. Their brothers would take pleasure in correction. It was all about excellence.

"Hey bro', what's going on today?"

"It's Wednesday."

"All these guys have on purple ties."

"Yeah. We meet today. But you can go home," I told him. "I'll see you later."

I saw Roland and give him some dap. "Hey bro', go check on Kareem and make sure he's getting that work done for Miss Johnson."

"OK bet," says Roland.

Bryan was curious. "What's he doing?"

"Oh, he's just checking on one of his Bro's," I explained. I don't tell him much other than that. I want to pique his interest.

"So what you guys doin' after school?"

"Hey bro'," I told Bryan, "That's Men of Majesty business. Get your own."

"Wow…man, what I gotta do to get in Men of Majesty?"

"You know, Round Two is coming up in a couple of weeks."

"Word? Fresh bro', just slide me right in there… do I sign up or something?"

"Listen, all that will come in due time. You'll get the notice at the same time everybody else does."

"Alright. Bet."

Bryan went home after school. He saw something: I had somewhere to be, and he didn't. I came home that night, and I saw Bryan sitting on the couch with a Bible open, reading.

"Hey, bro', you knocking out your homework?"

"No, I'm done bro'."

"Nice. What are you reading?"

"The Word," replied Bryan.

"That's whassup," I encouraged. Get it in broham!

"The Vision Keepers are cool, bro'. Do they accept young guys? 'Cause I'm only 16."

He had been a part of the Vision Keepers prayer session that we had just before church service. We were all pretty cool men, we had our individual styles and personalities. We encouraged and challenged one another to be better and had too much fun with jokes all the time! Above the cool or prestigious jobs and beyond the work ethic, we had one love: for the Lord. Bryan has never seen this before. He goes to the school, and sees this love. He goes to the church, and sees the same thing. Then he comes home and the same love and comradeship exist between the two of us.

Bryan began to grasp the connection. I was leading Men of Majesty at school, but I was also a servant and pupil of another Men of Majesty-like organization at church, the Vision Keepers. It's an adult version of Men of Majesty, if you will.

He followed through on his positive desire.

Bryan made the *Men of Majesty* cut. He could wear the purple tie and do the handshake, just like everyone else. He was proud.

*Men of Majesty*'s reputation is now circulating in a number of education circles in NYC. We began to receive donations and additional resources. One of them was tickets to the play, *Fences*. The play was written by famed African American playwright August Wilson and addresses the complicated issues surrounding the dynamics of the black family. Denzel Washington played the lead character.

The guys were excited. "Denzel? Denzel in the play? Remember when he was in Training Day and he was whippin' that old school Buick Regal, all around L.A. like he was God himself? This is gonna be crazy!"!

240

We emerged from the subway in midtown and walked up to get in line. Chad tapped me.

"Bro'," he says, "there go Will Smith."

I looked to my right. "Where?"

Will Smith was walking right past us. I had to keep my cool.

"Will Smith, what's up brother?"

Will's face brightens. "Good to see you brother!" He shook my hand. Just as if we'd just seen each other last week.

"You're a role model, man."

"Thanks man. Appreciate you."

The boys are going crazy. "That was Will Smith! Will Smith dog! 'I Am Legend.' 'Fresh Prince.'" They break out in the song: "Now this is a story all about how…"

Honestly, I was more excited than they were. After all, Smith was one of my role models too.

Then walked up Aretha Franklin. Lenny Kravitz. We were honored to be there.

# CHAPTER 16

## Class President

Mr. Rucker approached me before my first class. "The Sankofa Society is traveling to the Congressional Black Caucus (CBC)," he said. "You should go; you'll gain a ton of connections, you can take a few students, and I'm sure you'll bring something back to HLR."

With high anticipation, I agreed to attend the event. I had never heard of CBC Legislative Caucus Weekend. Apparently, this was a heavily attended annual conference filled with thousands of game changers. It takes place in September and it's like no other event I've attended. A year before I had volunteered for the largest sit-down dinner in North America, the NAACP Freedom Fund Dinner in Detroit. This was the largest consortium of black leaders I'd ever experienced first-hand. CBC's purpose is to propel black excellence through promotions and information exchange at the business expo, workshops, panels, speakers and specialists, the politicians and selling of an assortment of products. Solution-focused discussions, presentations, and heavy networking were front and center...not to mention exciting social and entertainment gatherings. Attendees are young and middle-aged and elderly, and the atmosphere is literally electrifying. Through every medium everything is oriented towards transformation, change and impact.

While sitting in on an education policy panel, I met a gentleman named Carlos Walton. Some people might describe him as a "militant," but Carlos was all about empowering young people. He was President of APEX, an organization that recruits and serves high-school students who are "bound for college." He is very strategic. His favorite saying is "Life is chess, not checkers." He's about 6'4", very cool, with a deep and resonant voice that he uses with authority and confidence.

Carlos told me about a college tour that he does every year. "Next time I do the tour, I want you to come and help chaperone."

"Sure," I said.

Six months later I received a call from Carlos.

"Hey Shawn, it's Brother Carlos. Good brother I'm still counting on you to go on the APEX HBCU tour!"

"Absolutely bro! I gave my word months ago," I said once again, thinking I had some time to prepare. "When is it?"

"Next week!"

*What?*

Next week meant during the *ENTIRE* spring break vacation, which I considered precious and needed down time. The thought of sacrificing my vacation to take a couple of my scholars on the tour with a gang of horny and anxious high school students who were not from my farm, was honestly both an honor and a dreadful privilege. But I promised, and so here I was. Bryan actually flew back to Michigan for spring break to go on a different HBCU college tour.

I had two students—Shawna and Chad—that needed to go on this tour. Shawna was the vice president of student government her 9th grade year, and Chad is one of the Men of Majesty leaders and currently the student body president. Chad was smart, definitely college material, but he didn't know it yet. He hasn't even applied to any colleges and it was almost April. He assumed he was just going to enroll in a community college. I had to pay for him to go. This wasn't an opportunity that he could skip. Shawna and her mom were already on it and paid as soon as I told them about it.

We made stops at Hampton, Howard, Morgan State, North Carolina A&T, North Carolina Central, Spelman, Morehouse, and Clark.

Carlos was an interesting guy. He gave kids a lot of autonomy and freedom to express themselves, but somehow he was able to keep a cap on it so they didn't get out of control. My chaperone style was a little different, but I respect his methods and watched the kids as they "raise the roof" with their voices all while keeping their behavior in check.

I met a fellow chaperone named Chris "Kazi" Rolle on the tour as well. "Kazi," the middle name by which he is known, is the Founder of the Hip Hop Project, an arts education organization that asks young people, "If you had the whole world listening, what would you have to say?" The young people who participated engage in artistic endeavors, community service, and activism. Kazi actually made a movie co-produced by Queen Latifah and Bruce Willis called *The Hip Hop Project*, which chronicled his life as an immigrant to America who traveled through reunion with his birth mother, homelessness, criminal activity and its consequences, and then connection with a master teacher who provided a channel for his unique voice and vision. Kazi has been supported by Jay-Z, Russell Simmons, and many others who believe in what he is doing. Really cool.

By the time we made it to the fourth school, the kids had a special name for me. They noticed my balance of preppy sweaters and bow ties mixed with my backwards snap back hats, Y3 sneakers, and my *Beats by Dre* headphones, they thought I was cool. "Yo, this guy right here, his name is Mr. Perfect!"

Mr. Perfect? Yes.

The ladies at the colleges we visited seemed to gravitate towards me, so the young men wanted to follow. "I'm rolling with Mr. Perfect!" they would say. I didn't really care why they were "rolling" with me; Given that they felt understood and genuinely safe prevented me with the capacity to teach and mold them. I utilized the opportunity to impart to them.

Kazi noticed. "This is the beginning of a good relationship Mr. Perfect!"

Shawna and Chad applied to virtually every school we attended. But the way Carlos worked was, once again, interesting.

Apparently, very few of the administrative faculty members at the colleges that we visited actually knew we were coming. But no worries: Carlos had an unorthodox yet organic method to his madness. He

245

mentored students in every single institution we visited. These students had also been participants in the APEX College Tour and wanted nothing more than to pass on the blessing that was given to them through APEX's exposure. It was those students who gave us the tours. And those students were nothing short of outstanding. They showed us everything, and told us everything, gave us their school's full history. At every school, there were college students waiting to see Carlos coming, literally straining their necks to catch him.

"Man, you have been putting in some work with these young hungry achievers," I told him. "Yeah," he responded.

I see it. Carlos gives his young people a chance to express themselves such that they know they have a safe space when they are with him. It was brilliant. It was effective. Chess, not checkers.

When we got to North Carolina Central, Chad was particularly impressed. The admissions officer told him it was "kind of late" to apply. "But let's see your scores," he said.

Chad showed them his scores, and Paul, the admissions counselor, sat up.

"You know Chad," he said thoughtfully, "I think we can get you in. But I don't know about the financing."

Chad brightened. "I can get in?" he said, eyes lit up.

You see, Chad was expecting to go into the Army or at best, a community college. For a legitimate four-year institution to tell him they'd be willing to admit him was a huge deal. It blew his socks off!

Shawna received the same feedback and was excited too. But she was a bit more prepared than Chad. She had a folder for every school and in each folder were her resume, recommendation letters, test scores—everything she would need to give each school a full, impressive picture of her credentials.

Nevertheless, Chad spoke very eloquently. He was such a natural-born leader that when he speaks, you believe him.

Neither Shawna nor Chad had some of the schools we visited on their radar. Particularly, North Carolina Central. They didn't even know the school existed!

Chad and Shawna were both accepted on the spot! We celebrated as if they just hit the lottery! This was the first acceptance letter for both of them!

Our final stop was the Atlanta University Center. Shawna's goal: Clark Atlanta University. We toured Morehouse, but couldn't get into Spelman. We ventured over to Clark, and once again Shawna pulled out her accordion folder with her resume and all the trimmings. Again: accepted on the spot. She was accepted to her dream school!

On Carlos's college tours, he throws the students a big party after the last stop in Atlanta. By the time we made it to Atlanta, the students have gotten to know each other pretty well, having spent several days together, getting admitted to colleges, learning more about college, laughing for hours and singing on the bus, and ultimately understanding that college was attainable. The students who were accepted to colleges on the tour received awards, and those who were not accepted received a promise for assistance in applying to schools back in New York. Everyone was inspired and had potential to be a future alumni from somewhere.

The students then made a video expressing how they feel about their experience. They were laughing and crying simultaneously. It was one of the most moving experiences I had ever seen: teenagers who were strangers just days ago were positively and freely expressing themselves without rigid boundaries. It was powerful.

We made it back to school after traveling on the bus for seven long days. I felt like I had a voyage alongside the story of creation. The creation of possibilities for a group of inspired young people. It was actually time well spent with Shawna, Chad, and every young person aboard, along with the chaperones.

Bryan and Chad were close at this point. This was the first time Bryan had a close friend, someone he hung out with every day who was the student body President and who also said: "I'm going to college."

---

I came home from work about an hour after school was over, and again, Bryan was reading his Bible. "Hey bro', I made food today," he said.

"Great. I appreciate it."

"Yeah. Let's eat together."

"Sounds good, I was hungry anyway. What are you reading?"

"I was just reading in Galatians."

"Galatians?"

"Yeah man. Just reading about the Spirit."

Bryan made two plates of baked sweet potato fries, grilled chicken breast, and vegetable fried rice with pineapples. Bryan loves vegetable fried rice with pineapples ever since we went out with my ladyfriend months ago. Unfortunately, only one plate had rice on it because we were running low. I went to reach for the plate without the rice.

"And what do you think you're doing bro'?" said Bryan. "The best plate is for you broham."

He smiled.

Interesting. When he first came, Bryan would have almost broken his neck to get the best plate or have the last seat on the bus or train. He is transforming.

So now the better plate is mine. He reads the Word of God on his own time. He began working out and lost 15 pounds. A number of his friends were going to college. He was a Vision Keeper—the youngest one—and an integral part of Men of Majesty.

You would think that he was becoming a little clone. On the contrary: he was simply becoming an individual.

And the scholars didn't call him "Little Shawn or Young Blanchard." They called him Bryan.

---

"My grandparents want me to go to freakin' Spanish camp in Minnesota. What the heck is Minnesota bro'? I wanna stay in New York."

Bryan was going to be gone the whole summer. He didn't want to leave New York, but such experiences are good for him to grow in his own environment with his own persona.

He went anyway, and he did extremely well. The break was nice for me, too. It's kinda rough being a 27 year old man in New York with a 16 year old attached to your every turn.

Bryan completed his junior year on an upward swing. He still had a long way to go, but so far "Round 2" has gone really well. His grandparents' goal was modest: "We just want him to graduate high school." I think we were on to something bigger and better.

---

When Bryan came back to start his senior year, the pressure to be an intellectual gentleman was weighing heavily on his mind. "My name was Pablo Escobar at camp," he told me. "But I've been thinking about some things. I want to change myself a bit."

"What do you mean?"

"This year, I want to achieve some big goals and track benchmarks."

"Is that right?"

"Yeah bro', by the end of the year I want to switch some stuff up."

"Care to elaborate on that?"

"Yeah. I got it written down. Watch. I want to take college courses in high school. I want to have a college to attend. And I got to be a leader bro'. People need to see that I'm a leader. That's how Chad got in school."

I had coached Chad to be president of the class, and he's now in college. He made sure that he told every admissions counselor that he was class president on the tour, and he then went to North Carolina Central. Honestly, that was one of many perks that accompanied Chad's package, but Bryan is making his point clear about what he wants to do.

"And I want to switch up the fashion game. I want to wear a tie to school, every day. Almost."

Bryan started wearing fitted clothes with complementing colors and a variety of fabrics instead of his typical baggy-matchy apparel. He looked like a fashionable New Yorker. He even purchased a pair of the same Marc Jacobs boots that he once despised.

"Ya know, not everyone understands these bro'! I like that. I don't even want to aim to be understood. I just like the idea of being me."

He continued.

"I want to turn my swag up, bro'. I want to be more spiritual. I want to be healthier and have a more sculpted body."

Bryan has already lost about 20 pounds at this point doing P90X among other work outs. He's caught the bug of understanding that he can be whatever he wants because of all of his small wins.

His mom and grandparents were happy.

"How do you plan on doing all this?"

"I told you: I wrote it down. But I need your help on all of this."

"What do you want me to do?"

"You know. Like you did with Chad. You wrote a recommendation for him, you helped him with his speech for class president, you put him on the college tour and coached him through the process. I need your help like Chad."

Clearly he was paying close attention.

What Bryan didn't realize is that he already, with his upbringing, had a huge advantage over his peers he attended school with. His foundation was impressive. He outscored everyone on practice exams and in mostly every class. He simply needed to focus.

"Bryan, if you really want to do this, you're going to have to do better than Chad. You've been blessed with an abundance of resources that Chad never had. Definitely give kudos to Chad for doing everything within his base of knowledge to make it to college. In addition to priming the pump to give you an idea of what you need to do. As for you, let's start with getting you signed up for an ACT prep course."

---

As a weekly ritual we pay the barber shop a visit, The Harlem Berry. When you visit this particular barber shop, be prepared to laugh, just like the movie *Barbershop*. Ron, my barber, is a weight-lifting muscle head who knows martial arts. He has a deep raspy voice, bald head, and always animated. Everything is passionate. Bree is about 5'4" and has jokes for days. He looks and dishes out comedy similar to Kevin Hart. Don't step foot in this shop if you've got somewhere to go quickly; you will end up running late from the hilarious conversations always floating around.

We walked in the shop and said hello to the beauticians and the women under the hair dryer on the first floor, then headed towards the back stair-well that leads to the barbershop on the second floor. As soon as we hit the steps there was laughter. Ron was talking about an incident that took place with a cab driver who almost hit him. Immediately, Ron ran to the driver side door and forced the cab driver out of the car. He helped him stand by grabbing his collar then knocked him to the ground and half of his body went under the car. Then he yelled, "Get in the cab!" Everyone laughed at Ron's gestures and animation. Adrenaline can make some interesting things take place.

A breaking story flashed on the television screen. It was a breaking story about a teenager who was murdered in broad daylight. The interviewees were talking about how kind and compassionate the slain young man was. The deceased young man happened to be Ron's good friend's son. The accused murderer's face flashed across the screen. It is Jimmy. One of my students.

Bryan pointed at the screen. "Hey that's Jimmy!"

Ron sees the face of the murder victim on the TV screen and recognizes him. "That's one of my man's sons," he says. Sad. "My man's gone be f--kd up over that."

Bryan knew Jimmy too. "Crazy," he says. He sees the Chads, but now he has seen the Jimmies too. He's not at Pioneer High School in sunny Ann Arbor any more. This is the concrete jungle. In Ann Arbor, they may fight, or sell a little weed, but this is a different world. Harlem. South Bronx. Detroit style. You can get murdered real quick. You can get taken out of the game in an instant. The entire span of human behavior is at our little school, and he was taking it all in.

The very next week, another one of my students, Caesar, was stabbed in the leg a few times. Not sure why. He ended up with a cane for a while but ultimately he was OK.

The same day a kid that I've never seen walked right past me in the hallway. He looked a little older. He wore a hoodie, and I told him, brusquely, to take it off. He complied. Ironically, I still didn't recognize him. My eyes suspiciously followed him down the hallway. He was walking toward a young man that was getting books from his locker further down the hall. Next thing I know…

Crack! Bang! Boom! The guy walking down the hallway put all of his body weight into a connecting 3-piece-combo and thrust his fist right in the other student's face! The first punch cracked his nose which lead to gushing blood as he started to timber towards the ground. On his way down he caught two more which helped him hit the floor with a thud. The guy who complied with my demand that he take off his hoodie grabbed his collar hoisting him sluggishly on the locker and commenced to the beat down to the likes of which I have never seen! He hit him repeatedly in the chest, and the victim's head hit the brick wall. I snapped out of my trance and ran toward the scene. Blood was everywhere!

I walked delicately. Carefully. I scooped the perpetrator up and moved him away from the scene. He was focused on his victim.

"Yeah m-----f-----, what's up now?" He yelled at his victim. I do not know this yet, but he is no longer worried about beating up anyone. The security guard arrives. "I'm good, I'm good," says the perpetrator. "He f--cked up now. What's up? Yeah, b--ch-a-- n----r, you robbed my twin brother!"

Turns out that he didn't attend HLR… He managed to find his way into the school specifically to do damage to the so-called robber.

There were smeared speckles of blood all over my shirt.

So: Jimmy murdered someone outside of school. Caesar got stabbed coming to school. This last bloodbath incident happened by someone who wasn't an HLR student. The school is in a good place, but the home life of many of our students wasn't. It's evident that mentorship simply needs to take place beyond the school day. It's days like this that I appreciate Roland always staying after school, always coming to my place for dinner with Bryan and I, coming to church on the weekend,

253

and overall turning his mentorship into a lifestyle. It was his choice to "opt in" and receive the teachings, letting the process mold him.

Forward movement was taking place with Men of Majesty, but at the same time all of these senseless acts of violence and misfortune were happening too. I realized that we were creating a culture within the school, but we have to take our guys with us once we leave school, in order to ensure that they don't fall into the outside culture when they left these newly-renovated academic halls.

There was more. Another student shot at someone from the top of an apartment building and caught an attempted murder case. Female students too: they come to me and want me to keep secrets. But I can't. They were cutting themselves. They wanted to kill themselves. They were abuse victims. Others would tell me they had STDs and ask, "What should I do?" We created a family atmosphere, so they treated us like we were their parents.

Bryan was prepping for the ACT and I was prepping for the law school entrance exam, LSAT. I served for five years and this was the last year. I was determined to go to law school. I told Mr. Rucker that this day was coming, but he didn't take me seriously.

That is, until I asked him to write me a letter of recommendation. "You're serious, huh?" he says. "You can't leave Blanchard! You're my MVP, man…you can't leave."

When he realized that I was serious, he changed his tune. "We gotta throw you a party now!"

We have collected stolen laptops, cleaned up the school *Lean on Me* style, created a family culture, taught rigorous academic topics, named and loved these scholars, visited their homes, and created programs out of thin air. But it's time for me to move on.

Bryan decided to seriously run for student government.

"I need a slogan," Bryan says.

"I can't do that. It's a conflict of interest."

"Why don't you just put on your bro' hat?" Then: "I know! My initials: BD. They'll stand for Bryan Dameron aka "Better Days." I like it.

Bryan's grandparents were coming to visit the same day that Bryan would be delivering his presidential pitch, and this is the perfect time for them to be thoroughly impressed with his confidence and growth, first hand. "Bryan: what are your core values as president?" I challenged him to cultivate a creative yet practical platform. "And think like Principal Rucker. Know your issues?"

"Hmmm… Uniforms are a big issue. Some of the students hate them and want more freedom of expression. We definitely need more dress-down days."

Folding his arms and placing his hand on his chin, he pondered and then said as his eyes widened:

"No! We need 'dress-up' days. Yeah! That's it! We need 'dress up' days! Administration would definitely go for that. We could even pay a dollar to participate as a fundraising effort."

I smiled. "Young bro', now you're thinking outside the box. Give students what they want in the form of what the administration wants."

Bryan repeated his slogan and pointed his finger for emphasis. "Better Days."

"You're on a roll… What else?"

"We need more field trips."

"That costs money bro'."

"Yeah. But not if we go to colleges that are right here in New York City. We need to do a local college tour. Just get on the train and visit. See who we know that could hook us up. You see what happened to Shawna and Chad when they personally went to the colleges to apply.

This would enable the students to understand what's going on in their own backyard."

"Better Days," he repeated, thrusting that finger into the air.

"Alright. Alright I see you Mr. Better Days."

"We need more parties in the school too, he continued. Bryan was on a roll now. "Yeah. We need fundraisers. We need to party with a purpose. We could do canned goods drives and because we are raising money and awareness towards key issues this would increase school culture. Rucker is always talking about school culture. He would surely let us have more parties. Better Days!"

So Bryan now had three key objectives to hang his presidency on. He had become creative as well as strategic, and even better, he had come up with these ideas by himself. I was proud.

He was fiercely writing on his notepad with a grin… He was crafting something… "Dress up days. Local college tours. Parties with purpose = Building more school culture. Raising funds. Exposing scholars. "How's that sound big bro'?"

What can I say? "Hey. Better Days."

It was time for Bryan to deliver his campaign speech. His grandparents and Mom were present—the grandmother and Mom who asked me to 'temporarily adopt' him for a time, and the grandfather who has said how much he appreciates my intervention. Bryan was nervous, and he was sitting in my classroom after he ate lunch. It was the final moments before he delivered his speech.

"You can't listen to my speech!" he declares. Do NOT come downstairs! You guys are not going to watch me do my speech; I'm going to do this speech by myself. I love you, but you gotta wait."

Bryan's grandparents and Mom stayed, as they were asked. However, he wanted me there for moral support. He kept repeating his slogan: Better Days. Better Days.

256

He received a standing ovation, and won the election hands down. A proud moment. Now, he could tell the colleges he is senior class President and making tremendous strides to better his community as opposed to formerly hurting his school community when he was in Ann Arbor.

His family was more than amazed. They were expecting no more than a possible high school graduate. The young man who stood before them now was not "just" a high school graduate, but a class President who scored a whopping 29 on the ACT test. He has tons of community service hours and leadership training through Men of Majesty. He served at church and had a host of mentors, many of whom are Vision Keepers. Moreover, he had hope. He was excited about life.

Bryan's grandmother and Mom cried. His grandfather was far more analytical. "Shawn, we couldn't have asked for anything better. You know, you did a good job. And I watched you in the classroom. You're so animated with the kids. You're so free with them. I mean, here are these kids, talking about math, but they're talking about life too… all at the same time. Yet they are productive academically. They get up and participate, too. How do you do that?"

"These are my little homies…It's all in the culture that we set."

We were heading to dinner to celebrate, and Bryan invited two Men of Majesty, Roland and Thadeus. Roland has one of the top three GPAs in the school, and Thadeus has become a perfect gentleman with college in his line of sight. They both had their bouts with shelters and their families living in one bedroom apartments. And now they were breaking the mold of family traditions and their immediate environment.

At the dinner, Bryan opened a multitude of acceptance letters from nearly every college where he applied! At this point we were just waiting to see who would give him the most money. Let the negotiation begin!

Round 2 was more like a Rocky Balboa rematch. God is good. My confidence in mentoring had become restored. Talking to my brother in prison often times haunts me as if I failed. This moment simply reminds me that mentorship is not about creating rock stars. It's about making others better off than what they would have been without you. Prison cell or college dorm, my mentees were definitely better off because of our encounters. Taking notes from this encounter, the process becomes crystal clear:

*Reach. Teach. Mold. Repeat.*

# CHAPTER 17

## The Gentleman's Code

*Buzz. Buzz.*

"Hello, this is Shawn."

"My man Mr. Perfect! This is Kazi from the APEX College Tour and the Hip Hop Project."

"My man! What's the word?"

"All is well and good brother, I want to run something by you. I'm curating an event called 'Straight Talk, No Chaser.' The audience will be all female, and you would be a key player among a panel of six diverse men. We're discussing relationships, and I want the women to walk away with some real honest answers from some real men."

"Count me in bro'! I'm always down to assist a good brother," I replied. "Is this TV show-style?"

"Absolutely."

I was down with that. I was once again single, and looking forward to mingling. My ex-ladyfriend was impressive, sweet, and beautiful, but the international tours were a bit much for me. We had to slow it down before we simply disliked one another because of the pressures involved with time constraints.

The event was held in mid-town Manhattan. I was one of six male panelists that Kazi strategically hand-picked. One brother was a music producer and a polygamist whose father had five wives. Another was a DJ. He had a girlfriend, but he wasn't married. Another was of an unknown age and occupation, but the ladies found him to be attractive and well groomed. Then there were two married brothers: one was a stay-at-home dad whose wife was successful; the second one was a comedian who had been married for more than ten years. All different personalities.

Then there's me: a single guy, educator, mentor and law-school bound. A Christian with a slightly different perspective. Pushing the envelope simply by being a gentleman. I find it interesting the way I'm depicted knowing that it was once a figment of my imagination, but now has become a continuous evolution.

The moderators, women, were interesting as well. Demetria Lucas worked for *Essence* magazine. Another, Shanelle Cooper-Sykes, is a famous motivational speaker and author.

The event began and all six of us, men, walked into a sea of women. Kazi had us all stand, collectively raise our right hands, and say:

"I declare that I will tell the truth, the whole truth, and nothing but the truth, so help me God."

"Alright ladies and gentlemen," Kazi began, "this is Straight Talk No Chaser. Ladies we have four rounds, hold your questions until the end. The moderator will ask questions and the ladies will be able to ask questions and chime in during Round Four. Brace yourselves ladies. We have got some really diverse men here and we're going to have some real talk. Let's get into the minds of these men tonight!"

We begin mumbling to each other. Almost with one voice, we say: "You see that reporter? She is baaad."

I was the only one who didn't see her... I panned the room and spotted her or at least who I thought was her. She was tall brown and elegant. Her smile penetrated my soul. I saw her last. And indeed, I agreed!

"First question," explains Kazi, "Is it OK to have sex on the first date?"

Everett, the music producer, earnestly grabbed the mic. Kazi repeats: "Guys, don't hold back. Say what you will. We already talked about this. Let these ladies know what's going on in the hearts of men."

Everett took the mic. "I got this one. I believe that, on the first date, a woman has to have sex because that's the only way I'm going to know if there's going to be a second date thank you." His words ran together just like that, and he gingerly passed the mic to the DJ to his left. Completely nonchalant and unembarrassed.

The women were squirming in their seats! They began mumbling and grumbling. I saw a few heads turn, lips smack, and eyes roll. Funny, I saw a few of them agree with Everett too. Kazi interjects:

"Excuse me, ladies, remember the rules: that during this portion you are to keep silent. The men are pouring their true thoughts out to you. No questions or comments during this part of the program. You can ask questions and talk in the later portion of the show. So: all ears ladies!

"Next up!"

DJ Boss is next. "I don't think there's anything wrong with that. Having sex on a first date won't keep me from date #2. If it happens it happens, but it's not my objective for the first night. You can build from whatever foundation you like, in my opinion."

Adonis agreed with DJ Boss. I was next.

"Shawn B., tell us what you think!" says Kazi.

"I think there is absolutely no way that a man should sleep with a woman on the first date," I began. A woman is too precious to deliver her goods to a man before she knows whether he deserves them. Time has to progress so they can see if they have a special relationship that would warrant them being together in such a way. We all make mistakes, but the objective is simply the objective."

A collective sigh—all the women—fills the room. The guys looked askance at me. "Thought we were keeping it real," they said. I whispered back, "I am keeping it real." They thought I was trying to impress the ladies. They didn't understand that I was simply speaking what I truly believed.

At the end of the show, Everett pushed his thoughts. "I'm a polygamist, my father is too, and as I see it, men should be able to have multiple wives. That's why women can be pregnant for nine months and men can impregnate several women at a time, while women can only carry one baby or two or three if it's a multiple pregnancy. We also know that a woman's biological clock ticks... Men don't have a biological clock." He was talking so fast that he barely gave the women—or any of us—time to properly respond either in nodding agreement or with outrage. "It gets really deep but I'll leave it at that."

Regardless of any of our comments—whether the ladies agreed with us or not—all of them wanted to connect with at least one of us for questions or actually exchanging information after the event. After the lines died down, the single guys huddled up.

Our conversation was straightforward and focused on the infamous Reporter. She was gorgeous, and we begin talking about who has "rightful dibs."

Everett says, "I saw her first."

Adonis says, "I kind of saw her first, really. I just didn't say anything."

"But I'm going to treat her the best," I offer. "I'm on the market for a ladyfriend and if she's proper... This could be long term."

We laughed, then decide on an old proven selection method: Rock Paper Scissors.

We all place our right fist in the palm of our left hand. Before we could begin I received a tap on my shoulder. At first, I try to brush the tap away because we were handling serious business, but then I realized:

It was the Reporter.

"Excuse me fellas," I said with a grin. "I'll be back."

I turned to the beautiful woman who has tapped me on the shoulder, the only woman in the room that our selective taste agreed on. "My name is Shawn," I begin. "So I know," she replies. "I just wanted to talk to you for a little bit. I want you to know that I found you very intriguing during the panel."

"Well, I want you to know that you made an impression on me as well from your beautiful aura, and elegance. While speaking to you during the interview you were captivating," I replied. "Funny, we were actually deliberating just now on who would have the rightful privilege to speak to you. You certainly had everyone's attention, specifically mine."

We exchanged numbers. "I'll walk you out," I offered, and walked her to her car. I came back in like a peacock. I couldn't help but smile given that I wanted to speak to her from the moment I panned the room looking for...the Reporter.

I gathered my belongings. "Fellas, it's been real have a good evening," I said. "Until next time."

"Mr. Perfect!" Kazi said with a laugh.

Everett said, "Let me get your number fam. You're a different kind of cat. Let's exchange."

We exchange numbers.

Demetria Lucas, the moderator from *Essence* Magazine said, "There is something special about you. We exchanged information for future collaborations.

Adonis and I kept up with each other over the years. He actually wrote a book about our encounters. It's called *The Gentlemen's Code*. I never knew our encounters would turn into a book. It's not published yet, but the excerpts are derived from our experiences simply hanging out. You'll see some of these experiences as you finish this chapter.

As I left the panel event, I had to reflect on what happened. I stood on the platform waiting for the C train heading uptown. I've always been

263

the type of guy that women may like in terms of aesthetics, but I like it much better when they like the core of the man—the person beyond the shell. Heck, I find it difficult to focus on more than a woman's shell myself most of the time. I was and still am a work in progress, and that's what I said, and the women liked it! That was not a humble plug, it was simply the truth. I may have been nicknamed Mr. Perfect, which made me laugh, but I'm my own worst critic. Yet I appreciated the nickname and the applause from the women; it let me know that I was doing something right. My readings, faith walk, and collections of mentors and "friendtors" were refining me.

Digging deeper, it was the character of the man that made the Reporter approach me. The other single brothers on the panel were also aesthetically pleasing to the ladies, and please believe there was a line for each of them. Mine was simply a little longer and included the Reporter. Most importantly, she sought after me. I am infinitely in the process of becoming the man I once hoped to be. The kind of man I would have looked up to as a child.

Adonis broke my pondering gaze on the C train platform as the train arrived:

"Hey bro', that event was nuts! You going to the event tomorrow? It's Valentine's Day and the perfect follow up."

"Sure."

"OK. See you there."

The next day, Adonis called:

"You on your way?"

"Yeah, I'll be there broham."

I hopped on the D Train Express at 145th Street to SOHO. When I got there, I saw Ian at the bottom of the steps. The venue was posh, just the way Kazi likes it.

"Nice boots bro'," he said.

"Thanks." We had similar wing-tipped boots on.

Kazi is a marketing genius, having another panel just before Valentine's Day.

"There's going to be a lot of ladies here," Adonis said excitedly.

That was a given, but I was only interested in one: the Reporter.

As we walked up the stairs, Adonis fell back and let me go first. When we got to the top of the steps, my expectations were right. The ratio of women to men was 5:1. I walked in and already see women gesturing towards me. Lots of pre-planning as they decided who they wanted to talk to. Many of them told me that they enjoyed my comments.

"See? I told you." One grabbed my hand and placed a small folded piece of paper in my hand.

"Call me."

I smiled. She was beautiful, but I still had one objective. I should have just called the Reporter instead of hoping for a surprise.

We saw DJ Boss on the 1's and 2's and again they started joking about the tap on the shoulder and the woman who just blatantly slipped me her number. "This guy right here... He grabbed the mic, "Shout out to my man Mr. Perfect-Romeo Edition."

"Mr. Perfect! You done it again." Kazi exclaimed.

"What do you mean?"

"Man, I have a lot of friend requests, and I'm not talking about Facebook, for you. Don't look now, but here comes one. Hey Zola!" Kazi said as soon as he saw her approaching.

Zola was attractive, but I was still looking for the Reporter. As I spoke to her, exchanged some smiles and laughs. In the midst of our conversation I peered over to Kazi, "Where's your reporter friend?"

Apparently, she wasn't coming tonight. Zola asked me a number of penetrating questions about what I did and where I worked, but I was distracted and ready to leave, even earlier than I thought I would.

Adonis said, "You're going to leave now? What about the ladies?"

"I gotta do my thing with my kids in the morning."

"OK. I'll take these ladies on myself. Bro', we gotta hang out more. How many numbers did you get?"

"I didn't grab any. Except for the woman who slipped her number to a brotha'."

What?

"Hey bro', if we talk to every beautiful woman we come across we would be talking for days and simply wasting time. I already picked a good one yesterday. I'll just give the Reporter a call tomorrow."

"Alright. I'm not a polygamist or anything, but it just seems like—I mean, there's a lot of women. I tell you what, just take your pick and I'll go get her for you. How about that?"

"That's just not my style bro'," I told him.

"OK, OK, I feel you. But what about this? Let's hang out this weekend. I'm just messing with you. Hahaha."

"OK. Cool."

"I attend church service on Saturday in Manhattan, you should come."

"Church? Aight."

I left quickly, saying goodbye only to Adonis, DJ Boss, and Kazi.

266

The very next day, Adonis called me after work.

"Yo. Bro'. The event was crazy yesterday."

"Yeah it was."

"I know, I know. "But the Reporter wasn't there," he said sarcastically. "But for real, let's hang out this weekend. Kazi's doing another event, there'll be a lot a people there, maybe even a *few* reporters," Adonis said, jokingly, but halfway serious. "We can have a good time; it's cool to hang out with good people."

"That's cool. By the way: I got some cupcakes today."

"Cupcakes?"

"Yeah. They were delivered to my school. Zola asked me where I worked, but I didn't expect her to send a gift to my school. You have to respect a woman who knows what she wants."

Adonis laughed. "Bro', you never cease to amaze me. You a funny dude."

"God bless bro'."

"God bless."

The weekend comes and Adonis and I met at the Union Square in front of Best Buy. Near the huge numeric ticker board on top of the building where I have no idea what those huge lighted numbers mean. Ian walks up.

"Yo man, this event is gon' be crazy!"

"Yeah. It should be good." I retort.

"You stay spiffy bro'."

"Yeah. You too bro'."

267

We were on our way to the Gansevoort Hotel in the meat packing district. There was a rooftop party. It was cold—February—but the area was heated and the view of the city was immaculate.

As we were walking we came across a seemingly homeless man that was tucked in a corner sleeping on cardboard and using an oversized sneaker as a pillow. For some reason, he struck me. It was one of those surreal moments that you can't walk by another human when you're bundled up with designer scarfs and gloves knowing that despite whatever that person has been through, no one deserves to live in such conditions.

I startled him as I approached; he flinched. "Here you go good brother." I gave him $20.

"Thank you! God bless you!"

"You too good sir."

At the party, we mentioned Kazi's name and skipped the line. Everyone seemed friendly, so I just said hello to every person I passed. At the bar, I asked for a cranberry and orange juice.

Adonis looks. "What do you put in your juice? Ciroc? Vodka?"

"No. just cranberry and orange juice."

"You see all these ladies looking at you."

"Well, I said hi, and people generally look at you when you say 'Hi.'"

Adonis takes a step back. "Bro'. Who the hell are you?

"What? I just said hello to people and asked for cranberry and orange juice."

"So now, you're coming from church, you don't drink, I saw what you did for the homeless guy, your swag is on 10,000, you don't take any random beautiful girl's info, you love the kids, and you know everybody!

That was the presidential walk and a mountain of self-control," chimed Adonis.

"I'm just chillin bro'. Just being the best I can."

A lady came over to us and introduced herself. I introduced Adonis, and we made small talk. Then I saw Kazi.

"Kazi, what's up bro'! In my best Kevin Hart comedic impression, I said, "Um…is the Reporter here?" By now, it's the running inside joke.

We all toasted to cranberry and orange juice.

Later, when I was in law school, Ian calls me. "Bro', I got a surprise for you."

It turns out that he had written a book…about me. Ian has been taking notes.

As we left the bar, Adonis asked me to hang out next weekend. I let him know that my mother was coming in, and invited him to come with us to dinner with a number of my close NYC friends. I was flying her in.

Adonis looks incredulous. "You're flying your mom in." Then sarcastically, "Yeah I want to meet your mom." Then seriously: "She must be pretty amazing."

"Well, let's just say that we've traveled the country together on interesting terms and she is an amazing entrepreneur. She pretty much handed me my love for fashion. She's the perfect mother for me good brother. She gave me a passion for life, and helped drive my life's mission."

# CHAPTER 18

## Ten Years Later

I picked up my mom from the airport. Seeing her put me in remembrance of our car accident when I was 15 years old. We were in Mom's brand new '97 Lincoln Town Car on Inkster Road making a left on Carlyle Street, heading to Aunt Corky's. My mom's boyfriend, Pops, was driving. We turned left and the front of a motorcycle helmet landed on the pavement from rough riding on the motorcycle's rear wheel. Instantly he smashed into the passenger side of our car, leaving a man-sized dent. It happened so fast I couldn't utter a word. He died instantly and broke every bone in his body. The bike was in pieces all over the street, his neck bone protruded from his lifeless body. His foot was still inside of his Jordan, but it was detached from his leg. He was twisted like a pretzel and his hands felt like jelly because every bone was broken. The Lincoln was totaled and my mother was sitting in the front passenger seat that received the most impact. I sat behind her and bruised my forehead from hurling my head into the window, but I was fine. The nerves on the right side of her body have been ruptured ever sense.

I greeted her at the gate she walked through the tunnel from the plane with a cane. I had a wheel chair waiting for her because she was going to need lots of rest for our planned excursions. Don't get it twisted: she was still hustling, even into her 50's.

We hop in the cab.

"Hey baby, look at you in New York City!" she says.

We drop her bags and headed to Time Square. She wants to sightsee and I take her shopping starting at Sephora. The irony: this was the first time I walked into a store with my mother to actually buy *her* something, instead of scheming with her to boost merchandise. *You better not take anything*, crossed my mind.

271

I bought her Dolce & Gabbana, Light Blue. I kept my eyes on her at all times. When she drifted off, I was two steps behind her. She was moving swiftly with that little cane.

"Hey! Don't take anything."

"I'm just sniffing," she replied. "But...if nobody's looking..." I smiled, then became deathly serious. "I'm not playing Ma."

We went to the movies, out to a dozen eclectic and cultured restaurants... She had an amazing time without a care in the world.

And to church. Over the years I'd made lots of friends in NYC, so when I announced that I had my mom with me, a line of people were waiting to meet her after service.

"You did such an amazing job with Shawn," they all kept saying over and over. "You are such a blessing to bless us with him, he's such a servant."

"Thank you," she says, nodding her head. "I bought his first computer."

Now this is where it becomes difficult. I think it was hard for both of us. More for me than for her, I think. I got a little perturbed with her taking credit for whatever I am today. And I'm still waiting on whatever computer she talked about. But I bit my pride and kept my mouth shut. Actually, I wanted her to have this moment and embrace it. I love her enough, now, to let her have that. After all, she, like me, didn't have a healthy universe full of mentors handed to her either. She was broken, as was I. At this point it was up to me to help her become better.

We didn't talk about that moment in church where she took credit for what God did for me. But, she gave me life, and that is enough for her to be honored. I think she enjoyed it.

I have made my peace with her. It happened in undergrad, when I began my serious quest to walk with God in a real relationship. Not a perfect walk; know that I have my own set of issues that I'm always attempting to wrinkle out. Starting that quest was a revelatory moment for me. Life is short. We must love what we have. How could I hold on to anger or bitterness from disappointment, when God loved me regardless of my shortcomings? I've been healed. I've been able to heal others.

It was time that I stopped tolerating my mother and started loving and healing her the best I could.

---

Bryan was starting to get letters—acceptances and award letters from the schools to which he applied. We opened the letter to Michigan.

*"CONGRATULATIONS Bryan—You're IN!*

*You've been admitted to the University of Michigan College of Literature, Science, and Arts for Fall 2011!*

*As a valued member of our freshman class we are confident that you'll continue to shape the tradition of excellence that keeps U-M a step ahead of the rest.*

*So how does it feel to be a Wolverine?*

*We are proud to present you with a full tuition scholarship including room and board! We know you're excited..."*

Bryan and I yelled at each other and ran around the living room in a circle arms flailing! We hugged, then read the other letters. Fordham was offering money, as well as other schools, but he couldn't care less about them.

Until we went on the Morehouse visit. Bryan was already admitted, we simply wanted to check out the acclaimed school where the likes of Martin Luther King Jr., Spike Lee, and even Fonzworth Bentley attended. While on our visit the administration liked Bryan so much that they offered him a full tuition and room and board scholarship! He was torn between Michigan and Morehouse.

273

Michigan: *Full ride.*

Morehouse: *Full ride.*

Decision time.

Bryan sat on his decision. We sat in a daze in the living room… "Bruh," I said, "This is a complete 180! You do realize your grandparents simply wanted you to graduate high school, Mr. President?"

At the same time, in a daze I mulled over being accepted to Wayne State Law School in Detroit. I was looking to make my way back home to Detroit to fulfill my mission of being an agent of change via politics, and a business owner in my native city. At this point I made my final decision to attend WSU Law after an encouraging phone call from Judge Edward Ewelle. During our call he expressed that he went to the University of Michigan for undergrad and Wayne State Law School as well. With this kind of alumni network and support I was convinced that this was certainly the law school for me. "This is a great stepping stone for politics and business," he said.

"Hey B! You realize that we have both set our eyes on a prize and now it's here? Hard work and dedication pays off. And you must admit… We had a great time in the process!"

"I'm proud of you too big bro'! I'm just trying to get on your level."

At school, it was no secret what was accomplished between Bryan and me. Our community was so much like family that everyone was supportive of the success of others. We also weren't the only people in the school with something to celebrate pertaining to college!

"My Brotha' from anotha' motha', I have something good for ya! ABC News wants to cover your story with Bryan." Ryan Glass contacted the news and sold them on covering our story: *Men of Majesty*!

"Do you realize…that Bryan has a full ride to Michigan?" I asked Ryan.

"Holy s—t!" replied Ryan. "That's amazing!"

274

*Bryan Dameron is a leader at Rucker High School.*

*"If anybody wants to be 'cool' the best way to do it is just to hit those books and stay in school," Dameron said.*

*Bryan Dameron is a senior, one of Rucker High School's best students, and was admitted on a four-year scholarship to Morehouse University.*

*To reach high school, and to find himself at the doorstep of a college career with a full scholarship, Bryan traveled from a very different path, one that could have led to very negative results.*

*"I was smoking weed. I was selling it, you know, just a lot of things that weren't me," said Dameron.*

*As a younger teen in Michigan, Bryan was mentored by Shawn Blanchard, who was then a university student. Shawn graduated and became a teacher at Rucker. When he left Michigan, Bryan's life went downhill.*

---

When the ABC reporter and television crew arrived, we regaled them with a mock *Men of Majesty* meeting. They shot footage of Bryan and me walking through the hallway. And of course they spoke to Mr. Rucker. Every student in HLR was given the hope of endless possibilities, we told ABC.

It was an exciting time. So exciting that when the story ran, NY1 News circled around and covered an additional story. They wanted a more in-depth perspective and decided to come to my apartment. "You started from where? How many brothers do you have? Wow…You really started from the bottom!"

Word got around at church as well and we followed through with a video testimonial.

Bryan said in the video, "Shawn displayed the unconditional agape love of God and enabled me to understand who I truly am outside of simply fitting in with others. I finally realized that being smart is cool!"

The *New York Daily News* piggy-backed and ran a story titled:

## "Two Lives Saved From the Streets"

Bryan and I laughed at that one. They didn't even interview us. They simply picked up the story from elsewhere and said we were both from the streets of Detroit! Honestly, you can live anywhere and have a street mentality, you don't have to be from the murder capital. Bryan knew many people from Ann Arbor that fit the description.

A good friend of mine, Jina, nominated me for *GQ*'s *Better Man, Better World* search. Thousands of people shared the story. I didn't win, but the exposure opened several doors.

It was Friday, a long week. Students shared different news stories from various papers, a few different news stations continued to run the story, and I interviewed with *People* magazine during lunch. At the end of the day, I was sitting in my classroom when the phone rang.

"This is Shawn Blanchard," I answered.

"Yes Mr. Blanchard," the lady on the other line answers. "I'm Marcia from Thomas Dunne Books. We're an imprint of St. Martin's Press, and we'd like to talk with you regarding your heroic encounters with Bryan Dameron and associated youth at your school. We saw you on ABC, NY1, and read several articles this week! We love what you've done with Bryan and in the lives of countless other youth. This is absolutely amazing!"

"Thank you. I appreciate that. It's an honor and privilege to serve people."

"Let me ask you. Have you ever thought about writing a book?"

"Well," I replied, I am a mathematician. I never thought about writing more than I absolutely have to. I'm going to law school next year, and..."

"Oh my God, you're going to law school too?"

276

"Well, yes."

"That is amazing. We want you to put a proposal together and write a book. I'll send you a mock example. Initially we wanted you to write about your adventures with Bryan, but the more interviews that I have read, we believe you should write a full autobiography! It would be absolutely epic and inspiring to all!"

I was stunned. After all, I didn't ask for this. I didn't promote myself, or talk myself up to anyone. But the opportunities kept falling in my lap. I don't believe in coincidence. God is funny.

*For promotion comes neither from the east, nor from the west, nor from the south. But God is the judge: he puts down one, and sets up another.*

~Psalm 75: 6-7

"OK. Let's meet." As in all things I will need to ask God for wisdom and I know He will put the proper vessels in my path to take advantage of this opportunity that is clearly ordained.

The following Wednesday was my final *Men of Majesty* meeting. All of our seniors—we had about 12—were graduating and going to a post-secondary institution:

Kariem

Yogi

Roland

Bryan

Thadeus

Brian H.

Arjenis

Derick

277

Jermaine

Ty

Julio

Jordy

"All of you gentlemen have been striving," I told them. "Now look where you are. I am so proud of you."

"Hold on now," says Ryan. "Let's take a look at what's going on with you, Head Master Blanchard. The book, the news, the magazines, headed to law school, you're leaving a legacy with HLR and on the hearts of the members and co-founders of Men of Majesty... You are about to return to Detroit and reign as a supreme servant! This is monumental!"

The air became thick, my nose twinkled, and my eyes watered. My grandfather always pressed that a man wasn't supposed to shed tears. That was something I lived by ever since my grandmother died. I'm sure I could have counted on two fingers the amount of times tears have fallen from my eyes since that conversation with M.C. Higgins when I was 12 years old. This was my last collective meeting with these beloved young gentlemen as their M.O.M. leader. I was heading back home—where I know I need to be—but leaving this place on the East Coast that has been so good to me, allowing me to make a real impact on young men's lives. It was a surreal moment.

"You're right," I replied hoarsely, trying to keep it together. "Listen, I only wanted to be a good teacher/mentor/brother/father figure for all of you guys. Now all these people and the universe believe in my mission, and want me to be an author and expand my platform."

I continue. "But I want you to understand my origins. You already know this: I started with drugs in my system. With parents who were not the best role models. No real role models like you guys have now. I had a host of "really good bad examples" or people that I simply paid

278

no mind. You have so much more. So if I can sit here…and all these good things are taking place, that means that every last one of you better be doing something amazing.

"Or I'm taking back all these purple ties!"

Laughter all around. Mostly everyone was wiping their eyes.

I looked around the table and saw:

100% graduation.

75% college-bound.

Class president.

Top three ranked males academically.

Captain of the basketball team.

Prom King.

Prom Prince.

"You guys have to dream bigger," I urged them. "All some of you wanted to do was graduate from high school, and look where you are now. You can do so much more if you live life purposefully! Place the image of excellence in any given moment in your mind… Trust me, you all know I'm speaking from experience, fellas. This is what I dreamed, and look!

Graduation is upon us. "I love you all," I told the guys, choking up a little more than I expected. This was my fifth and last year too. I'm not coming back next year to bring another group of guys through the process. The majority of our members are seniors and were about to disperse throughout the country. Some of them will go on to become successful. Some will bump their heads. Others are not quite there yet. But they are all on the road to something greater than what we started upon their entry of our mentorship program.

Bryan had his whole crew out: his mom, dad, uncles, cousins from New York, and the grandparents who helped raise him for so many years. It was a "full circle" for me: a couple of years ago, my brother Doug was graduating from Robichuad High School right outside Detroit and I was about to go to New York; now Bryan was graduating from a New York High School and I am about to go back to Detroit. Once again, It feels…surreal.

And now I get to meet Bryan's father. Interesting.

I actually did not meet his father until graduation day. I had spoken with him by phone. I had my own thoughts about who he might be. Was he like my dad? Cool? Maybe not. Did he care about Bryan? I knew that Bryan liked him a lot. Is this warranted? Is it only because he is Bryan's dad?

Bryan's dad, Lee, was 5'9", brown-skinned, medium build, with a bald head and a deep voice. Surprisingly, he was charismatic. Smooth. Similar to Bryan. I had always thought he picked up those traits from his mother.

"Hey, man…this is an amazing moment. Thank you." Lee stated. "Can I talk to you for a second?"

"Sure," I replied.

"Thank you, man." His eyes were intense and searching. "I watched him walk across the stage, and I see how excited he was, and how excited you are."

He looks down.

"I just feel like I wasn't there to do what you did for my boy. I couldn't be what you are to him. I humbly thank you for fathering my son."

I was speechless. I never knew what this moment would be like. I found myself respecting him.

"I'm your number one fan, man," he continued. "We are family bro'. If there's anything I can do for you..." his eyes began to water..."We family."

We bro-hugged. This was a moment. Big for him and big for me.

Bryan talked to his dad at least once every couple weeks during his New York stay. I never could gauge the depth of their relationship. I was always focused on the present moment. Bryan's father was actually more of a father to Bryan than my own was to me. He was, after all, the one who told Bryan, "You are going to New York." He knew a good opportunity when he saw one. Even though he was not in the home, he still cared about...loved...his son. His main goal: for Bryan to change the trajectory of the Dameron name. He believed that Bryan had the potential to alter the family legacy. He wanted to know more about me as well.

"Where you from, bro', you from Southfield? You went to one of the private schools? U of D Jesuit? Cranbrook? Country Day?

"Nah." I told them the details of my background. Bryan's dad and uncle, who was also present, were shocked.

"Man! You know how to do this! You know what?" they continued. "We got a nephew and some other dudes you could work with...we'll just slide 'em over to you and you can do your thing," they declared. Come on back to the 'D' and let's get this pipeline going. Hahaha!" They laughed, but they were totally serious.

"If I could give you a dollar amount for what you did for my son," the dad continued..."man, there's no measure."

He was starkly different than my perception of him.

We hung out that night. I wondered: "Why didn't you do this?" I found out he had gone to community college on a basketball scholarship but didn't make it academically. He was a ladies' man, with a few children. He came back and tried to make enough money to support them.

We stayed up talking until about 4 a.m. We talked about Bryan, his life, my life. It was a great conversation.

The *Men of Majesty* members helped me pack up my belongings in my apartment. We reminisced about the speed dating event, the singer/celebrities who presented their craft, the plays, and the restaurants.

"I got something," said Roland. "The bathrooms."

The bathrooms?

"Remember all the places we went: Landmark, Bar 89, The Hudson? In every one, the bathrooms were immaculate! You can always tell a well-run establishment by the bathrooms!"

The bathrooms?

I let them take some of my smaller things: the Foreman Grill, pots and pans, blenders, and even my bedroom set. I gave the two who stayed behind—Roland and Thadeus—$200 a piece just because. I felt like I owed them more along their individual journeys.

"You really 'bout to leave," they said.

Roland said, "What am I going to do tomorrow?"

"Remember when you took the ACT exam in October?" I reminded them. "I told you guys: This same time next year, you'll be in a completely different place. But we'll stay connected. Those words are true. You guys are going to be just fine. I guarantee that. I'm a text and phone call away."

Both Thadeus and Roland were going to Johnson and Wells in Rhode Island in the fall as roommates.

Bryan was excited about his Michigan letter, but ultimately decided on Morehouse. It was a difficult decision for him. Everyone he saw graduate from the University of Michigan was "doing it big." But his grandmother felt he needed more structure. More role models that look like him. Although she taught at Michigan, and was excited at his admission, I think she helped sway his opinion.

There was another factor. Honestly, this was the most important factor at the time. Bryan stated, "I want to chart my own course," he said. "I don't want to be in anyone's shadow."

---

Morehouse-bound.

Bryan showed up on campus with a khaki-colored suit jacket with custom gold buttons, green tattered army fatigue shorts, and a button-down shirt, the neck button open with a dangling skinny tie, a fitted hat, and New Balance sneakers. Definitely making his own style. He was living in Graves Hall.

"Martin Luther King stayed in this hall," I told him. As we continued walking, we noticed a sign.

"No purses, high-heels. No skirts in this facility."

"What? I asked. No girls allowed in the school building? I can understand the dorm, but wow! That's messed up."

Bryan already knew the drill. "No bro'," he explained. "That's telling the dudes they can't wear that stuff. That's for the cross dressing guys..."

I looked at him quizzically. "You know, you can always go to Michigan."

"It's OK," he replied. "I'm straight. I love all people. It's all good."

I was proud of him.

"Listen bro'," I said. "Try and keep your room clean, 'cause your roommate is going to be pissed." I continued. "If I can leave you with anything it is this: whatever you do, be your own man. Stick to your own path. You've done a great job so far. You've done tons of community service. You're a great leader. You're smart. Leverage who YOU are."

"I got you, bro'," said Bryan.

"Man," he continued, "thank you so much." He teared up. "We been together for a long time. Tomorrow, we're going to be in different states; it's going to be like this for a while." He shook his head. "I couldn't have done this without you, bro'."

"What I did for you," I reflected to Bryan, "I needed that myself as a teenager, but God always has a plan. Somehow I didn't get what I thought I needed and that same "void" made me who I am. There is no such thing as a coincidence; we met so I could pour into you from my former lack. You feel me?"

I felt like I was dropping off my own son.

As I boarded the plane flying back to Michigan from Atlanta there was a nostalgic feeling. I was turning a page, closing one chapter of my life and opening another. The thought of leaving my mentee after he graduated from high school was unnerving due to my last encounter with my brother, Doug. I knew that Bryan's future will be determined by how he leverages what he has been taught and internalized.

Staring out of the airplane window I smiled as I thought about what ten years can do. Ten years before, I was on the news for the first time with a one piece orange jumpsuit, no smile, mugshot, and termed, "A Thug." Ten years later I was on the news several times and termed a savior, blessing, and mentor. Ten years ago I was in trouble with the law and now I have a Bachelor's Degree in Economical Mathematics, a Master's in Secondary Math Education, and I was on my way to law school.

# CHAPTER 19

## Homecoming

*Follow your curiosity and you will arrive at the doorstep of your passion.*

"New York City Educator Comes Back to Detroit to Attend Law School at Wayne State University"

-Detroit Legal News

I studied Criminal Law during my first semester of law school. It was my favorite class. I was in Section 1 along with one hundred of my peers: two African American men, two African American women, and one Nigerian. Everyone else was white.

The criminal law professor, Professor Henning, entered the class stating, "Today's topic pertains to case law dealing with police raids. In a raid, what happens is: the police come to the door and begin to knock. If you don't answer the door, they will enter given they have a warrant to enter the premises. They won't tear up your place, and if they do, they put everything back accordingly. They are mainly concerned with whatever evidence or persons they are searching for."

*What?* Clearly this man has never been in a police raid around my way. I have been privy to a half dozen raids, and at every encounter, the police have torn up furniture, tipped over televisions, disrespected innocent citizens, used unnecessary violent force and every time I've been present they never found whatever they were searching for. Then they leave and go home. These police are not angels. That was the biggest hunk of crap I had ever heard!

But I decided not to say anything. I didn't want to be perceived as the stereotypical black guy in class. I have brothers in prison and brothers who are dead. Thus, criminal law is very intriguing. This professor was usually sharp, but today the professor was describing something that was assuredly not my experience.

One day professor Henning caught Robert, the other African American student, and me, and whispered:

"When I ask you two to come down, just make your way to the front of the class and flank my sides."

We had no idea what he was planning.

"Ladies and gentlemen," Professor Henning began, "Let's consider 'what's a crime.' When does something become an offense?

He walked up to one of the female students in the front row of the stadium-style lecture hall.

"Hey. You got five dollars?"

He came within a foot of her as he said it.

"Was that an offense?" he asked. Everyone in the class agreed that this scenario was not an offense. After all, he just asked a question.

Then he came closer, and asks the question again. Again, the class agreed that there was no offense.

Then he snaps his finger for Robert and me to flank his sides as he asked his question. We all lean in to the young female (white) student. Then he asked the question again.

"Hey. You got five dollars?"

"Now. Is that a crime?" the professor asks.

The room was silent. It's clear that our classmates didn't want to offend us. After all, we were the only African American males in that section.

"OK," the professor continues. He then pulls up his shirt slightly to reveal a plastic pistol. He once again asks the young lady if she has five dollars.

"That's an offense!" interjects one of the students as he raised his hand.

The professor looked around. "Why did you guys get so silent when the two black guys stood next to me? Did you not want to be offensive to them? What if they were white guys? Would it be an offense then? In fact: how many people thought it was an offense when these young men stood next to me and I asked for five dollars?"

A few people were honest and slowly raised their hands.

"Exactly!" the professor responded. "There is an array of subjectivity that plays a role on our decision-making process when it comes to criminology," he explained. He unveiled the essence of subjectivity in criminal law, explaining that some crimes were measured weighing heavily on human perspective.

Interestingly enough, Trayvon Martin was killed a few months later. Once again the subjectivity of the law was apparent and Professor Henning's perspective was proven.

No matter what topic was covered, I had a first-hand connection—a connection that no one else in section one experienced. I had been in jail. I had visited family members locked up in the county, state prison, and federal prison.

You would think that I had a burning desire to practice law. I was much more focused on the doors that law school could open. Still fascinated by my example-mentor Kwame Kilpatrick, I wanted nothing more than to work in city government. Outside of that my constant desire to build wealth shaped my mind toward entrepreneurship. Reading cases and being in an out of court was not my forté. Nevertheless, the education was a great journey that would eventually open many doors.

Robert was studying to be an entertainment lawyer. He asked me one day:

"You ever think about modeling or acting? I could hook you up. I know people. Really, I know people who know people."

Ironically, the same day, I talked to Demetria Lucas from *Essence* magazine. We caught up on how life was progressing since the "*Straight Talk No Chaser*" panel. Excited about the developments taking place between law school and all other highlights that have transpired since our last encounter, she offered me a feature as the *Essence Magazine* "*Single Man of the Month.*"

I was also in conversation with Shaun Derik, a producer who was a good friend of Kazi's, about filming an episode for a web series titled "Journey Me." He strategically correlated the release of my episode, titled "*Run This Town*", with the feature in *Essence*.

"Journey Me" captures dreamers who are in the process of making their dreams come true. The title *Run This Town* came to life from Shaun's understanding my reason for coming back to Detroit to assist my native community and family.

While filming I visited the house where I grew up on the west side of Detroit, 9960 Ohio Street. Pulling up I drove past houses that were once full of life, but were now many of them burned down, leaving in their wake vacant lots, boarded windows, and teddy bears tied to street lights, indicating where a child was murdered. It wasn't the best place in the world when I left in year 2000, but this 2011 version wasn't even the reality I once had.

I walked up the driveway into the backyard of my old house. The backyard was sort of run down, evidence of Grandad's lax upkeep after he became ill. There was a man near the garage next to a rusted conversion van staring intently at me while I stared the house up and down and walked up the driveway. He didn't understand my sense of entitlement.

"Hello sir," I said. "You mind if I walk in? I used to live here. Actually, I grew up here until I was 18."

"No," he said. "The house isn't together, it's not really clean."

That was an understatement...

I persisted. "What if I just take a look at the basement? That's where my bedroom was."

"Ummm… Alright, Alright. But it ain't clean down there either." he said reluctantly.

He let me in through the side door and I walked directly into the basement. He never did notice the HD camera that the videographer was carrying the entire time. The doorway leading into the basement seemed smaller. The ceiling appeared lower. And it smelled like cats and sewage. They knocked the diving wall down that separated my room from the utility room. It was one big space. In the far right corner I saw my closet cabinet; apparently they kept it. Wow… The door to the closet hung from the hinges.

I had spent 18 years in this house and 10 years away. It was eerily strange going back into that basement. I felt completely disconnected from what it once represented. I remembered cursing my Mom out when I was taking up for my younger brother when I was 15, taking Doug in and setting up his bed near the basement entrance. Even the floor, though peeling and reeking of mildew and fungus, was the same black paint that I painted years ago.

We traveled to my high school, Mackenzie. There, I jumped into the broken window that led to my high school's security office. Parts of the ceiling were caved in and lights hung from the intact parts. Tile on the floor was jagged, and the furniture that was left in the building was warped and tipped over. It looked like World War II took place directly inside Mackenzie High School. We walked through the rubble to the classroom where my first high school math class met. I thought about my good friend Taheed, who had been recently released after 12 years

289

in prison. I thought about Mrs. Carpenter, who made me fall in love with Mathematics. In all that rubbish, I found a piece of chalk. And the chalkboard was oddly in flawless condition as if someone just cleaned it after a long day of learning. It was the only item in the classroom that managed to remain untattered.

And so I wrote my name: M-R-. B-L-A-N-C-H-A-R-D.

I suddenly had a feeling of deja vu come over me. Memories began to flood my mind: walking through the classroom door first period… finding out my brother, Mike, was shot and killed, and weeks later, when I walked through the same doors first period and I learned my father had died. I sat in the front of the class and Mrs. Carpenter didn't know what was going on in my life, but she was a mother figure that believed in me and often called on me to present before the class.

Staring at my name on the chalkboard I had an epiphany: "I have officially made it to the other side of the desk." I was no longer bound by ignorance and a lack of exposure. Memories came in like a flood, but I was no longer in a hopeless state of mind. I could now aid others in being strong with my wisdom that I've accumulated and desire to gain more.

I smiled.

And drifted somewhere else in my mind. Somewhere peaceful.

But like the chalkboard, I was ready to be used with a clean slate in the midst of chaos. Ready. Like the chalkboard, I would have to find a way to make myself useful in this place, this place where I grew up, lost a lot, and gained a sense of self in the process.

A physical place can hold so much, and I felt all of it in this ragged and abandoned classroom that I had come to love when it was vibrant and full of learning. Pain intermingled with growth so intimately that you can't tell the pain from the growth. Now, the physical place was about to be bulldozed. But the memories can never be taken away. The spirit is strong in this place.

My passion to serve was all the more intense when I came back to Detroit. Every chance that I could step away from my books I would go to a school and speak to young people in the city and surrounding suburbs. Due to the local and national publicity I received, I began getting tons of speaking requests for career days and other high school and college events. More and more articles were written for simply doing what I was going to do anyway…

I recall going to Romulus High School to interview with a host of students for their school newspaper. For the first time I saw a young person cry because they were going through a similar struggle that I once endured throughout high school. Death, drugs, and a lack of guidance plagued the lives of a few students who listened to the interview. A young lady broke down into tears of pain due to her circumstance, yet hope because she met a tangible example of what her life could be. Through her blood shot red eyes and tears she said, "I know I can do great things because you exist." Some of her friends cried as well. They told me their dreams which were limited due to their lack of exposure, but surely relevant. "I want to be a lawyer." "A doctor," said another. "A music producer," said another. "A pro basketball player," said another. They knew they could do anything despite their current position in life. "I'll still probably do the rapper thing," a young brother said, "but now I think I'll go after the astronaut idea that I threw away. Don't get me wrong… I'll still rap. I'm going to be the first rapping astronaut. I might spit some bars on Mars!" We laughed, but there was no pun intended with the truth of knowing that anything is possible with your skill set.

I was still on an emotional high from actually having the opportunity to attend such a great law school, but I couldn't deny my true passion of serving young people.

It was finals time. Anyone that knows anything about law school knows that you study the entire semester and get graded based upon your performance on one final exam at the end of the semester. In most first year courses, finals determine 100% of the final grade.

I was in the basement with my books spread across my L-shaped glass desk, studying my life away. In the middle of doing practice exams I received a call from an unknown 917 number: New York.

It was Adonis, "Yo! Just checking in on you fam, seeing how things are going."

"Great to hear from you, bro'! I'm smooth, just getting down on the books for finals. I need a quick break anyway. What's going on?"

"I just wanted to tell you," Adonis said, "thank you. I got something for you. Since you left, I reflected on the times that we hung out and the influence you had on my life. I wrote a book about our adventures bro'. Straight up!"

He continued, "I have never seen a dude maneuver the way you do with a balance of integrity and cool. I know how a lot of celebrities move and even rich people without the fame, still I've never witnessed anything quite like you. What you're about is what you're about. You don't waver. So I wrote about my experiences with you."

"Bro', I didn't do anything special."

"That's exactly what I mean bro'! You're simply authentic."

I guess he was paying attention, I just never attempted to impress; I was simply being what I once only desired to be. Adonis always made comments about my clothes and how I interacted with people. He observed me giving…to Bryan, to my mentees, to the homeless. I was always fixated on bettering myself such that I forgot that people see me in the same manner that I saw Keith Campbell.

"You really have an effect on people. You have had an effect on me."

He emailed me the book.

I took a break from studying, and read the book from cover to cover. It took approximately two hours. Adonis's word power surged an energy through me that propelled me to keep studying. If I could have this kind of impact on grown men and people in general at this young age, 28... Where could I go from here? My conscious mind was racing. It's apparent that God has big plans.

It hit me like a ton of bricks.

I finished the last final. In law school, you just write until you can't write any more. Everything you remember finds its way to the infamous electronic blue book

Trying to get some air, I walked two miles down Anthony Wayne Drive to the New Center One building and walked inside. I was mentally exhausted, and absent-mindedly went up the escalator without a destination. I saw a man coming out of one of the doors at the top of the escalator. .

"Shawn Blanchard?" He recognized me. "Sebastian Jackson."

Sebastian emailed me a couple weeks ago. He was in the process of opening a grooming shop on Wayne State's campus. He called it "The Social Club Grooming Company". He was a young entrepreneur on the rise seeking to build an eclectic community beyond the typical barbershop. He esteemed me in the same regard after seeing my *Journey Me* episode, *Run This Town*.

"I work at Kaplan," he explained. "Frankly, I can't stand it and today's my last day. What about you? I see you're doing the law school thing, you want to be a lawyer?"

"Actually, I don't. Although I just finished my first semester of law school, my goal is to be a politician, maybe even the mayor and absolutely a business owner." I said. "Law school is my vehicle that will make that happen."

"The 'vehicle', I can respect that..."

We became good friends quickly. I needed some positive energy outside of the law school bubble. I left Detroit as a 17-year-old hustler and returned as a refined professional with hustle. Sebastian was my first friend outside of law school. I could sense that his refined hustle was strong.

I switched barbers to Sebastian. I believed in his vision sort of in the same manner as Mr. Rucker. Both visions were in process upon meeting both of them, but you can be certain to bet on the jockey (the person successfully living their dream with integrity) and not the horse (the dream itself). I left a well-polished barbershop and started getting my hair cut in a small dusty and windowless room sitting on a crate in the back of a shop-in-progress. It wasn't ready for mass patrons, but a few of his good friends came by to get things rolling in the interim.

"I need to meet more people bro'," he said. "My network is not where I want it to be here."

"Hmmm… In New York, I was invited to something called a 'Power Brunch,'" I explained. "My 'friendtor', Keith Campbell, invited me and introduced me to an A&R at Sony, a VP from Marc Jacobs, and another entrepreneur who hosts celebrity events. Great connections were made. I'm not sure how they selected their guests, but we should innovate that concept here," I continued. "Hey—I'll invite six, you invite six. Keeping it spiritual with that magic number—12—that started *Men of Majesty*."

Sebastian added, "I like that concept. The individuals that are invited are not allowed to invite others. This will be willful and deliberate. Only strategic partnerships will be allowed that can ultimately benefit everyone that attends the event."

It was settled, we decided to host intimate "Power Brunches" to purposefully expand our network. We discussed ideas and visions with our mastermind group. We invited a Michigan alum, Greg White, who was working on his PhD in Education. A fellow three-year law student, Josh Kush, who owned his own insurance company. Brian Kelly, a photographer who freelances for *Time* magazine. Jerami Roy, a high fashion clothing store owner. Shel, who wanted to create tin container buildings made of recyclable materials. Armond Harris, a WSU football

294

player who developed a scholarship program for his high school. He was in a program called Bizdom, created by Dan Gilbert of Quicken Loans.

I stayed in touch with everyone and especially built a rapport with Armond. He seemed to be a powerful young brother who needed to channel his energy. In doing so I figured he would surely become an influential brother. Through mutual friends I was placed in contact with a lawyer named Terrance Reeves who also has an intriguing story. This brother went from a high school drop out to passing the law school exit exam, the bar, in the top 1% in the nation. He's sharp to say the least. He also graduated from WSU law school.

Terrance and I were both runner enthusiasts and decided to go for a run in downtown Detroit. There was a stark contrast between running the streets of New York and running in downtown Detroit. There was no one else around with running shoes. We pretty much had the entire Detroit Riverwalk to ourselves. It was clean, but absent human life, it was an untapped treasure.

"Dude, there's nobody here. Dismal."

We talked about it with some friends over brunch the following weekend and commiserated about the dearth of people downtown. It was a ghost town. Additionally, at the time Detroit was considered the 5th most obese city in the United States!

"Why don't we start a group?" urged Terrence. Everyone else agreed.

"Shawn, if you create it, we'll join in," said Terrence and all parties included.

Done. I'm always down to create intentional events that are beneficial to others. I decided to name it "Run This Town." The name had a dual-meaning: I had gained a substantial amount of weight in law school, 15 pounds to be exact, and wanted to run it off. And, frankly, "Run This Town" aptly described my aspirations as a change agent.

I crafted the language and overall execution strategy as a lesson plan. Similar to mathematics there is a need for differentiated instruction. If we intended to invite a host of professionals to network and work out we should make the environment inviting for all fitness levels: power walkers, joggers, and runners. The overarching theme will be the concept of "personal best"—Collaboration over competition. And we'd make it every Tuesday throughout the summer.

May 8, 2012 was our start date. I posted an event on Facebook. I invited Armond and a few other gentlemen to assist Terrence and me as we carved out the trail, but only Armond and Terrence actually came to set the trail. With that said, our collaborative partnership was formed.

Thirty-five people came the first day. The next week, 50 people came. Then 75. Then 100. Then 200. Then 300. Before we knew it we attracted the attention of reality shows and local news who came to film us. We added circuit training—outside, then indoors when inclement weather started. The bonus: I lost the weight I had gained in law school. Hence, the event turned into a movement that benefited thousands of people in metro Detroit.

Eventually, we expanded to other cities such as Chicago and Kalamazoo. In Detroit alone after our first year there were over 20 people who lost over 50lbs and hundreds of people dropped at least 15lbs.

The very next day after *Run This Town* began, I received an email from ABC's *The Bachelor*:

*Hi Shawn,*

*My name is ------, and I'm a TV producer working on casting the upcoming season of ABC's* The Bachelor. *We're looking for an outstanding eligible man to be* The Bachelor *on our new season, and ------- at* Essence *magazine gave me your name.*

*You seem like you could be an awesome fit for the show, so please email back or give me a call at the number below if you're interested in talking about this! Info attached.*

*Thanks!! Hope to hear from you soon.*

Wow! Craziness. Was this one of those scam emails?

It really was authentic. I received a call after I responded to the email.

"How did you find out about me?"

"Oh, it wasn't random at all," they explained. "You were *Essence* Man of the Month, and we asked them to recommend some good guys for the show. Yours was one of the first names they mentioned.

This would be a first! There has never been an African American "Bachelor."

"What do you think?" she asked.

"I'll need a little time to digest the offer."

I was determined not to be a cartoon or caricature of what people think black men are. Plus, I've never watched the show. I didn't want the show to turn into "For the Love of Shawn B"!

"Let me watch the show first to make sure the direction lines up with who I am."

A few days later, they called back. I had looked on YouTube and had pretty much decided. It was ridiculously tempting, but this was not the show for me. It actually had a great deal of class to it. However, I'm not trying to group tongue kiss a bunch of women, or have a group of them in a hot tub with me. That's much too much like the life I've been running from for years. Now if I was asked 10 years ago when I was 18, my bags would have been packed, quick! Then again, they wouldn't have looked my way 10 years ago for multiple reasons. I didn't want my life to be edited for me.

I explained all of this to them. They told me I didn't have to have sex, but may have to "kiss a few every now and then." The woman said it jokingly, but I'm sure she was serious!

Just in case I did want to entertain the option I met with them, even did the interview. One question really tempted me:

"What kind of women are you attracted to?"

To a law school student who was tired of reading endless cases and writing about them, that frankly seemed like a wrapped-up Christmas present. What do I want in a woman?! I was basically given a menu for the perfect woman and asked what kind of trimmings I wanted! Whew… The struggle is real!

But then, back to reality. I do not want anyone to edit my life. I will edit it myself, thank you. I told them as much. I just couldn't bring myself to do it.

So much for Christmas.

I began a legal internship at DTE Energy. I preferred to work for a non-profit, but that wasn't available through the summer internship options. Indirectly, it turned out to be a dream job for me—at least I think. I had an office, with a view of the city landscape and the Detroit River in the distance, no less.

I was given a stack of cases to read: mergers, acquisitions, and internal company documents. My duties entailed crafting briefs and memos from a host of cases for a team of supervisors.

There was minimal human interaction. Just me, my computer, an office, and stacks of documents. I couldn't help but stare out of the window and gaze at the birds passing. This was the first time I ever felt like I had a job. Being an educator was so deeply rooted in my life and passion that I never noticed that I was working a 9-5. But this…Oh boy! I shook off the desire to stare at the sky and the birds.

I spent more time thinking about how much I loved running and Run This Town, because we were changing lives.

I managed the workload and built really great relationships with my supervisors. I was introduced to a VP that wanted me to speak to a host of students that were in an undergraduate summer program. I was asked to speak to them about my background and mentorship. That was a pleasure.

The same supervisor noticed my passion and appreciated my career path. She kept me tapped into what I loved to do, impact lives.

"Shawn, I would love for you to present at a Career Day for my sister's school."

I showed up at Eman Hamilton Academy. I delivered a speech to the students, and they were in awe. The students requested that I return and the administration requested that I speak at their promotion ceremony and provided an honorarium. I believe it was $300, for 30 minutes. I accepted the opportunity to impart into the youth with gladness.

I finished my DTE stint and moved to the Federal Courthouse for the second part of my internship. Different kind of office—no windows or view this time.

At the time one of my example-mentors, former Detroit Mayor Kwame Kilpatrick was on trial. Oddly, approximately ten years ago, I was at my brother's trial in this very same courthouse. He was a sponsor-mentor for many years of my life. Now my brother is serving a life sentence in federal prison and Kwame Kilpatrick was up against similar odds.

Did you catch that? At this point: Kilpatrick has been indicted. My brother is in federal prison serving a life sentence. And I am doing an internship under the same roof. It was surreal. I do believe my brother will come home one day, but the thought of his current situation blows my mind.

299

Damn.

A few interns and I walked down the hallway touring the federal court while cases were in session. A prisoner caught my eye as he walked down the hallway. His hands were cuffed and linked to an extended chain that shackled his feet. He wore a one-piece orange jumpsuit. It was reminiscent of a personal encounter I will never forget. He was flanked by two Federal Marshalls. As I moved closer, his eyes were blood shot red, as if he was about to cry, but he managed not to let one tear fall.

I've been there before, I think. My brothers have been here before, too.

For an infinite moment we locked eyes.

"What's up bro'?" I asked.

My fellow interns were talking about golfing after work and laughing about last week's scores. They paid him no attention.

He looked at me as if to say, "Dumb question and you wouldn't understand anyway."

He stared at me with a smirk as if I was attempting to provoke him.

I wish he knew how well I understood the moment. I wish I could've talked to him.

He was strong in the moment, reminiscent of my brother as the judge struck the gavel and took him out of the court room away from Detroit for life.

Later, I was meeting with a few judges for lunch.

"You know, you seem like a smart young man. We were just talking about you. I teach law at Wayne State. I'm Judge Rosen. Check out my class when you get a chance. I teach evidence."

Judge Rosen. At the time, Chief Judge of the 36th District Court.

I went home; something urged me to take a look at my brother's case. The name of the judge?

Judge Gerald Rosen.

Interesting, I knew he looked familiar. I remember him. I sat in court when he said to my brother, "You are one of the most dangerous men I've ever seen in my life," as he hit the gavel. Now, he wants to "do lunch" with me.

Like the prisoner, he didn't know who I was. In either situation it didn't matter.

Connections were everywhere. My mentor at Wayne State Law, his mother was the judge in my brother Doug's trial—the one that sent him to jail for 12-20 years. It wasn't her fault. Right?

I tried to make sense of it all. What was being communicated to me? I don't believe in coincidence.

I sat at home for the evening and received a phone call. My mother had fallen and hit her head on the hood of a car. After the routine check-up they found a cancerous tumor behind her eye. Stage Three.

At this point I didn't care to be in anyone's court. I left my internship, aided my mom, and prayed for my brothers. At this point I have almost 50 nieces and nephews and they all need guidance. I'm just glad I'm in Detroit to be a light for them.

Speaking of guidance, Bryan came home from Morehouse. He didn't do as well as expected, and lost his scholarship. He needed a bit more guidance before he was left to his own devices.

When Bryan was completely free at Morehouse, he had an opportunity to choose his friends. He was the "cool guy," and that attracts certain kind of people. Those people chose Bryan. They were balanced, but Bryan wasn't. When he lived with me in NYC, I chose his friends. I determined his schedule. I regimented him to the hilt. At Morehouse: different story. A story Bryan wasn't ready for.

301

He came home to live with me, in my downtown Detroit brownstone.

We decided to take the community college route. There was a program at Washtenaw community college that can lead to a transfer to the University of Michigan if specific classes are taken accompanied with a stellar GPA.

Roland, on the other hand, did extremely well at Johnson & Wells College. I told him about the summer program that Bryan was in, and Roland decided he wanted to participate too.

Then my niece called. "Hey Uncle Shawn. Can I stay with you this summer? Just until school starts."

One week ago, I lived alone, a happy bachelor in a downtown brownstone. Suddenly, I was a caregiver to my mother and "father" of sorts to two mentees and my niece. Still running *Run This Town*, doing speaking engagements, in the last half of my internship program.

I decided to stop the Federal court internship. It was all too much. It was a great opportunity, but I had a bit too much on my plate. Something had to give.

Returning to law school I was done with the monotonous first year courses. I decided to take Teaching Law in High School and Voting Education Law, all while maintaining my overall focus of business and education law. After the summer I would only take law courses in line with my passion.

I received a call from one of my mentors. "Shawn, we have a teaching position here at Michigan. I would love for you to teach in the mathematics department."

I saw where this was going. My passion was calling me. It was my pleasure and duty to answer the call. I accepted the position.

It was a week later that I decided to put the theory of my voting education law course into action. I volunteered on a political campaign of a gentleman running to be the next mayor of the City of Detroit. I met with a friend of mine for dinner at Andiamo's off the water in downtown Detroit. We sat outside until a gentleman tapped on the window. He was the prospective co-writer that I was considering as a partner to write this book.

He wanted me to come inside the restaurant to meet few thought leaders. He introduced himself as my prospective co-writer.

"Shawn, this is former Michigan Supreme Court Justice Conrad Mallet," he began. "And this is Ken Harris, President of the Michigan Black Chamber of Commerce."

"And this," added Justice Mallett, "is the next mayor of the City of Detroit: Mike Duggan."

Ken Harris kindly jumped into the conversation. "Gentlemen," he interrupted, "let's understand what's going on here. This is Shawn Blanchard. Shawn hails from Mackenzie High School on the west side of Detroit. This brother went to the University of Michigan and obtained a degree in Economical Mathematics. From there, he went to New York City and obtained a Master's degree in Secondary Math Education, where he was a pivotal force in revitalizing a school from the bottom up. He started a successful mentoring program and mentored dozens of young men and even adopted one. Came back here and continued his great work with the City of Detroit as a founder of a huge community organizing effort that helps hundreds of citizens called "*Run This Town.*" This is Shawn Blanchard. A future/current leader right here in Detroit."

"Thank you, good brother, you're too kind."

I met Ken once before and didn't realize how much information he had gathered. I was impressed with his recall.

"Let's give Shawn a card," said Mallett. "We'd like to connect you with our team."

I was excited about the prospect of getting involved. This was an opportunity to participate in a grassroots campaign. This could potentially lead to tons of impact and connections with good people. Before I jumped the gun I did my homework and spoke with a number of political minds that I respect. I prayed about it.

The decision was made.

With Duggan, I visited over 60 homes and heard him speak and watched him listen to the citizens say what they wanted for their city. By the time we finished, Duggan was the new mayor and I was appointed as the Director of Youth Services.

The stars align when you do the work. I continued as an integral founder of *Run This Town*, taught math at the University of Michigan, delivered dozens of speeches, all while writing this book, and serving in the Mayor's Cabinet.

It's an honor to serve.

---

I know my calling. I see it through the lives of my mentees and mentors. I've seen their success, their struggles, and their triumphs. I'm a mentor to many and a firm believer that you don't have to create a gang of rock stars: instead simply plant seeds and enable them to be better than what they would have been without you. You will see their growth.

I see such things when I look at the life of Roland. He's a mirror image of myself. I was to him what Ms. Champion was to me. He now has a full ride at the University of Michigan.

Today, my reality is that I walk through the Mayor's office doors with a brief case like Marcus Graham, a gentleman like Will Smith in *Hitch*, a politician like Barack Obama, walking through the same double doors as Kwame Kilpatick. My suits fit like James Bond, I'm even a co-owner of a custom suit company "SnapSuits." I continue to give and give and give the way that we all should as reasonable servants on earth. I'm always seeking to be better. Do better.

Our life trajectory is heavily weighted by the three phases of mentorship. These three phases of influence that we experience can propel us as we transcend from unconscious mentorship, to conscious mentorship, to creating consciousness.

In order to get the life you want, you must be purposeful, willful, and deliberate. So write your vision down. Make it plain. Gather gurus (mentors) around you. Create a healthy universe. Repeat. Give.

When I was a kid I never met anyone like myself until I became myself.

How 'bout that for a crack baby?

# EPILOGUE

## Leveraging Mentorship

We are mentored from the moment we open our eyes to this world. Mentorship is the process by which we are influenced or guided by individuals, ideals, and/or society. We are all students to some teacher, but we have the fortune of choosing at least some of who these teachers may be. I strongly urge that you choose wise gurus to propel you forward. Here are some helpful tips to guide you through this process.

Remember! Be *Purposeful, Willful, and Deliberate* with your life. Be honest with yourself about your current state of consciousness and identify your current phase.

**Phase 1**: This is where you identify your good, bad, and really good bad examples.

**Phase 2**: This is where you take control of your life and begin to build a healthy universe of informal and formal mentors. Live your life such that you always live in a healthy universe.

**Phase 3**: This is where you bless others with your gifts by being a mentor to others. You can serve as an example, director, or sponsor.

## PHASE 1
# UNCONSCIOUS MENTORSHIP

In Chapters 1-10, I am being led and influenced in an unconscious way as I learned from some **"Really Good Bad Examples."** That was, in effect, all I knew. Nobody asked to be here. No one chooses their environment or the actors within it. You see, we are all students to some teacher. In fact, the moment we begin to breathe life in this world we start the process of being mentored.

*Mentorship is the process of being influenced by individuals, ideals, or society. For simplicity we will use the term "mentorship" and the term "influence" interchangeably.*

Think about it: initially we find ourselves in an unconscious state of mentorship. This means we are students to teachers that we have not personally selected. Imagine living life believing the world is everything you see through a pre-set lens. The pre-set lens often cripples our ability to choose our own set of influential forces and actors.

Those that life smiles upon will be born into a world with a pre-set lens that's saturated with **"Good Examples."** Truthfully, that's not the reality for most humans. Most of us have a pre-set lens that has a distribution of **"Good Examples"** and **"Bad Examples."** Honestly, even those with a heavily weighted distribution of **"Good Examples"** can have an attractive set of **"Bad Examples"** that can nullify the most optimum distributions, ultimately making it difficult to leverage the *good* into a successful life.

However, there is beauty in struggle and the ability for us to learn from even a **"Bad Example."** We will call these **"Really Good Bad Examples."** In this case we may not know what to do, but we definitely know what *not* to do. With that said, we can learn from every aspect of our pre-set lens. This phase of life, which impacts our free will, is called **"Unconscious Mentorship."** We will all live in this phase until we decide otherwise.

# CONSCIOUS MENTORSHIP

INFORMAL
MENTORSHIP

FORMAL
MENTORSHIP

1. NETWORK - FRIENDTORS
2. SOCIAL MEDIA
3. MAGAZINES
4. BOOKS
5. BIBLE
6. CHURCH
7. MUSIC
8. ART
9. HOBBIES
10. MOVIES
11. TELEVISION SHOWS
12. MOTIVIATIONAL SPEAKERS
13. NEWS MEDIUMS
14. FAVORITE WEBSITES
15. SOCIAL GROUPS

SPONSORS

DIRECTORS

EXAMPLES

In Chapters 11 and 12, you can see it's certainly time for me to make some adjustments in life. I was learning not to be controlled by life's pre-set lens filled with influences and actors that can stunt life's trajectory.

Once you move beyond **"Unconscious Mentorship,"** it's time to take control of your life by understanding "**Conscious Mentorship**." We have free will. We have the ability to create a healthy universe filled with our own set of influences. Let's expand upon the concept of "**Good Examples**" by creating two influential models that will take your life to the next level: Informal Mentorship and Formal Mentorship.

**Informal Mentorship**

We know that mentorship is simply the process of being influenced by individuals, ideals, and society. In the realm of **Conscious Mentorship** we take advantage of the opportunity to choose that which will guide us. Furthermore, we can immerse ourselves in the life that we want to live and let faith, combined with the law of attraction; guide us toward our desired life outcome. Here are three key rules to follow:

**Rule #1: Check your network!** You ever hear the saying, "If you show me who your friends are I'll show you who you are"? How about this one, "If you hang around nine fools you'll be the 10th one." The same applies for "If you soar with the eagles, that's means you're an eagle too." In life people will do one of two things for you. They will help you excel, or help you decline. The people that you call friends are the people that will give your life energy. Some energy may be positive while other energy may be negative. Look at your friends as "**friendtors**."

### Friend + Mentor = Friendtor

Your network is rich and filled with greatness all around you. I guarantee that everyone you hang around has something unique about him or her that you admire. Adopt their good traits and soar with the eagles.

**Rule #2: Gather your belongings!** Pack your life bag and stuff it full of positive energy that will travel with you for the rest of your life. This includes numbers 1-15 on the informal mentorship chart. Gather everything and be deliberate with every element that you enable to influence you.

## Formal Mentorship

The concept of formal mentorship is vague. What exactly is a mentor supposed to do for you? What are you supposed to expect from a mentor? How can you make sure that you are truly learning and gathering everything you need from the Gurus?

There are levels to mentorship. Below you will find clarifying definitions for each of those levels. This includes how mentors should interact with their mentees and key tips on how to initiate mentor/mentee relationships.

## Example Mentor

You most likely don't have a personal relationship with this person. You see them in passing and may say hello to them or have small talk in person. You follow them on social media, have read their bio, believe in their mission and want to align yourself with their brand or create your own brand in the same lane as theirs.

## Director Mentor

You have a personal relationship with this person. You at least have this person's email address and can meet for an occasional lunch to catch up. This person provides you with direction and believes in your potential.

## Sponsor Mentor

You have an intimate personal relationship with this person. You have their phone number, can call for advice, and most likely have been invited to dine at this person's home. This person believes in you and

312

will co-sign for you, will open their network for your personal gain, and will most likely provide some kind of recommendation for you.

**Rule #3: Assemble the Gurus**! Your mentors are gurus and it's your duty to assemble them to guide, direct, and fight for your success. Accumulate examples, directors, and sponsors. In order to assemble the gurus it will take patience, consistence, and persistence. Gurus become sponsors when they believe in you, which takes a bit of time, trust, and some understanding of your excellence.

To thoroughly reap the benefits of having mentors, it's best to have a clear sense of what you need from them. In other words you need a clear understanding of your ideal self. Make a commitment to yourself to set aside time for the proper research to build the concept of your ideal self. This is the only way you will merge toward actually becoming your ideal. This process is purposeful, willful, and deliberate. You must be honest with where you are currently in comparison to where you want to be. This includes understanding your unique gifts.

Imagine a kid that's a mathematician, charismatic, possesses great oratory skills, and has an innate ability to make sales. What if this kid attempts to be a drug dealer instead of a chemist that's destined to find the cure for cancer? DON'T LET THIS BE YOU! Enjoy your hobbies, but never disrespect your gifts. I often think my brother Mike could have been the man to create the cure for cancer, but he never left Phase 1. He accepted his environment along with the influences and actors within it. Let this very real scenario serve as a "**Really Good Bad Example**" as you decide to leverage both formal and informal mentorship in your life.

*R.I.H. Big bro', Mike. I appreciate every lesson you provided with the knowledge that was available to you.*

# CREATING CONSCIOUSNESS

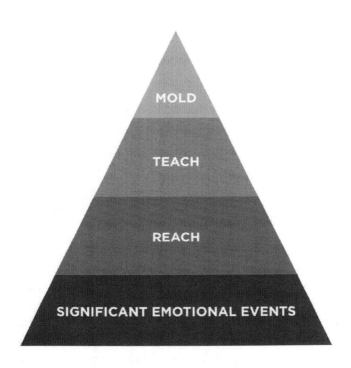

Once we hit Chapter 13…well, for me, that's when the excitement begins! As we set out to better ourselves by cultivating a healthy universe through informal and formal mentorship, we will perpetually build upon **Conscious Mentorship**. Phase 2 never stops! Catch that, because it's vital to your continuous evolution. However, we are blessed to be a blessing. The only reason we reach a level of **Conscious Mentorship** is to ensure that others have the opportunity to transition beyond the **Unconscious Mentorship** phase. This allows us to enter into Phase 3, which is **Creating Consciousness** in others.

To effectively teach means to have mastered one's craft. After we become masters of a craft we tend to believe that we can simply provide others with information and they will grasp the teachings and live life happily ever after. Sadly, this is not the case. Before we teach people we must reach them. The minds of people (particularly young people) are often closed until they have a reason to trust the leader. Before we reach them we must understand them by tapping into their **Significant Emotional Events.**

## Significant Emotional Events (SEE)

There are key events that are unique to everyone's life that affect their thought process, interactions, and overall worldview. The people that need the most help often endure **Significant Emotional Events** that can form mental barriers that prevent heightened levels of learning and connection with others. These barriers are often formed due to perceived or actual abuse or neglect.

## Reach

Due to the lack of trust that's developed from **SEE**, the mentor must reach the mentee by displaying genuine acts of understanding and care. This may be in the form of vulnerability of expressing similarity and/or through clearly going above and beyond to connect.

## Teach

Once a safe space is created through understanding and care, the mentee begins to open his or her mind. Once the mind is open, the coast is clear for the mentor to pour from their knowledge pool of mastery.

## Mold

Mastery of a craft is never enough when we want to ultimately help a mentee transition from **Unconscious Mentorship to Conscious Mentorship**. This means there is more to **teach** outside of the subject matter presented during the typical school day. True behavior modifications occur in the absence of the mentor as their lessons become embedded in the mentee's day-to-day decision making. An effective sign of a mentor's lessons **molding** the actions and mind of a mentee is **independent selection**. This is crucial! When a mentee begins to select mentors themselves, based on the mentor's expertise, experience, or wisdom, the mentee shows themselves to be wise, and they are able to bond even more effectively with the mentor they select. In the event that a mentee is paired with a mentor, the mentee's willingness to reach out beyond the scheduled appointments with the mentor is evidence that they are engaging in **independent selection.**

As mentors it's not our duty to create rock stars. It's our duty to create a safe space and plant seeds in the lives of others. Our simple purpose is to make the life of someone else better than what it would have been without us.

*Luke 6:38 – Give, and it will be given to you. A good measure, pressed down, shaken together and running over, will be poured into your lap. For with the measure you use, it will be measured to you.*

*R.I.H. Denise L. Thomas, Mom – Thanks for your unconventional teachings, love, and wisdom.*

## About Shawn Blanchard

Shawn KNOWS what it means to turn test into testimony. Blanchard is a firm believer that we never lose; we simply win or gain wisdom. Throughout his humble beginnings he has applied these simple truths, evolving into an upstanding gentleman and exactly what he needed as a child to many.  Through co-founding a successful mentoring program—which extended to legal guardianship of a teenager, obtaining multiple degrees; leading a math department to the top 5% in New York City; teaching mathematics at the University of Michigan; co-founding a fitness movement (Run This Town/Networkingout); being featured as *Essence* magazine's *Man of the Month*, on CNN's *"Impact Your World"*, and most recently as *Black Enterprise* magazine's *"BE Modern Man"*; he has defined what it means to be a modern day "Renaissance Man."

Blanchard was appointed to the City of Detroit's Mayoral Cabinet as the Director of Youth Services. During his tenure he successfully launched a citywide elementary soccer league and provided nearly 5600 jobs, heading the *Grow Detroit's Young Talent* youth employment initiative.  He also served as the Detroit Mayor's Office Liaison of President Barack Obama's *My Brother's Keeper* (MBK) initiative. Currently, Blanchard is the CEO and Founder of Shawn Blanchard Productions and the Style Advisor and Co-Owner of SnapSuits. He's a member of a number of boards, including Real Life 101 and MBK Detroit and was selected as the 2015 University of Michigan Emerging Leader and a *Michigan Chronicle 40 Under 40* award recipient for his leadership and dedication to community service. Most recently he received the President Barak Obama's Volunteer Community Service Award. In sum, Shawn uses his life experiences to enable people to live life to the fullest with a winning perspective.

317

Made in the USA
Lexington, KY
23 March 2017